THE SOURCES OF HISTORY:
STUDIES IN THE USES OF HISTORICAL EVIDENCE

GENERAL EDITOR: G. R. ELTON

THE SOURCES OF HISTORY:
STUDIES IN THE USES OF
HISTORICAL EVIDENCE

GENERAL EDITOR: G. R. ELTON

The purpose of this series of books is, broadly, to present to students and readers of history some understanding of the materials from which history must be written and of the problems which these raise. The books will endeavour to bring out the inescapable links between historical sources and historical reconstruction, will help to define promising lines of fruitful research, and will illumine the realities of historical knowledge. Each volume will be concerned with a logical span in the history of a given nation, civilisation or area, or with a meaningful historical theme, and it will confine itself to all the primary materials extant for that sector. These materials it will consider from the point of view of two crucial questions: what can we know, and what have we no right to expect to learn, from what the past has left behind?

G. R. ELTON *England, 1200–1640*

T. H. HOLLINGSWORTH *Historical demography*

C. L. MOWAT *Great Britain since 1914*

IAN R. JACK *Medieval Wales*

KATHLEEN HUGHES *Early Christian Ireland*

CHARLES H. CARTER *The western European powers, 1500–1700*

WALTER ULLMANN *Law and politics in the Middle Ages*

WILLIAM R. BROCK *The United States, 1789–1890*

DAVID KNIGHT *Sources for the history of science, 1660–1914*

BRUCE WEBSTER *Scotland from the eleventh century to 1603*

The Sources of History:
Studies in the Uses of Historical Evidence

England 1200–1640

by

G. R. ELTON

THE SOURCES OF HISTORY LIMITED

IN ASSOCIATION WITH

CAMBRIDGE UNIVERSITY PRESS

CAMBRIDGE · LONDON · MELBOURNE

Published by the Syndics of the Cambridge University Press
The Pitt Building, Trumpington Street, Cambridge CB2 IRP
Bentley House, 200 Euston Road, London NW1 2DB
296 Beaconsfield Parade, Middle Park, Melbourne 3206, Australia

First published in association with Hodder and Stoughton 1969
Published in association with the Cambridge University Press 1976
Reprinted 1977

First printed in Great Britain by
The Camelot Press Ltd, London and Southampton
Reprinted in Great Britain
at the University Press, Cambridge

ISBN 0 521 21452 1 hard covers
ISBN 0 521 29152 6 paperback

Contents

Introduction

By what right do historians claim that their reconstructions of the past are true, or at least on the road to truth? How much of the past can they hope to recover, are there areas that will remain for ever dark, questions that will never receive an answer? These are problems which should and do engage not only the scholar and student but every serious reader of history. In the debates on the nature of history, however, attention commonly concentrates on philosophic doubts about the nature of historical knowledge and explanation, or on the progress that might be made by adopting supposedly new methods of analysis. The disputants hardly ever turn to consider the materials with which historians work and which must always lie at the foundation of their structures. Yet, whatever theories or methods the scholar may embrace, unless he knows his sources and rests upon them he will not deserve the name of historian. The bulk of historical evidence is much larger and more complex than most laymen and some professionals seem to know, and a proper acquaintance with it tends to prove both exhilarating and sobering—exhilarating because it opens the road to unending enquiry, and sobering because it reduces the inspiring theory and the new method to their proper subordinate place in the scheme of things. It is the purpose of this series to bring this fact to notice by showing what we have and how it may be used.

G. R. E.

Preface

Four and a half centuries are a long period, and though I hope to show that thanks to the predominance of official sources they possess a unity based on the nature of their historical evidence, the period they form is also sufficiently diverse. No one can have first-hand experience of all the types of material that survive, and I certainly make no claim of that sort. I am, indeed, very conscious of my rashness in straying so far outside the years to which in the main I have devoted my professional labours. Nevertheless, it has proved a risk worth taking: I have learned a lot and can only hope that I may be able to convey this better understanding to others. I shall be astonished if my errors should all prove minor ones and grateful for corrections from the experts. To two such experts, Mr Philip Grierson and Dr R. S. Schofield, who have helped me to look in the right places and to avoid mistakes, I am already most grateful. Many others have assisted me through their writings; if I have in some way misused them, I beg their pardon. One thing that I certainly suspected I have found to be entirely true: far more history than is written remains unwritten. We are still a long way from the evening of our labours.

Clare College   G. R. ELTON
Cambridge

April 1968

CHAPTER 1

Narratives

No matter how refined and penetrating the study of original materials may have become, historians would be in a bad way if they did not have the work of their predecessors to guide them. Although the middle ages did not regard the study or writing of history with any great respect, they nevertheless practised it. Curiosity about the past and a desire to perpetuate the memory of the present are universal human attributes, while from ancient Rome, that general fount of learning, there survived examples to act as instructors. Some men devoted themselves seriously to the study of the past and deserve the name of historians. Others were content to note whatever came to their eyes and ears; bare chronicles and mere annals—lists of events ordered by years—are plentiful. The later middle ages yield quantities of such writings, of very varied competence and extent. In general, however, there was a decline in quality from the work of the twelfth century, and the fifteenth descended to a point little higher than that reached in the dark ages of the Danish invasions. However,

BIBLIOGRAPHY. The chronicles for the last three medieval centuries are listed, together with notes of discussions about them, in the bibliographies of three volumes of the Oxford History of England: F. M. Powicke, *The Thirteenth Century* (1953), 730–5; M. McKisack, *The Fourteenth Century* (1959), 543–9; E. F. Jacob, *The Fifteenth Century* (1961), 730–5. For the Tudor chronicles see *Bibliography of English History: the Tudor Period*, ed. C. Read (2nd ed. Oxford 1959), 25–9. There are two standard series of editions: the Rolls Series (R.S.), officially called 'Rerum Britannicarum Medii Aevi Scriptores', published from 1858 onwards and now obtainable from Her Majesty's Stationery Office; and the still progressing 'Medieval Classics', edited by V. H. Galbraith and R. A. B. Mynors, published by Nelson (N.M.C.). This latter series prints the original and a translation on opposing pages. Many chronicles, however, have appeared independently from these

towards the end of that century historical studies received a new impetus from the influence of Italian scholarship which, in the hands of learned humanists, had revived critical methods and improved, without profoundly altering, the characteristic chronicle style of the middle ages. The humanists still wrote consecutive narrative, still thought largely of purely political history, and still tended to organise their matter by years, though they usually managed to give a better shape to their histories and to investigate cause and effect a little more searchingly. Tudor historical writing was influenced by these innovations through the work of Polydore Vergil, an Italian resident in England for many years from 1502 onwards, who wrote a big history of his host country down to 1537. The narrative sources for our period therefore fall into three groups: the last set of serious chronicles of the medieval type, the scrappy and often primitive aftermath of this activity, and the reinvigorated chroniclers of the sixteenth century.

The first group of writings, covering the thirteenth and four-teenth centuries, is both quite full and largely continuous. At the Benedictine abbey of St Albans, something like a tradition of historical enterprise established itself with Roger Wendover in the early thirteenth century. He was succeeded by Matthew Paris, the most prolific and idiosyncratic historian of medieval England; and after some lesser names and a partial lapse the tradition came

series; some are listed in the footnotes to this chapter. A good introduction to the medieval histories is provided by J. Taylor, *The Use of Medieval Chronicles* (Historical Association: Helps for Students of History No. 70; 1965). For medieval scholarship see especially two lectures by V. H. Galbraith: *Roger Wendover and Matthew Paris* (Glasgow 1944) and *Historical Research in Medieval England* (London 1951). On Tudor historiography see F. J. Levy, *Tudor Historical Thought* (San Marino, Calif., 1967) and F. S. Fussner, *The Historical Revolution: English Historical Writing and Thought 1580–1640* (London 1962). Two valuable studies of individual historians are: R. Vaughan, *Matthew Paris* (Cambridge 1958), and D. Hay, *Polydore Vergil: Renaissance Historian and Man of Letters* (Oxford 1952). (P.S. The N.M.C. series is now published by the Oxford University Press.)

to an end with Thomas Walsingham in the early fifteenth century.[1] For just over two centuries, English history thus benefited from the labours of men who were sufficiently close to the centre of affairs to escape the purely parochial. Other monks, too, assist us. At Bury St Edmunds, Jocelin de Brakelond's fascinating account of Abbot Samson—an attempt at general history which turned into a biographical monograph—seems to have inspired the keeping of a chronicle which terminated in 1301.[2] A Yorkshire monk, Walter of Gisborough, variegates our knowledge in a work once ascribed to Walter of Hemmingburgh (and so cited in the older books);[3] this ends early in the reign of Edward II. Matthew Paris ran down to 1265; from then on the Norwich chronicle of Bartholomew Cotton fills the gap.[4] The fine work of Gervase of Canterbury, so important for the twelfth century, was brought down to 1207 by Gervase himself; a valuable continuation was kept at Canterbury to the death of Edward I.[5] All these are general chronicles, well aware of the world at large. More specialised information comes from a less usual source, two narrative poems. William the Marshal, the great knight and administrator, inspired an enormous piece of 19,214 lines in rhymed French, while Simon de Montfort moved an Oxford Franciscan to an ecstatic admiration embodied in a much shorter Latin poem.[6]

Even larger in number though inferior in quality are the recorders of the fourteenth century. The insufficiencies of the St Albans

[1] The St Albans tradition is discussed by Galbraith and Vaughan in the works cited in the Bibliography on p. 14. See also V. H. Galbraith, *The St Albans Chronicle 1406–1420* (Oxford 1937) and 'Thomas Walsingham and the St Albans Chronicle 1272–1422', *English Historical Review* (1932), 12–30.

[2] Both these works have appeared in N.M.C.: *The Chronicle of Jocelin de Brakelond*, ed. H. E. Butler (1949); *The Chronicle of Bury St Edmunds 1212–1301*, ed. Antonia Gransden (1964).

[3] *The Chronicle of Walter of Gisborough*, ed. H. Rothwell (Camden Series, vol. 89; London 1957).

[4] *Historia Anglicana*, ed. H. R. Luard (R.S. 1859).

[5] Gervase of Canterbury, *Chronicles*, ed. W. Stubbs (R.S. 1879–80), vol. 2.

[6] *L'Histoire de Guillaume le Maréchal*, ed. Paul Meyer (3 vols; Paris 1891–1901); *The Song of Lewes*, ed. C. L. Kingsford (Oxford 1889).

series before about 1380 are compensated for by the works of two secular clerks from Oxfordshire. Adam Murimuth covers the years 1303–47; Geoffrey le Baker is useful for the years 1320–56.[1] In the many-authored *Flores Historiarum*, building up on Matthew Paris, a Westminster monk, Robert of Reading, wrote a section which provides an original contribution on the reign of Edward II.[2] Even more valuable is the anonymous *Life* of that king, written by a monk who had meant to compose a general history but came to deviate into biography.[3] The military exploits of Edward III are recorded by Robert of Avesbury[4] and at greater length in the remarkable chronicles of the layman Jean Froissart who in his history of fourteenth-century wars and chivalry concentrated mostly on France and Burgundy, but of course recorded the deeds of the invading English and in consequence incorporated some internal English history.[5] More domestic matters form the mainstay of an exceptional contribution from the mostly silent north, the Anonimalle Chronicle of the abbey of St Mary's, York, important especially because it incorporates newsletters received from the south.[6] For the last quarter of the fourteenth century and the first of the fifteenth, we possess in addition to Walsingham the writings of another two secular clerks of notable ability, Henry Knighton and Adam of Usk.[7] There are other lesser accounts, some very petty but some adding significantly to knowledge.

As we move into the fifteenth century, this abundance is

[1] Adam Murimuth, *Continuatio Chronicarum*, ed. E. M. Thompson (R.S. 1889); Geoffrey le Baker, *Chronicon*, ed. E. M. Thompson (Oxford 1889).

[2] *Flores Historiarum*, ed. H. R. Luard (R.S. 1890), Vol. 2, 137–235.

[3] *Vita Edwardi Secundi*, ed. N. Denholm-Young (N.M.C. 1957).

[4] Added by Thompson to his edition of Murimuth (above, n. 1).

[5] The Tudor translation of Froissart by Lord Berners, still the best complete version in English, was republished by W. K. Ker in his series, Tudor Translations (6 vols, London 1901–3).

[6] *The Anonimalle Chronicle 1333–1381*, ed. V. H. Galbraith (Manchester 1927).

[7] *Henry Knighton's Chronicle*, ed. J. R. Lumby (2 vols; R.S. 1889, 1895); *Chronicon Adae de Usk*, ed. E. M. Thompson (London 1904).

replaced by real dearth.[1] Though some monastic establishments continued to keep chronicles, these rarely now amounted to anything much; like that very belated example, the register kept by Butley Priory in the early sixteenth century,[2] they confined themselves much more exclusively to the affairs of the house that produced them. Equally localised were the interests of the town chroniclers who multiplied in this century. But because London was already very much the centre of affairs, the lively chronicle tradition of that city contributes something of value to the general historian. However, what was done in the main part of the century was scrappy and recorded little except city affairs.[3] Work in this tradition improved a great deal in the reign of Henry VII and led straight to more serious historical efforts in that of Henry VIII.[4] By the side of this poor material we can put little except the English *Brut*, a vernacular set of annals terminating in 1479 which after 1333 includes original contributions; before that, the English *Brut* is a translation from a French original which owes too much to legend and fable.[5] Altogether, the *Brut* is so poor a source that it is used only for periods not described in better books. The fifteenth century produced something like a new phenomenon in the lay antiquary William of Worcester, an ardent collector of materials, some of whose notebooks survive; however, these do not significantly contribute to knowledge.[6]

[1] See C. L. Kingsford, *English Historical Literature in the Fifteenth Century* (Oxford 1913).

[2] *The Register of Butley Priory, Suffolk, 1510–1535*, ed. A. G. Dickens (Winchester 1951).

[3] *Chronicles of London*, ed. C. L. Kingsford (Oxford 1905).

[4] *The Great Chronicle of London*, ed. A. H. Thomas and I. D. Thornley (London 1938). The introductions to the works mentioned in this and the preceding footnotes provide the best account of the London chronicles, extant and lost.

[5] *The Brut or the Chronicles of England*, ed. F. W. D. Brie (2 vols; Early English Text Society, London 1906, 1908). The work is called by this name because it begins with the popular fairy-tale of England's colonisation by one Brutus, eponymous hero of Britain.

[6] K. B. McFarlane, 'William of Worcester, a preliminary survey', *Studies Presented to Sir Hilary Jenkinson*, ed. J. Conway Davies (London 1957), 196–221.

The increasing number of writings not of the chronicle type will be considered in the appropriate place.

After this two things happened to historical writing in England. One was the arrival of 'humanist' historiography in the hands of Polydore Vergil, scholar and papal tax-collector; this has already been mentioned. The other was the invention of printing. History sold, and history therefore served the printing presses well; in supplying the new reading public, the popular historians tried to abstract and transmit the work of their medieval predecessors, as well as to continue it into their own time. The work produced falls into two main types. On the one hand we have books that deal with a relatively short period of history and even make a theme of it. To this category belong Edward Hall's account of the triumphant emergence of the House of Tudor and William Camden's history of the reign of Elizabeth.[1] Apart from these largely original compositions, on the other hand, there appeared vast compilations covering either all or most of England's history. Of this profitable literary enterprise, Richard Grafton, the printer, was the first exponent; Ralph Holinshed composed the largest and most read collection; John Stowe's chronicle was the most careful.[2] Both Grafton and Stowe published abridgements of their mammoth works, an idea in which Matthew Paris had preceded them. These chronicles embodied both the London tradition and the best known medieval chronicles, especially those of St Albans; though they learned both matter and manner from Polydore, they reacted against his criticism with a chauvinistic attachment to the *Brut*; for their own time, they added much detail, some of it resting on careful research. Between them, Polydore and the native Tudor chroniclers really established the outline of the traditional 'kings of England' type of history. The

[1] E. Hall, *The Union of the two noble and illustre famelies York and Lancastre* (best edition: London 1809); Hall finished his work down to 1532, but the remainder to the death of Henry VIII rests on his notes. W. Camden, *Annales rerum anglicarum et hibernicarum regnante Elizabetha* (best English edition: 1688).

[2] First editions and best editions: Grafton 1568, 1809; Holinshed (1577), 1587, 1807–8; Stowe, many editions starting in 1580.

sixteenth century also witnessed a more sophisticated continuation of the biographical tradition going back to Asser and Jocelin: Thomas More's one-sided *Life* of Richard III was used by Hall, but the better book on Wolsey by George Cavendish remained unpublished and unknown until the nineteenth century.[1] There are a few minor diaries and chronicles of independent value.

One exceptional work, however, which clearly belongs to the narratives, deserves special mention: John Foxe's *Acts and Monuments*, or, as the popular term has it, his *Book of Martyrs*, one of the most influential books ever to appear in English. Excessively hostile criticism nearly demolished Foxe's credit in the nineteenth century, but modern scholars have come to the conclusion that he was a careful worker whose unquestioned bias did not destroy the reliability of his research. Although Foxe told the story of Christian martyrs back to the foundation of the Church, his important contribution covers the persecution of English dissenters from the early fifteenth century to 1558; and for this period and topic he remains indispensable.[2]

Thus, while there was plenty of history written in these centuries, by no means all the period enjoyed equal benefit. The first thing to note is that none of the writers mentioned can be said to have been outstanding historians. An exception should probably be made for Camden, a man worthy of regard in any company, who in his narrative writing, however, concerned himself with only a very short piece of history. Polydore Vergil scored in the main by a degree of independence, a product of his foreign birth and humanist training, but he did less with these advantages than might be supposed; he cannot compare with other Italian historians like Bruni or Guiccardini, brought a second-rate mind to his

---

[1] Best editions: Thomas More, *The History of King Richard III*, ed. R. S. Sylvester (New Haven 1963); G. Cavendish, *The Life and Death of Cardinal Wolsey*, ed. R. S. Sylvester (Early English Text Soc., London 1959).

[2] Best editions by S. R. Cattley and G. Townsend (8 vols, London 1837-41) and J. Pratt (8 vols, London 1870). For a discussion of Foxe's scholarship and influence see J. F. Mozley, *John Foxe and his Book* (London 1940) and W. Haller, *Foxe's Book of Martyrs and the Elect Nation* (London 1963).

systematisation of the past, and showed little objectivity in his treatment of his own time. Hall was honest and just capable of organised thought; Stowe's industry and care were not matched by his control or by a sufficiently critical sense. As for the medieval chroniclers, even Matthew Paris cannot be mentioned in the same breath as such real historians of earlier times as Bede or William of Malmesbury. This lack of intellectual distinction was aggravated by the primary principle of medieval and Tudor historiography. In his study of the past the historian's first duty was to collect the best accounts and transcribe them as accurately as possible, not to analyse and reconstruct them; how could he, who had not lived through those events, know better than those who had? He applied criticism only in the most limited sense, that is in deciding which past statement was the better and more trustworthy. 'Original composition was the last refuge of the historian.'[1] Most chroniclers reached a long way back—to the Creation or the Fall or the Flood, or at least to the arrival of Brutus in England. But what they had to say about the times before their own is readily identified as more or less verbatim borrowing from their predecessors.[2] The Tudor chroniclers were no better in this. Men like Grafton or Holinshed collected; they did not study, analyse or compose.

Naturally, this method failed the historian when he came to his own time; there, reluctantly, he had to make his own contribution to the common stock. For the modern student of these centuries, all the writers really matter only when they are writing contemporary history. Here again their quality and usefulness vary widely, but it should be understood that the amount of sheer knowledge that they convey is considerable. One can distinguish two main methods employed: either the chronicler assembled the facts and events of one year after another (as was the habit of Matthew Paris or Edward Hall), or he wrote a series

[1] Galbraith, *Historical Research*, 6.
[2] See, e.g. Luard's edition of Cotton's *Historia* (15, n. 4) which very illuminatingly uses different type to distinguish wholesale borrowing from original writing.

of individual and distinct stories (as did Roger Wendover or Henry Knighton). Both types, however, really proceed straightforwardly through the years, as indeed they were bound to do when describing contemporary events, a fact which inhibits these writers from ever achieving a structured narrative. Fundamentally, they record only. Analysis and explanation are very rare, a criticism which must apply even to Polydore who at least does tell the story. But even in their mere record the differences are marked. The very brief and scrappy notes of the Bury St Edmunds chronicle, for instance, which give even to the striking events of 1258 a mere few lines squeezed between a remark on the weather and a note on the election of a local prior, would seem to suggest what many believe—that monkish chroniclers could not be expected to know even what went on in their own time outside their immediate vicinity. But a few pages later the chronicle blossoms forth, and the Barons' War gets a very full treatment. The St Albans chroniclers lived in one of the lively centres of England, met many travellers, and (as Matthew Paris records) made it their business to learn all they could; here the events not only of England but of the greater world, too (pope and emperor, France and the Levant) find record. Knighton gives a long and personal account of Wycliffe and Lollardy which fills over forty pages in print; Adam of Usk tells the story of the 1388 Parliament from personal experience and in vivid detail. The newsletters incorporated in the Anonimalle Chronicle preserve not only a good account of the 1381 Peasants' Rebellion (this one might not wonder at) but also the inside story of the Good Parliament of 1376 in a manner not matched again until Edward Hall, a burgess of the Reformation Parliament, came to describe events there. The contemporary parts of these major chronicles are therefore always as important to the historian as the rest is negligible.

This means that for the thirteenth, fourteenth and sixteenth centuries we possess a reasonable account of events which can be reconstructed from the words of contemporary writers. The fifteenth is in a much less happy condition: no writer of significance recorded its annals, and what there is is heavily parochial and extremely patchy. Yet the history of that century has long been fixed in as firm a mould as that given to the thirteenth by Matthew Paris or to the reign of Elizabeth by William Camden. The trouble is that in this case the mould was shaped later: the standard account of the fifteenth century, with its dynastic strife and Wars of the Roses (a term invented by Sir Walter Scott), was put together in the sixteenth, partly by Vergil and partly by Hall, both of them concerned to play up the Tudor dynasty under which they lived. Taken over by Holinshed and embedded in Shakespeare's plays, the structure became very strong and still sometimes exercises its formidable hold over the less discriminating historians.[1] It is because no sound contemporary history exists for this age that its shape and meaning are so much in dispute now. Of course, it does not follow that the Tudor historians were wrong, but at least the obvious purposes they meant to serve in, for instance, denigrating the achievements of Richard III, have rightly called forth a critical reassessment. Unfortunately, the lead in this has been taken by amateurs as heavily committed to the other side. It should be stressed that the narrative material does not permit much scope or depth to reconsideration, and those who have tried to rewrite fifteenth-century history from the narratives alone have been beating the air.

The contemporary narrative tradition is not complete; in so far as it exists, can it be trusted? Certainly, the chroniclers and historians claimed to tell the truth, and the more serious of them went to a deal of trouble to prove their veracity. In particular, they often cited at length from documents, sometimes tacitly but more often explicitly. Matthew Paris even invented the appendix of documents, so familiar in seventeenth-century historical works and an indispensable feature of modern doctoral dissertations: he produced a whole volume of 'additions' (*liber*

[1] In his *Bosworth Field* (London 1966) A. L. Rowse 'proves' the accuracy of Shakespeare's interpretation by using only Shakespeare's sources and using them trustingly.

additamentorum) to which he cross-referenced his text. Though neither he nor others were above altering the documents they preserved, sometimes tendentiously,[1] the material as a rule stands up well enough to critical examination. An historian who produces his evidence deserves respect. Of course, these men were limited in the archives they could consult. The St Albans chroniclers used mostly such things as papal letters to the abbey, royal writs to the sheriff of Hertfordshire, and so on, while a Norwich monk like Cotton cites his royal letters from the files of the sheriff of Norfolk. But many chroniclers obtained less localised materials, often of a surprising kind. Thus Murimuth describes the battle of Crécy in a Latin letter which the king's confessor had sent to the London Dominicans, while Robert of Avesbury transcribed a French account composed by Master Michael of Northburgh, a member of Edward III's council who accompanied the king during the campaign. Altogether, the chroniclers preserve much original material now lost and do so with quite as much accuracy as some eminent historians of more recent times.

The humanist inventions of the later fifteenth century did not in this respect improve matters; in some ways they made them worse. The demands of art and style discouraged the simple copying of documents: Polydore has none. Although the medieval writers had occasionally invented set speeches for their characters, the new history inherited an ancient tradition which regarded the invention of appropriate orations as one of the historian's more legitimate literary devices. It was fortunate that Hall owed so much to native example and was a careful reporter by instinct; as a source for the modern historian, his chronicle is greatly superior to Polydore's. Even Holinshed occasionally went to the trouble of discovering the full details of something that interested him; we know this because when he did it his pride of achievement moved him to record the fact. In general, the better writers applied enough proper standards of honesty and evaluation to their contemporary evidence to enable the modern scholar to

[1] Vaughan, *Matthew Paris*, 132.

use them with confidence, provided that he in his turn treats them with rigorous criticism.

Such criticism must in the first place apply to the possibility of prejudiced bias. Traditional sneers at 'monkish chroniclers' not only forget that many of them were not monks but those enemies of the enclosed orders—friars, secular clergy and laymen—but also seem to assume much too readily that anything written by a cleric must automatically be weighted in favour of the Church and the cloister. This is much too simple; each author worthy of the name requires individual assessment. On the other hand, such assessment is rarely difficult. Wendover did regard King John as an enemy of the Church and abominated him accordingly. The author of the *Vita Edwardi Secundi* manifestly favoured the king; Robert of Reading, describing the same period, displayed a strong bias in favour of the king's Lancastrian opponents. Both Polydore and Hall, for different reasons, very much disliked Wolsey and left a one-sided picture which even today is more influential than Cavendish's loving biography, obviously prejudiced in the cardinal's favour. No chronicler stood forth more plainly than Matthew Paris, that Tory squire dressed up as a monk. He hated change, disliked and distrusted all foreigners, and—monk or not—had grave doubts about all popes. Since he was free with comment on his facts, his prejudices everywhere pervade his history, but they are plain and can be allowed for.[1] Less obviously, one can learn from Adam of Usk why on the whole he leaned towards King Richard II when he tells a story of his student days at Oxford. He had there led the Welsh students in riots against the northern men and had narrowly escaped conviction before a jury, an experience which, he says, left him with a permanent respect for the King and his law. The main bulk of the lesser chronicles were compiled by men whose personality neither appears from the work nor affected their gathering of often unrelated and usually undigested fact.

Discovering the historian behind his history is a necessary task in all historiography, and one much practised at the present time.

[1] See Vaughan, *Matthew Paris*, 125 ff.

More difficult is a more general question: for what purpose did these men write? Modern historians write to be read generally and widely, and once printing was invented this was true of earlier historians, too. And although the circulation of even the most copied manuscripts was much more restricted than is print, an appeal to a wider audience clearly underlies much medieval writing, too. Matthew Paris referred the readers of his abridgement to his larger work and all his readers on occasion to the collection of materials which, he said, could be inspected on demand. Such popular annals as the *Brut* or the *Flores Historiarum*, of which far more manuscripts survive than of all the rest, no doubt served a wide audience. But a good many of these writings, and certainly the occasional brief effort from some religious house or other, looks like being intended to satisfy only local need, and this is especially true of civic chronicles with their careful list of local dignitaries. Such works therefore concentrate on what was important or of interest locally and mention events from the great world only occasionally, almost by accident, as news came through or someone on the spot was affected. If the greater chonicles, with their annalistic arrangement, resemble nothing so much as an annual register,[1] the lesser pieces often read like the files of a local newspaper.

One kind of bias and purpose is worth singling out for a special word. The general chroniclers wished to record history in general, whether the whole of it, as in Ralph Higden's popular *Polychronicon* which made the whole known world its province, or such of the whole as came to the undiscriminating attention of the reporter. The writers of monographs constructed their works around a narrower, better defined, and much more propagandist purpose. Thus the authors of the poem on William the Marshal or of the *Song of Lewes* came to praise; here there is no nonsense about impartiality, and both the Marshal and Earl Simon were fixed in images which may be quite misleading. Modern criticism

---

[1] A better title than history for even so massive a work as Matthew Paris's *Chronica Maiora* might be 'Annual Register, or the year's events with a personal summing-up by our resident grumbler'.

has done something to reduce Simon to a more believable figure;[1] the Marshal, perhaps justly, remains very much as his admirer described him.[2] That this is so because for the history of the one there are plenty of other materials, while for the other very little personally illuminating evidence survives, should act as a warning; criticism can be effective only if it has tools with which to operate. But as a rule there are some tools available; internal analysis can help when no external evidence exists; and, speaking for myself, I find the poem's William thoroughly convincing—a solid and efficient operator set firmly in the conventions of his time, a man of light and shade and no sort of plaster saint.

A proper use of the critical faculty, directed at three main points (what can the writer have known; what was his personal bias; what purpose did he mean to serve?) makes possible a very thorough appraisal of the worth of the information purveyed and enables the modern historian to extract a great deal of reliable history from these very varied works. Of course, he is better placed when the chronicles are fuller and thicker on the ground; it has already been explained that the deficiencies in quantity, skill and learning which mark the fifteenth century, account in large part for the muddle which hangs over that period. Yet there is a sense in which the virtues of the medieval historian become drawbacks in the eyes of his modern user. Do we really want good historians from whom to reconstruct history? The more the chronicler resembles the historian, the more problematic becomes his product; the more he serves up the raw materials only, the fewer difficulties he poses to the interpreter. This becomes particularly manifest when one moves out of the middle ages proper. If even to this day English historical narrative has not entirely escaped the often misleading authority of Polydore Vergil and his Tudor successors, this is because they were so much

[1] See the discussion and bibliography in C. H. Knowles, *Simon de Montfort 1265–1965* (Hist. Ass. Pamphlet; London 1965).

[2] E.g. Sidney Painter, *William Marshall, Knight Errant, Baron and Regent of England* (Baltimore 1933).

more like real historians than most of their predecessors; but since they were still historians of at best modest quality and in particular unaware of the vast masses of material available to the modern student, their schemes of narrative and interpretation are nowadays liable to pose an obstacle to understanding. At any rate, we still need a good deal of work on the massive survivals of narrative sources. Despite the work of such splendid scholars as Stubbs, Kingsford or Galbraith, a good many chronicles still need sound editions; in particular we badly need modern editions of the sixteenth-century writers who, with the sole exception of Polydore,[1] have been not so much edited as merely reprinted. Further we need to know a lot more about the sources and materials used by all these writers and in many cases more about the men themselves. The sort of work that has been done on Matthew Paris and Polydore Vergil is probably not possible for most of these obscure men, but an investigation of the historical writing of the period as an example of the intellectual attitudes characteristic of the time is badly needed. Froissart, for instance, absolutely cries out for treatment.

Still, though more could be done, there are certainly reliable ways of using the old narratives and extracting sound history from them. Much less tractable is the fact that their interests were in many respects so different from ours. 'Since,' as Galbraith points out, 'we no longer ask the same questions about the past, the answers we seek are not forthcoming.'[2] The main, almost the exclusive, subject matter of this kind of history comprised public events—the doings of the great in State and Church. War and peace, appointment to high office, internal disturbances, great trials at law, politics and parliaments and taxation—on such things the chroniclers have something to say. They were interested in individual people but as a rule only in the outstanding ones, and even there they were given to conventional descriptions. A really personal portrait, like that of Edward I painted by

---

[1] *The Anglica Historia of Polydore Vergil, A.D. 1485–1537*, ed. D. Hay (Camden Series, vol. 74; London 1950).

[2] *Historical Research*, 46.

quite a minor chronicle, is rare;[1] ordinarily one finds persons so described as to embody the cardinal virtues or vices. This was one of the things that historians inherited from ancient Rome. Nor were the Tudor chronicles much better in these respects; humanist historiography, too, concentrated on politics and affairs, and described people in conventional terms. Polydore's very influential picture of Henry VII, the ageing miser, is a case in point: a figure from a morality play, not a living creature. The many questions which the modern historian likes to ask about the economy, the institutions, the ideas and civilisation of a past age, not to mention the generality of men, find virtually no answer in all these narratives. Very occasionally one may pick up an accidental allusion, especially to the conventional convictions of a period. A lucky exception like the Anonimalle Chronicle's account of the 1376 parliament (which has helped the institutional historian to a surprisingly clear understanding of that body at a very early date) was not, of course, intended as an institutional study at all. To tell a story—that is the ambition of the good chronicler; his inferior brother simply listed events.

Nor should one forget that the concerns of men may change. It was not simply idiocy that confined past historians to certain themes, even as it is not necessarily proof of intellectual distinction if a modern historian rejects 'political history'. Yet some of those past interests, informative in themselves, were exasperatingly peculiar. We should gladly sacrifice Froissart's lists of noblemen or even some of his spirited battlefield conversations for some detailed information on the raising of armies, the effects of war upon the economy and the people, or the inner politics of the day. Edward Hall must annoy the modern student with his long and loving descriptions of every bit of pageantry—royal weddings and revels, the meetings of kings—which absorb space that he could have used in a more careful account of events in Parliament or to give facts on the cloth trade, with both of which he was familiar. However, it is not much use pining after what is not there. In itself, the focus of an historian's interest says something

[1] Cited by Taylor, *The Use of Medieval Chronicles*, 18.

about the concerns of his age; a re-reading of the chronicles would usefully remind historians that in thinking about the later middle ages they would do well to remember wars and dynasties, rather than press their own passion for agrarian problems or population change. New questions should, of course, be asked concerning any past age, but trouble ensues if they are asked without any understanding of that age's own intellectual and emotional preferences.

The chronicles are products of the past which we study, and they thus offer a key to that past's mind. This, however, is not their chief service to the modern historian. The purpose for which they were written has not ceased to exist, and their first and greatest achievement is to have provided a vast quantity of facts, accurately dated in a general chronological framework. If it were not for this, we should be quite unable to begin to write the history of those centuries. We are nowadays so well equipped with textbooks and handbooks that we are only too likely to overlook the fundamental difficulty of reconstructing a sequence of events through time. The historians of those centuries, like their predecessors and, for a long time, their successors, made no such mistake. They were struggling to create the chain of dated events which we take for granted. They did other things useful to us by preserving documents, describing personalities, recording opinions. In many of their works there is the quality of life and subtlety which records cannot possess; there are art and skill, humour and anger, all the qualities which give fascination to the past. But these are incidentals, a bonus to the modern historian which he is glad to have, not a necessity for his own work. True, if we had nothing from which to reconstruct the history of those years except the writings of the old historians, chroniclers and annalists we should have to content ourselves with a very limited history, restricted in its questions, uncheckable in its answers, a primitive product by and large. But if we had all the rest of the materials to be described in this book and lacked the chronicles, we should be reduced to hopelessness in the face of the task of fitting facts into an unknown chronology. Without the chroniclers, we could not write this history at all.

CHAPTER 2

Official Records: the State

The many records produced by the King's government form both the largest and the most systematic part of the evidence for the centuries under discussion. In any historical investigation of the period they must stand at the centre of things; the historian who does not know them or cannot use them cannot write this history. Their quantity and variety is so overwhelming that they cannot possibly be described here in full. There is room only for an outline introduction, but the reader should get some impression of what is available. Furthermore, plentiful and often continuous as these materials are, they also pose all sorts of problems, both in understanding and employing what is there and in managing to do without that which either is lost or never existed. The public records test the historian's skill and knowledge severely, but the keys which skill and competence provide unlock the door to an unexpectedly full knowledge of medieval and early-modern England.

BIBLIOGRAPHY. The main part of the official records are preserved at the Public Record Office in London: they are listed in the *Guide to the Public Records* (2 vols; London 1963). The archives are described in greater detail in hundreds of lists and indexes. Fifty-five of these were printed (now reprinted by the Kraus Reprint Corporation); the List and Index Society (c/o Swift Ltd, 5–9 Dyers Buildings, Holborn, London E.C.1) distributes photographic copies of many more, at the rate of twelve a year, to subscribers only. The P.R.O. also publishes occasional handbooks explaining selected record classes. For all official publications (lists, calendars, etc.), which are published by Her Majesty's Stationery Office, see the current edition of *Record Publications* (Sectional list no. 24). Some of the material is found elsewhere, at the British Museum (for which see the catalogues of the Cotton, Lansdowne, Harleian, Stowe and Royal MSS collections, plus the continuous series of Additional Manuscripts, now catalogued up to 1935),

(a) THE ROYAL SEALS

The nerve centre of the administration in any state lies in its secretarial offices where the decisions of the government are embodied in orders to the executive agents, and where reports are received from the parts of the realm as well as from abroad. In medieval England, the royal secretariates were organised round the royal seals, the instruments with which the Crown authenticated its letters. Of these, the great seal, kept by the chancellor and served by the sizeable staff of Chancery clerks, was both the oldest and the most important; a great many things carried authority only if done under that seal. The privy seal, however, which had acquired a permanent keeper and staff by the early years of the fourteenth century, acted throughout the later middle ages as the seal with the greatest originating power: it was in this office that the instructions were really formulated, while the Chancery commonly acted only upon orders, most of which were sealed with the privy seal. Out of several lesser seals employed in the fourteenth century, the signet, the third royal instrument, emerged in the reign of Richard II. In importance it always remained inferior to the other two, but it was the seal kept at court (by the principal secretary), and in the fifteenth and sixteenth centuries

---

in local County Record Offices (many of which publish lists), and for Wales in the National Library at Aberystwyth. Samples from many classes are in print, often with useful introductions; see the bibliographies listed in the note on p. 13. The records of the Chancery have in part been published by H.M.S.O., usually in the form of 'calendars' or abstracts; for those of the Exchequer, the Pipe Roll Society has made a start. These publications are noted below, in the appropriate place. The difficult legal records are best approached through the publications of the Selden Society (SS) which include volumes of selections from them, with translations and introductions; see the *General Guide to the Society's Publications* (London, Quaritch 1960) which describes the first seventy-nine volumes (1887–1961). A great many public documents were printed by Thomas Rymer, *Foedera, Conventiones, literae et cuiuscunque generis acta publica* . . (best edition: 10 vols, The Hague 1739–45).

it was therefore often used to initiate the King's actions. All the seals did independent work of their own, not connected with each other, but in the commonest use, the disposal of the King's patronage, a chain of command had developed by which the King ordered signet letters to the privy seal which in turn copied these orders in warrants to the great seal. Only the document which then issued out of Chancery gave legal force to the grant made.[1]

In the sixteenth century, one royal secretariate outstripped all others. This was the office of principal secretary, soon called secretary of state, frequently after 1540 shared by two men. Although the secretary commanded the use of the signet, and although signet warrants and letters to other departments controlled a good deal of government under the Tudors, the characteristic development was away from the archaic use of seals altogether and towards replacing them with letters signed by the secretary and other councillors. The seals continued in use, the more so since certain tasks of government could be carried out only through them, but the secretarial work of the seals offices increasingly concentrated on routine duties, while dynamic and original action came to be embodied in the letters we call the State Papers.[2]

The documents produced by this medieval organisation thus record the active work of government throughout three centuries, and they survive in profusion, even if much is also lost. The Chancery, in particular, kept its records very professionally, with much system and care. From the historian's point of view, the great moment came early in the reign of John when the newly appointed chancellor, Hubert Walter, apparently instituted the regular recording of documents passed under the great

[1] For the seals see H. Maxwell-Lyte, *Historical Notes on the Use of the Great Seal in England* (London 1926); T. F. Tout, *Chapters in Medieval Administrative History* (6 vols; Manchester 1920–33); J. Otway-Ruthven, *The King's Secretary and the Signet Office in the XV Century* (Cambridge 1939); G. R. Elton, *The Tudor Revolution in Government* (Cambridge 1953).

[2] Below, 66ff; and see F. M. G. Evans, *The Principal Secretary of State* (Manchester 1923).

seal. The office may before this have kept file copies, but these were easily lost and very few survive. From 1199 the King's letters were regularly transcribed on to parchment rolls, made up of membranes (skins) sown end to end to make up a strip sometimes forty feet long. Soon the mass of matter was seen to be too great to be contained in one series, and separate rolls were introduced for different kinds of documents. The following are the most important classes. 200 Charter Rolls (1199–1516) have copies of the most formal and solemn exercise of the royal bounty.[1] Much more voluminous are the Patent Rolls on which letters patent (issued open, with the great seal hanging from them) were recorded; about 2,900 rolls cover the years 1201–1640.[2] Letters sent folded and sealed are called letters close; these form the main content of approximately 3,300 Close Rolls surviving for the years 1200–1640.[3] The Fine Rolls preserve record of all money payable to the Crown for grants made under the great seal, payments allegedly voluntary but hardly so in practice; 553 rolls fill the years 1199–1648.[4] Orders for payment from the royal coffers, if authorised by the great seal, were enrolled on the 148 Liberate Rolls, extending from 1200 to 1436.[5] Special rolls were kept for matters touching the King's possessions in France (Gascon Rolls, 1254–1468; Norman Rolls, 1200–6 and 1417–32); the Chancery was also responsible for some records of Parliament which shall be mentioned in the proper place. There were many

[1] Printed in full for the reign of John (Record Commission, 1837) and calendared from 1217 to their cessation (6 vols; H.M.S.O. 1903–27).

[2] Printed in full for the years 1202–32 (Record Commission, 1835; 3 vols, H.M.S.O. 1901–3); the calendar, which takes over from there, has so far achieved sixty-seven volumes and the year 1572 (H.M.S.O. 1906–66). For the reign of Henry VIII they are included in the general calendar (see below, 66n).

[3] Printed in full for the years 1204–72 (2 vols, Record Commission, 1833, 1844; 14 Vols, H.M.S.O. 1902–38) and calendared so far to 1509 (48 vols, H.M.S.O. 1892–1963).

[4] Printed in full for the reign of John and in long extracts for that of Henry III (Record Commission, 1835–6); calendared to 1509 (22 vols, H.M.S.O. 1911–62).

[5] Printed in full for 1200–4 (Record Commission, 1844); calendared for the years 1226–72 (6 vols, H.M.S.O. 1917–64).

other, lesser series of this kind. Although some of them ran on well beyond the time of this survey (the Patent Rolls are still kept up, though now in books), it will be seen that others petered out in the decline of medieval government in the late fifteenth century; on the other hand, as late as the reign of Elizabeth the old archival practice was good enough to deal with the consequences of the Reformation when the Dispensations Rolls (recording dispensations and other ecclesiastical documents whose issue was transferred to the Chancery in 1534) were instituted.

These rolls register the output of the Chancery; the other main category of its secretarial archives consists of warrants received by it. These were supposed to be carefully preserved, but a comparison with the rolls shows that many were lost. Even so, 1,796 files of documents survive from 1217 to 1485, and something like 150 bundles of monthly files for the rest of our period. Here are found orders from all the various departments that could authorise the issue of letters under the great seal: warrants under the privy seal and signet, letters under the royal sign manual, petitions to the Crown endorsed for action, orders from the Council, the lord treasurer, officials of the Royal Household, the law officers. Most of them resulted in letters patent and can therefore be found duplicated on the rolls, but many others are known only from these files.

Among the secretarial material of the Chancery two more classes may be included. The Crown could, by great seal commission, order a great many enquiries known as inquisitions, and the returns into Chancery make up another vast collection. The biggest part of these are the inquisitions *post mortem*, taken by an officer called the escheator (one for each county) on the death of a tenant-in-chief in order to establish what he died possessed of and what rights, royal or private, existed. From Henry III's reign to the end of the feudal tenures in 1660 there are 1,874 files of these, or thousands of documents giving invaluable information on individuals and families, not to mention landed property all over the realm. Various other inquisitions add greatly to the possibility of knowing about people not connected with the royal administration, about the state of the law, the rights and activities of corporations (for instance, towns), on such political events as rebellions after which the government might institute an enquiry into the forfeited possessions of defeated opponents. Secondly, the so-called Chancery Miscellanea—in fact an accidental collection deriving from several government departments —contain thousands of documents on details of the medieval administration, the working papers of a very active bureaucracy. They are, naturally, neither systematic nor complete, but it is never safe to suppose that details as various as the strength of a military expedition, the enclosing of some waste lands, or the debts owed by a visiting Italian merchant cannot be known. The Chancery Miscellanea are an untidy muddle in which anything to do with the life of the nation may have left record.

It should also be noted that the records of the Chancery find a complement, very much smaller in size, in those of the lesser Chanceries administering palatinates and franchises: Lancaster, Chester and Durham all provide extensive survivals similar to those already described.

The archives of the lesser seals are very much less massive. They kept no rolls. Indeed, the main part of what we know of the activities of privy seal and signet comes from the files of Chancery warrants which preserve the works of these other clerks. The privy seal itself kept files of warrants received by it, mostly but not exclusively from the signet, but a good deal of these has disappeared. The Signet Office now contains nothing before the year 1584 when the docquet books start, registers of all the documents to which the smallest seal was affixed. One or two earlier such registers survive haphazardly, none before 1540. The activities of the lesser seals have also left record in the archives of the Exchequer because from the fourteenth century this department usually paid money on privy seal warrants, and one may on occasion find originals in local or private depositories. In the main, however, the products of privy seal and signet have suffered severely from the wastage of the years. Since they never kept office copies of out-letters, knowledge of what they did is bound to be markedly unsystematic.

A sketch of this kind can hope to give only a hint of the masses of record material produced by the royal secretariates in these 450 years and still extant. What can the historians gain from it, and in what way are these records either deficient or useless? In the first place, of course, the Chancery rolls provide very extensive information on the disposal of the royal patronage and the exercise of the King's governing power. The Charter and Patent Rolls list the gifts of land, money, offices, ecclesiastical appointments, licences, monopolies and all the other favours which the Crown poured into the ever waiting hands of the ruling classes. The Fine Rolls tell of a few more such grants and add administrative action on behalf of the Crown's fiscal concerns with their lists of writs touching rights over tenants-in-chief, lands forfeited for felony or treason, debts, appointments of local revenue officers. The King's right to demand unpaid service from those on whom he conferred his authority resulted in an endless stream of commissions to selected persons of which the commission of the peace, regular from the end of the fourteenth century, is only the most familiar. These were supposed to be enrolled on the dorse (back) of the Patent Roll, and a great many are, though the Chancery could be negligent in this respect. Royal payments appear on the Liberate Rolls; some part of the royal revenue on the Fine Rolls; but these, of course, are merely ancillary to the main mass of financial records to be discussed in the next section.

Even more informative are the Close Rolls, at least until the emergence of the lesser seals robbed the Chancery of the task of writing and authenticating the King's ordinary letters.[1] While 'open' letters expressed formal exercises of the prerogative and embodied matters to be protected at law (as for instance the passage of Crown lands or offices from hand to hand) the closed letters were letters in the ordinary sense—the King's administra-

[1] From the middle of the fifteenth century, the Close Rolls carried few royal documents; from 1534 there are none. For the non-royal use of the Close Rolls see below, 142.

tive correspondence with his servants, wherever they might be. In the thirteenth and fourteenth centuries, when these documents really do describe the government in action, the most frequent correspondent was the sheriff, followed at a distance by the escheator, so that the control of the counties from the centre appears as the main task of government; but representatives abroad or foreign princes, household officers, treasury officials, and private persons also received letters from the Crown. The contents of the Close Rolls cannot be summarised any more than any busy man's correspondence can; it is a vast mixture. Thus on 2 November 1229 two letters were sent and enrolled. One ordered Roger de Clifford to see to it that the earl marshal got the four wild boars and four wild sows out of the Forest of Dean which the King had given him as a present. The other dealt with the King's grant of the wardship of William of Mulethorpe's heir to Anquetil Mallon: the sheriff of York was ordered to put Anquetil in possession of all William's lands lying within his bailiwick. In September 1230 the sheriff of Staffordshire received a command to suspend the hearing of a plea touching the custody of certain lands because one of the parties required the presence of a man then serving the King overseas. These are totally random examples; anything at all involved in the business of governing England and running the private affairs of a monarch may appear on the Close Roll.

Naturally, this mass of letters provides also an enormous amount of information on people other than the King. Not only can one construct lists of office holders and landowners, or trace quite a few lives through their main stages, but thousands of individuals parade through these parchment membranes. This is information vastly augmented by the inquisitions files: the King's right to hold enquiries at which local men answered searching questions concerning their neighbours has left an immense amount of detailed historical knowledge behind. The knowledge naturally concentrates on the wealthier classes; nothing was so likely to get a man into the record as possession of land. Merchants in a sufficiently large way of business to have engaged in foreign trading are another group to make it. But it would be wrong to think that lesser men do not appear. Even from the secretarial files of the Chancery, the peasantry is not absent, though (as we shall see) there are other records where they turn up more regularly.

However, this mountain of evidence (for one kingdom of perhaps two and a half million people rising to five before the end of our period) is not quite so comprehensive as this description may have made it appear. In the first place, while we have the government's out-letters, we have almost none in return. The archive class called (in despair) Ancient Correspondence, extending in sixty-two volumes of bound manuscripts from Henry II to Henry VII, does contain some, but in the main it, too, provides evidence of government action. Thus we mostly lack documented knowledge of the springs of action: we can learn little of the pressures upon government, the information it received, the conflicting influences behind the steps taken. One side of any correspondence on its own is always a somewhat frustrating thing, and by and large this is what we possess for the King's government in the middle ages.

Furthermore, even this side is by no means complete. It is certain that not every letter under the great seal was enrolled, and it has already been said that of the massive work of the lesser seals only a fraction survives. Letters patent issued on behalf of private persons were enrolled for a fee, and while most people may have been willing to pay in order to get their title deeds into the record, some were not. Enough unenrolled patents survive in warrant files, in private collections, or enrolled in the Exchequer to warn one against overestimating the efficiency of Chancery.[1] Some of the missing documents may be found elsewhere, and grants of the royal bounty in particular stand a good chance of surviving. By the later middle ages, the procedure for making them could involve the grantee's petition, a signet letter, a privy seal

[1] E.g. Twenty-nine patents for the year ending in November 1337, which the Chancery's financial department recorded as having been issued, are not found on the roll (Maxwell-Lyte, *Great Seal*, 363–5).

warrant, the great seal patent, and enrolment, all in identical terms—five possibilities of record. In addition there was the practice of getting old grants confirmed at intervals, especially at the start of a new reign; these new patents, call '*inspeximus et confirmavimus*', recite the original grant in full and thus preserve not only some unenrolled patents first granted after 1199 but also quite a number of documents first issued before enrolment began. But whatever is not on the roll does not survive systematically; we can never know what is missing, a fact which hampers all argument from the absence of such evidence. It is usually taken for granted that matters advantageous to the King were enrolled, but the important commissions are certainly not complete.

As for the Close Rolls, there is really no telling how faithful enrolment was. The documents copied on to them entirely excluded all writs meant to be returned with an answer, because these could be filed (those that survive are not at present accessible) but that is a small matter compared with the irregular exclusion by failure to enrol. Surviving originals are very few indeed, and there is no other place where the letters may be found. However, for the years during which the Chancery acted as the King's real private secretariat we do at least have a very large number of such letters; from about the reign of Edward II onwards, as the lesser seals with their inadequate archives began to take over, knowledge decreases, and in the dead ground of the fifteenth century, between enrolled letters close and Ancient Correspondence on the one hand, and the State Papers on the other, the actions of kings and ministers become markedly less well documented.

Nor can these materials always be taken at their face value. The Patent Rolls were not made up from the finished product; the clerks used the warrant or a draft, and late changes, which can occasionally be shown to have occurred, do not appear in the office copy. There are, of course, clerical errors, double entries, some enrolled documents never actually issued.[1] No clerical

[1] Maxwell-Lyte, *Great Seal*, 359–60.

organisation is perfect, and England's medieval secretariats were more fallible than most. That indolent clerk of the privy seal and barely competent versifier, Thomas Hoccleve, shakes hands across the centuries with successors who find the office as boring and the pub as attractive as he did.[1] Inquisitions *post mortem* are well known to be unreliable. At the enquiries which produced them the King's interest clashed with the heir's, and the jury were under temptation or pressure to minimise the Crown's entitlement. Dates cannot always be trusted. At first the Chancery often transcribed the date of the warrant on to the patent, thereby backdating grants by months. This abuse was remedied by an act of Parliament of 1440 which ordered that the date on the patent should be the day on which the warrant was delivered into Chancery; thereafter, dates on patents are realistic. On the other hand, the privy seal seems to have continued the practice of copying the date from the warrant received, a fact which has bewildered one scholar who found privy seals addressed to Sir Thomas More as chancellor but dated some months before he held that office.[2] On the other hand, the framing of all these documents followed such fixed rules that (if one considers the vast output of the offices) major inaccuracies are very few.

Yet these fixed rules themselves produce the most serious limitation of all this material as historical evidence. These are all

---

[1] He took time off to express his feelings in the midst of his *Regiment of Princes* (c. 1411):

> What man that three and twenty year and more
> In writing hath continued, as have I,
> I dare well say it maketh him full sore
> In every vein and place of his body . . .
> And if it happened on the summer's day
> That I thus at the tavern had be,
> When I depart should and go my way
> Home to the privy seal, so moved me
> Heat and unlust and superfluity
> To walk unto the bridge and take a boat.

[2] H. Schulte Herbrüggen in *The Times Literary Supplement* of 20 January 1966 (48).

formal documents, so much so that the enrolments cut the introductory and concluding formulae to a mere word or two.[1] Nothing whatsoever can be gathered from their phrasing. A signet letter might address itself to the King's trusty and well-beloved cousin, or to someone right trusty and well-beloved, or to someone merely trusty and well-beloved, but these are only formulae, governed by the standing of the addressee: in this case, respectively an earl, a baron, and a commoner. Patents would invariably declare that the King was acting of his own 'mere motion' or for 'certain knowledge' of the grantee's service and goodness. None of this means anything, and, as the Fine Rolls occasionally reveal, the chances are that the King was acting for a substantial consideration. All these documents are essentially impersonal, and this goes also for the so-called private correspondence in letters close or signet letters. It is even hard to know how far these allegedly royal letters represent the King's personal action. Not until the fifteenth century was the sign manual (the royal signature) commonly added to signet letters, and in the reign of Henry VIII routine documents and warrants often received it by means of a stamp. These out-letters of the King's government embody decisions, record action, and preserve innumerable facts of the life of the time, but they tell nothing about personality, motive, or politics. The record is formal and therefore remarkably neutral.

It has to be remembered what purpose these documents were meant to serve. One purpose certainly not in view was the writing of history, and the historian must always remember the limits which this sets to his ability to reconstruct the past. Letters patent were intended to give the recipient proof of title and to the Crown a record of what it had granted—no more, no less. The how and why were of no concern to the Chancery. The administrative orders of the Close Rolls and the lesser seals cover a fairly wide range, but the competence and concerns of medieval

[1] E.g. a patent of Edward III's would open with the words '*Edwardus dei gracia rex Anglie et Francie et dominus Hibernie, omnibus ad quos presentes littere pervenerint, salutem.*' On the roll this would appear as '*Rex omnibus etc.*'

government were relatively limited; large areas of the nation's life hardly came within them. Thus facts of the economy, such as the use of land or the manufacture of cloth, might be touched on, but only if the King's fiscal interest was involved, and often only if some private interest succeeded in mobilising the King's officers. A *post mortem* inquest would try to record with care what lands a man had died possessed of and of whom they were held, interesting information in itself. It was not concerned with the crops grown or improvements made, with the late tenant's family history or even his age at death. If such points do get mentioned, they cannot be regarded as reliable and certainly not as exhaustive.

The records of the seals are very numerous and very informative; above all, they are, in the Chancery at least, very continuous. They tell much about government, about the King's possessions and rights, about the fortunes of lesser men, about the day to day administration of the realm. Even in these respects they are often patchy, and where the King had given away his rights, as in the great palatinates and franchises, knowledge is much reduced. As for many other interesting questions about the people of England of all ranks, this vast accumulation of parchment and paper can tell things to the enquiring mind that the recorder was not even aware he was putting down. But their use is limited by their original purpose, by their formality, and by the deficiencies of survival. Even so, it should by now be clear that the kings of England disposed of a secretarial machine which preserved for posterity an amazing amount of raw material for the recovery of dead lives and past events.

(b) FINANCE

Whatever else governments may do, they collect and spend money, and whatever else they may record, they are most anxious to know where to find money and how they have spent it. The age under consideration was certainly no exception. The main financial office of England's medieval monarchy, the

Exchequer, was also the oldest properly organised department; as early as the reign of Henry II its complex and sophisticated organisation and methods were, happily, described for posterity in a handbook composed by its treasurer.[1] The materials accumulated by it over the centuries are far too large in quantity and too diverse in kind to be described here: the *Guide to the Public Records* devotes sixty-nine pages to what is little more than a list. In addition there is material on the Crown's finances in the Court of Wards, the various palatinate archives, and the Duchy of Lancaster. The mass is so enormous that research on it will never end; the information is so multifarious that nothing, one feels, that happened in the realm could possibly have escaped record; the technical difficulties are such that very few scholars have ever mastered more than a part of these sources; and compared with the Chancery, very little has so far been done to make the records accessible in print.[2]

However, the historian might as well react with gratitude rather than despair to this massive supply of working materials, and if he values the result he will be well advised to acquire a systematic knowledge of what he may expect to find there. Despite all their variety, the records can be usefully divided into two categories: accounts of revenue, and documents subsidiary to the accounts. The second group again divides into materials directly connected with the keeping of accounts, and materials more casually collected either as aids in administering the finances or as by-products of the accounting process. All of them tell

[1] Another volume in this series considers Richard Fitz-Neal's 'Dialogue of the Exchequer' (see C. Johnson's edition, with a translation, in Nelson's Medieval Classics).

[2] For financial administration see the works of Tout and Elton cited above (p. 35); also J. Willard and W. A. Morris, *The English Government at Work 1327–1336*, vol I (Cambridge, Mass. 1940); S. K. Mitchell, *Taxation in Medieval England* (New Haven 1951); A. Steel, *The Receipt of the Exchequer 1377–1485* (Cambridge 1954); W. C. Richardson, *Tudor Chamber Administration* and *History of the Court of Augmentations* (Baton Rouge 1952, 1961). F. C. Dietz, *English Government Finance 1485–1558* (University of Illinois 1920) and *English Public Finance 1558–1642* (New York 1932) contain much of value but also very many errors and misunderstandings.

much; all of them pose serious problems of which the least result from deficiencies of survival or inefficiency in record keeping. The worst obstacles to understanding are built into them by the business methods of the department.

The Exchequer consisted of two departments. The Lower Exchequer (or Exchequer of Receipt) was responsible for the collecting, storing and dispensing of the revenue; it kept rolls of receipts and issues in which its activities were written up. The Upper Exchequer, or Exchequer of Account, audited the accounts of receivers of revenue and acquitted those charged with receiving the King's money. Its rolls are many and majestic.[1] The oldest master record of all was the great roll of the Exchequer or Pipe Roll, continuous from 1155 to the abolition of the office in 1833, which at first dealt with all the King's money.[2] From about 1300 onwards, the bulk of the Pipe became so large that the so-called foreign accounts (those rendered by anybody except the sheriffs) were gradually split off into separate rolls, such as customs accounts, accounts of subsidies (direct taxation), accounts of the butlerage (duties on wine) or the Royal Household; the re-organisation was completed in 1323–6, and from 1368 there is an annual roll of foreign accounts, accompanied by special series for separate items. Further changes in the Exchequer's revenues and machinery produced from 1550 onwards (isolated examples survive for the previous fifty years) a new series called Declared Accounts; these differed in book-keeping practice and are more easily understood, but they provide a similar detailed picture of Crown finance. Masses of accounting documents, subsidiary to the final statements, survive in a class called, despairingly, 'Accounts, Various'; it took a folio volume of 351 pages to list the main bulk of them. There are numberless files

[1] In the Upper Exchequer (and the law courts) rolls were made up by laying membranes (rotulets) on top of each other and sewing them together at the head; they were then folded rather than rolled up.

[2] About 480 pipe rolls survive for the period down to 1640; of these the Pipe Roll Society has so far (in eighty years: 1884–1964) published seventy-five, covering the years 1155–1216. That for 1189 was published in facsimile by the Record Commission.

of writs for payments, and archives of papers produced by in-
vestigations. Add to this that Exchequer practice often involved
the keeping of duplicate rolls by officers supposed to control one
another, and it would indeed seem that these records make possible a complete and relatively easy account of the Crown's revenue
and expenditure, of the basic financial problems of government.

Yet no one has yet composed the obvious tables, for these rolls
need to be analysed and recast before such questions can be
answered. The rolls of the Lower Exchequer are not, despite their
names, simple statements of receipts and issues. Rather they were
meant to be registers of tallies, those notched wooden sticks which
the Exchequer used in lieu of receipts and upon the keeping and
matching of which the whole accounting process turned. They
were supposed to be issued when money was paid in and produced
as proof of payment when the account was audited, but the process
was nothing like so simple. Tallies could be used as credit instruments, in which case their issue represented an anticipation
of revenue yet to be received, but if that revenue never material-
ised (a common enough occurrence) creditors received new tallies,
a practice which resulted in duplicated book-keeping entries on
both sets of rolls.[1] The clerks of the Receipt never totalled their
rolls: they knew well that such totals had no meaning. The
modern scholar wanting to know what came in and what went
out finds himself frustrated at the very point where he would
have expected success.

Nor are the rolls of the Upper Exchequer easily used to establish the Crown's balance-sheet. The auditing methods of the
Exchequer arose from the nature of Crown revenues. The main
part of these were thought of as 'certain' or fixed, and so far as
they were concerned the Exchequer's interest therefore concentrated on getting in known and expected items of revenue. The
result was a method of book-keeping called 'charge and dis-
charge': the question put to the accounting officer was not 'what
did you collect and what did you spend?' but 'what happened to
the following sums of money which you are supposed to collect?'

[1] For these complications see Steel, *Receipt of the Exchequer*.

Each year, the clerks effectively copied out an established list of charges for a given account, in a document prepared before the audit;[1] to the resulting series of questions, item by item, the accountant would reply by producing tallies (proof of delivery into the Receipt), by claiming 'allowance' (cancellation of the item because payment out had been authorised in advance or because the source had ceased to exist), or by a regretful shrug of his shoulders. If he did the first or second, the item was 'discharged'; the rest stood to his charge for ever until he could produce it. These unreceived moneys—technically debts owed to the Crown by the accountant, not by the ultimate payer of due or tax—appeared on the charge of subsequent accounts as 'arrears' and were added annually as though freshly occurring, a practice which greatly swelled apparent totals. Furthermore, audits commonly closed years after the event, so that the apparent completeness of the transaction entirely disguises the fact that the year's money was never available at the actual time, and the technicalities of the process led to all sorts of technicalities on the rolls which must be fully understood before the record yields correct answers to sensible questions.

The existence of these 'debts' (outstanding items) led to the creation of two further record-keeping departments, the offices of the king's and lord treasurer's remembrancers with their separate series of Memoranda Rolls.[2] These documents may be said to record unfinished business transacted in the department: such matters, that is, as would continue to affect later business. In their early days they consist in the main of orders made by the presiding officers, the barons of the Exchequer, in the course of passing the accounts;[3] later the bulk of these rolls is filled with

[1] For 'uncertain' (irregular) revenues, the charge was made up on the basis of certificates prepared elsewhere in the Exchequer.

[2] About 480 king's remembrancer's Memoranda Rolls cover the years 1216–1640; *c.* 650 treasurer's remembrancer's rolls the years 1216–1640. Those for 1199–1209 were published by the Pipe Roll Society (1943, 1957); the first volume contains an important account of Exchequer records by H. G. Richardson.

[3] E.g. in the Michaelmas Term of 1230 one finds orders to sheriffs to put off

cases at law in which the King's financial interest was involved. However, since their main purpose was to remind the Exchequer of outstanding business, their contents are miscellaneous and illumine all sorts of matters connected with the revenues. They are vital to any analysis of what went on, but they are also exceptionally difficult to use.

For establishing what happened to the King's revenues the master records are thus only a start; they need informed analysis, and they need to be helped by the many subsidiary documents. Lesser or partial accounts, writs and warrant for payment, receipt bills issued by the tellers (responsible for the cash) and records kept by them and their co-ordinating officer (auditor of the Receipt) can all be used to work out the royal finances, though the important tellers' records become available only from the reign of Henry VII. Such documents are in any case much less well preserved, with more gaps than coverage. There are lucid moments. From 1504 to 1552, the Exchequer made annual and quite straightforward declarations of income and expenditure; it is unfortunate that this period coincides with the time when the Exchequer was eclipsed by other revenue departments. From the reign of Elizabeth onwards, half-yearly declarations were compiled by two separate officers in the Receipt; the series are incomplete. The new 'Declared Accounts' for revenue not collected by sheriffs, which begin properly about 1550, were kept on more rational book-keeping principles and do give totals (often wrongly added up and still including the misleading 'arrears'). But while the sixteenth century yields a novel mass of various records, it also displays much confusion; the old master records are more patchy and less meaningful than ever, the new ones emerge only gradually and are not clear-cut before the reign of James I. The state of the records reflects the history of government: in this case, that administrative revolution which replaced the personal royal government of the middle ages by the depart-

payments, a writ summoning a jury to determine a dispute over lands claimed by the Crown, a note that defendants had arrived with evidence in a case, orders to pay arrears, and so on.

mental administration characteristic of subsequent centuries.[1]

Above all, it should be noted that even if we had all the records of the Exchequer and the other established departments, and understood them aright, we should often still be some way from knowing such fundamental things as the total income and expenditure of the Crown. This is because throughout the middle ages and down to about 1536 important parts of the King's revenue never passed through the Exchequer but were handled in departments of the Royal Household, in the Wardrobe down to 1307 and later at times in the Chamber. Chamber administration of a virtually unrecorded kind was especially characteristic of the years of monarchical recovery (about 1470–1530).[2] While earlier medieval Household methods of this kind left some deposit in the records of the Exchequer, the methods employed by the Yorkists and early Tudors left none; the story has had to be reconstructed, with some uncertainty and much controversy, from records which are neither systematic nor complete. In the 1530's, the organisation of new courts, mostly short-lived, improved matters; the revenues taken from the Church by Henry VIII are well documented in the archives of the Courts of First Fruits and Augmentations, whereas darkness attends upon the Crown lands, administered till 1542 in an insufficiently organised department.[3]

Thus, despite the abundance of materials, despite the care with which the governments of these centuries went after their revenues, tried to prevent corruption, and endeavoured to control expenditure, the history of the royal finances—with all that this involves for policy, resources, general activity, and the general history of the country—remains essentially incomplete.

However, this should not hide the fact that the amount of historical knowledge provided by the records of financial administration is enormous, very varied, and in many cases systematic

[1] See my *Tudor Revolution in Government*.

[2] See especially Tout, Elton and Richardson (above, 46, n. 2); also B. P. Wolfe in *English Historical Review* 1956 and 1964. Richardson's book on *Chamber Administration* contains a valuable analysis of the sources.

[3] W. C. Richardson's *History of the Court of Augmentations* contains a useful analysis of those massive departmental archives.

enough. In the first place, of course, the material makes possible an extensive understanding of Crown finance, though we shall always be better informed about the what than the why. Direct evidence for financial policy is rare. Next, the Exchequer records provide much evidence for economic history, as for instance a great many price data. The customs accounts are vital to the history of trade, though that of industrial production profits little from documents which record only what passed through the ports— mostly exports, some imports. Quite apart from the tiresome and insoluble problem of smuggling, internal trade in manufactured goods escapes the net. But reliable statistics of exports can be constructed.[1] The fact that the Crown was the largest landowner makes its financial records most useful in any study of agriculture, rural society and estate management; there is still an enormous amount to learn about this. It is likely that governments touched more people as collectors of revenue than in any other capacity; hence names, and sometimes details, survive for tens of thousands, though nearly always not very far down the social scale. The by-products of financial activity can be particularly revealing. Thus, because the Crown had a profound interest in lands held in feudal tenure (on which heavy death duties were payable) we possess an Exchequer series of inquisitions *post mortem*, supplementing those preserved in the Chancery. During its existence (1540–1643) the Court of Wards gives a very full account of the landed classes, and—since its 'livery books' recorded the inheritance of all land held in knight's service—not only on condition that a man's heirs entered their inheritance still minors.

By the side of the systematic records produced by administrative process, one finds the casual and unpredictable. Collections of precedents and of office memoranda, such as the Red and Black Books of the Exchequer,[2] contain, among other things, admissions

[1] E.g. the splendid tables of *England's Export Trade 1275–1547* compiled by E. M. Carus-Wilson and Olive Coleman (Oxford 1963).

[2] Named after the leather in which they were bound. The Red Book was edited by H. Hall in the Rolls Series (3 vols, 1896); the Black Book edited by Thomas Hearne (Oxford 1728) is not the record now so described at the Public Record Office.

to office of departmental officers, aids to dating, casual poems and drawings, transcripts of charters, information concerning feudal rights and tenures. In the sixteenth century, some of the office papers of lesser officials survive. As long as one is looking for something that in any way touches the King's fiscal rights and interests—and that includes a very large part of the nation's life— it is unsafe to assume that no information exists in these multi-tudinous records. To cite a last example: that ancient record office, the Treasury of the Receipt, preserves among other things 284 miscellaneous volumes of books. Of course they include a preponderance of financial papers (which themselves range very widely) but also such things as the renunciation of the papal supremacy signed by all the clergy of England in 1534 or a fourteenth-century register of papal bulls. Most of what we know of the Elizabethan stage comes from the papers of a Household department, the Office of Revels, preserved in the Exchequer. What H. G. Richardson says about an earlier period—'In the records of the Angevin kings . . . there are few aspects of medieval life that are not in some measure illuminated'—is truer still of later times. The history of the people of England, high and low though more the relatively high, is deposited in the materials arising from the efforts of her kings to finance their governments.

Nevertheless, let us end on a note of caution. This seeming universality has its limits. Those who were of no fiscal interest to the Crown—the landless, the vagrants, most women, most children—do not appear; the record grows manifestly fuller as one works upwards through the social scale. And studies demand-ing systematic records are usually handicapped, either by loss of evidence or, more seriously, by the fact that the ages in question were not interested in the statistics which the modern historian wishes to extract. I have already noted this with respect to in-dustry and trade; the point is even more important when historians are tempted by the survival of tax records to attempt population studies. Now and again, there may be some firm ground; but the slightest incautious step will send the investigator into the morass, to disappear with bubbles of conjecture as sole reminders that once there was here an historian.

(c) COURTS OF LAW

To the King, government meant the exercise of power and the conduct of policy; from his point of view, secretarial and financial records loomed largest. To the subject, however, the main purpose of government was to maintain order and protect rights: litigation and the obtaining of justice provided that contact with the King's officers which he desired. In this period, all institutions of government were, in fact, liable to be thought of as designed to arbitrate in disputes, as courts of law. Suits at law absolutely require the keeping of an artificial memory—a case must be recorded while it proceeds—and a system in which law grows through precedent demands that decisions and arguments be preserved. In addition, the King's monopoly of justice, essentially complete by the beginning of our period, offered a consistently profitable source of revenue. It is thus no wonder that the records of his justice exceed in bulk even the records of his Chancery. They also pose many difficult technical problems. Quantity and difficulty account for the fact that they remain very inadequately exploited by historians.

One obvious distinction among the King's courts is between those sitting at the centre of government, at Westminster, with a jurisdiction covering the whole realm,[1] and those held in a locality and competent for a limited area. The latter may again be subdivided into permanent courts set up for special regions, regular courts created by royal commission, and occasional courts.[2]

The central courts included the courts first developed out of the original all-embracing royal court (*curia regis*) of the twelfth

---

[1] Until 1536 local 'franchises' (areas of special privilege) could sometimes exclude the central courts, but in general the King's writ ran everywhere.

[2] The best concise description of the courts is found in W. S. Holdsworth, *History of English Law*, vol. 1 (7th ed, London 1956).

century—Common Pleas and King's Bench—as well as the Exchequer in its judicial capacity which had moved out of the *curia* by the reign of Henry I at the latest. They further include the courts later produced by the justice-dispensing power of the King's Council, remaining there after those regular courts had achieved institutional independence: Parliament (in the reign of Edward I), Chancery, Star Chamber and Requests. Lastly, they include the financial departments created by statute in the sixteenth century (Augmentations, First Fruits, Wards) all of which were much engaged in hearing litigation arising out of the revenues in their charge.[1]

The permanent local courts were the franchisal courts of Durham, Lancaster, Chester and Wales. To these the Tudors added the Councils of the North and of the Marches of Wales, local counterparts to central conciliar jurisdiction. Of permanent local commissions that of the peace must take pride of place, but the work of the coroner, reduced in the fourteenth century by the justices of the peace from an earlier wide competence, should not be forgotten. Occasional courts, many of them frequent enough to be thought of as almost regular, were created by special instructions. The judges of the central courts travelled the country out of term to settle disputes and enforce the law (general eyres, commissions of assize), and the criminal jurisdiction of the justices of the peace was subordinated to the work of special commissions of gaol delivery and of oyer and terminer which conferred the full power of the King's courts to punish felons and traitors.

These lists are long enough, though not exhaustive, and all these courts have left some memory in the record.[2] From the

---

[1] For Star Chamber and Requests, and all sixteenth-century courts, see G. R. Elton, *The Tudor Constitution* (Cambridge 1960).

[2] Outside the ordinary system, there stood some specialised courts in which the law administered was essentially the Roman (civil) law of the continent and whose practitioners were doctors of law, called civilians: the high courts of Admiralty and of Chivalry. Both of them have a medieval history but virtually no medieval records; both of them were fully organised only from the later seventeenth century; and in consequence both of them are here

point of view of historical sources, these institutions are best divided into those which used the common law methods of trial (procedure by writ) and those which employed the less formal procedure by complaint or bill. This is not a distinction to be made with perfect simplicity, if only because the same court sometimes used both methods, nor is it a very important distinction from the point of view of legal history because all these courts administered essentially one body of law, the changing, growing, uncertain body of the common law. But it is a very important distinction if one is to discover what the records of justice reveal to the historian and what their deficiencies may hide.

On the one side stand the common-law courts proper, distinguished by the fact that they kept plea rolls—rolls, that is, on which the daily business of the courts was entered as of record (capable of being cited as a lawful precedent in another case or in another court). The number of such rolls is staggering. There are 226 in the undifferentiated *curia regis* (1193–1270), 1,657 in King's Bench (1272–1640), 2,456 in Common Pleas (1235–1640), 573 in the Exchequer of Pleas (1235–1640). Apart from these massive collections, one finds lesser items like the 48 rolls of the Exchequer of the Jews (1218–87) or the 28 of the Court of the King's Household (1282–1400). The palatinate courts are less well served, but even so 38 judgment rolls survive for the Bishopric of Durham between 1504 and 1537, and 363 plea rolls in the archives of the County of Lancaster between 1400 and 1540. A great quantity, difficult to add up because of their variety and patchiness, record court business in Chester and Wales. The activities of central jurisdiction in the localities yield over 1,200 various rolls of general eyres, assizes and courts of trailbaston (crimes and trespasses), 267 coroners' rolls, and 802 rolls and files for sessions of gaol delivery, but all this material, which mostly begins about the middle of the thirteenth century, ceases by about 1480. On the other hand, the records of the courts held by justices of the peace (quarter sessions) begin patchily after 1540; though ignored. It should, however, be noted that the Admiralty produced records which throw much light on maritime and colonial history after 1524.

more carefully preserved from the reign of Elizabeth onwards, they are never very complete in the era here considered. Unlike all the rest listed, they are entry books, not plea rolls, and are found locally, now usually in County Record Offices.

Plea rolls and rolls supplementary to them do not exhaust the records of the medieval and early-modern courts of common law. For example, the King's Bench preserved also something like 100 bundles of indictments taken and tried elsewhere but returned into the court (Ancient Indictments); these include the well-known state trials of the sixteenth and seventeenth centuries. In Common Pleas we find that vast depository of knowledge, the documents known as fines or final concords, records of agreements concluded between parties and blessed by the court.[1] A number of lesser series start in the reign of Elizabeth, to remind us of the reorganisation which took place under the Tudors. In addition, there are preserved in hundreds of sacks, unlisted and unsorted and at present effectively inaccessible, thousands of writs sent out by the courts in the course of actions and returned with replies and endorsements which, if they could be used, would greatly amplify and deepen the knowledge to be derived from the plea rolls.

On the other side stand the courts which did not keep plea rolls because they did not try actions started by writ but, borrowing from the practice of the Church courts, offered ostensibly no more than to hear complaints brought by petition (bill) and arbitrate equitably between the parties.[2] Though the original informality of these courts (Chancery [as a court], Star Chamber and Requests) quickly gave way to relative precision and formal rigour, their record-keeping never followed suit. In none of them are the archives very satisfactory, but that does not mean that they are not large. Procedure involved two stages: the exchange of written charges and denials between the parties (followed up by examining witnesses upon written interrogatories) which

---

[1] See below, 143f.

[2] The Exchequer of Pleas kept plea rolls, though actions were there started by bills.

were produced by the parties and put into court, and records of decisions taken which were produced by the court itself. The former are known as proceedings, and they compose the bulk of the surviving material. In the Chancery, something like 4,000 bundles survive from the late fourteenth century to 1640; 1,397 volumes and bundles account for Star Chamber (1485–1640: but very few before *c.* 1515 and hardly any after 1625); Requests is content with 829 bundles for the same period. Each of these bundles contains between 150 and 300 case files. On the other hand, the court's own records of their doings are much less well preserved. In Star Chamber the books of orders and decrees, which were once kept, have completely disappeared; in Requests, there survive 210 various books mostly from the reign of Elizabeth onwards. The oldest of the three courts, Chancery, was curiously enough slower to adopt this kind of record: only from 1534 did it begin to enrol its decisions (decrees) and only from 1544 did it initiate a series of books in which orders made in cases were entered day by day.

This very inadequate account, confined to the main items in the archives, will give some indication of the quantity of information obtainable from the records of the King's courts. However, two problems arise. These records are naturally, since they deal with the law, exceptionally technical; even less than other government archives can they be understood without help and training. And secondly, in part because they are technical, in part because they do not always form continuous series, and in part because they have a special built-in bias, the question what they can and cannot tell requires careful consideration.

The records are technical in part because all law is technical; they can be understood only if the law behind them is understood, though in turn much law can be learned only from them. In this context, however, this is a marginal problem; it matters more that they are technical and shaped by formality in themselves for which reason they hide a good deal that one would like to know. Though the plea rolls of the common-law courts contain at first much casual informality, from about 1350 at the latest they are fixed in rigid form. By then they have in effect become registers of the essential procedure of the medieval common law which centred upon the issue of writs and process. They effectively record only the regular sequence of instruments under which actions were started (original writs) and the trial of cases was conducted (process out of court). In the Exchequer, these stages (which might or might not come to a final conclusion) were at least entered consecutively, in one place, for every suit, no matter for how many years it might drag on; in Common Pleas and King's Bench the business was written up day by day, so that one has great difficulty in tracking the history of a given case through the rolls. All entries follow common form and tell almost nothing of the personal or individual facts behind a case: one will be told the names of the parties and usually their employment or status, and one is likely to discover the cause alleged in dispute, but that is all. The plea rolls were not meant to be law reports but registers of the court's action in the history of a litigated case (which means that if the case was compromised, the record might simply cease in the middle of nowhere), and it is therefore pointless to expect from them details of either fact or law as they emerged in the course of litigation. Private evidence for such things can occasionally be found,[1] but not in the records of these courts.

A similar formality hides much knowledge concerning the Crown's criminal jurisdiction. Once process by indictment or presentment (nearly identical) had become virtually universal— again, from about the middle of the fourteenth century—and once it had become established that an indictment could be defeated by finding technical fault with it, these instruments became of necessity absolutely formal, alleging offences in identical terms and hiding whatever peculiarities a case might have. Every felon did this or that contrary to the peace of the lord King and the statutes in such cases made and provided; all we are told is what indictable crime he has committed, not how or why or in what circumstances, and if it is decided that an alleged murder was self-defence the chances are that we know this only

[1] See below, 169ff.

because a pardon has survived on the Patent Roll. The record for a successful trial for treason, murder, rape or such like is always briefest where it is most intersting: at the stage of trial in court. We get long lists of indicting juries, accounts of arraignment procedures, and much to show the difficulties involved in bringing trial juries into court, but where the case becomes real it will say no more than this: the accused put himself upon the country (asked to be tried by jury), the jury were summoned (and came, sometimes after several attempts), they found him guilty, he has no chattels (that is, nothing accrued to the Crown by way of forfeiture), he was sentenced to be hanged. Or, of course, the jury found him not guilty and he was dismissed. What was alleged or argued or proved, or how it was done, cannot be discovered. We know that by the fifteenth century at the latest witnesses commonly appeared to testify, but of this there is nothing in the records of the court. These provide no more than the merest bones of the case, but they provide them in ordered and complete sequence.

In theory, at least, the less formal archives of the other type of court ought to supply more specific detail and inside information, and as a rule they do. The bills which initiated action in Chancery, Star Chamber and Requests had to follow certain formal rules, but the complainant was left free to elaborate the details of his grievance. Thus we get extraneous matters, histories of disputes, personal data, vivid description of events, recorded speech—a great deal of specific if necessarily unsystematic information. One difficulty arises from the fact that these proceedings are often very hard to date; I have not been able to establish approximate dates for more than half of the Star Chamber cases in the reign of Henry VIII (that is, out of perhaps 5,000). Besides, formality imposed its limitations on these records, too. Thus after the first exchange of bill and answer, nothing new was as a rule introduced in the further documents, and such restraint was obligatory from the reign of Elizabeth onwards. Witnesses' depositions must not be treated as though they gave the sort of information one expects to find in the transcript of a modern trial, and this is not because those people were fools but because procedure imposed conditions. In these courts, witnesses did not appear before the judges to be examined and cross-examined. Their testimony was taken privately and in writing, in answer to prepared interrogatories supplied by the contending parties who also named the persons to be examined. Combined with a tendency to turn speech into the set forms employed by the examining clerks, this reduces, though it does not abolish, the lifelike quality of their statements and certainly restricts the range of the information they supply. Common form appears also in the rest of these seemingly casual documents, whether in the conventional self-abasement of complainants seeking the court's aid in their destitute or permanently damaged state, or in the regular allegations of violence and riot required, for instance, to give the Star Chamber jurisdiction in the cases in which no such events may have taken place at all. It is the essence of all settled jurisdiction that it should adopt standard procedures and regular forms in order to give coherence, continuity and certainty to its working, and medieval courts and lawyers paid a great deal more attention to the precision of procedural detail than to the human details of a case. At any rate their records did, and while casual evidence here and there may show that circumstance and the particular were not always ignored, this is well hidden in the formal records which survive in such quantity.

All this limits the amount of knowledge one may gain beyond the mere fact that litigation was engaged in, or that a crime was committed and punished. The student must certainly remember the formality of his information, though learning and understanding will enable him to extract the maximum of real knowledge from the common phrases of rolls and proceedings. What he cannot overcome are the gaps in the record, and these are large. In even the most continuous series of rolls—those of the central courts at Westminster—some are missing. Much worse are the deficiencies of the records produced away from the centre. When the general eyre ceased in about the middle of the fourteenth century, the historian lost a most valuable source of information on everything that went on in the shires—civil and criminal cases as well as general administration. We have seen that the assize and gaol delivery rolls, on which our knowledge of local events in great part depends, peter out in the reign of Edward IV, and even before that they were not kept very conscientiously. Since it was a rule of the common law that crimes must be tried in the shire in which they were committed, the central records cannot supply these gaps, and though in due course quarter session records came to replace the medieval rolls, it has already been remarked that in our period they nowhere survive complete.

It is therefore to be noted that the difficulties of knowing about crime and law-enforcement are greater in the sixteenth century than the thirteenth; in the Tudor period it is difficult to speak with confidence even about so drastic an offence as treason. Though an act of 1542 ordered the standing and special commissions which handled most of this work to report their activities to the King's Bench, it seems to have been entirely ignored, and almost the only cases which came to that court (and therefore have survived in the record) were those in which the accused escaped because he had obtained a pardon or could prove a technical deficiency in his trial. The Tudor rolls of King's Bench, at least their criminal sections, are not records of law-enforcement but virtually records of acquittals, and a fact of this kind can be understood only against the background of our knowledge that they were bound to be so. What actually went on in criminal trials all over the country is in great measure lost.

As serious in their own way are the physical deficiencies of the records preserved by the conciliar type of court. This is in part because the word 'preserved' can be a trifle relative. As has been said, the archives of these courts consist of proceedings and entry books (or their equivalent). The proceedings carried no validity as records in the technical sense of being citable in any court as precedents or record of action taken. Once the case was over, they therefore ceased to be of interest, and in consequence they were very poorly kept. Before the reign of Edward VI, the proceedings of Star Chamber and Requests are in a sorry state, with few complete files and the documents of a single case often scattered among the bundles. Even thereafter the files often enough lack some part of what should be there. Things are a little better in the Chancery, but not much. Thus the proceedings often provide only a glimpse—perhaps only a set of interrogatories or merely a defendant's formal answer. Worse, there is absolutely no telling what proportion of them may be completely lost; at best they enable us to calculate the minimum number of suits brought into court, never the total. Other evidence of a haphazard kind, found here and there, makes sure of this. Thus we know for certain that the 194 cases in Star Chamber preserved for the reign of Henry VII represent a small part of what ought to be there and presumably once existed, nor is there any reason to think that the decline from 312 bundles for the reign of James I to one for that of his son reflects anything except different habits of preservation. The court remained extremely active down to 1640.[1]

One would feel less aggrieved by these insufficiencies if the 'real' records, the entry books, were continuous and well kept. Unfortunately only the Court of Requests possesses anything like a reasonable series. In the Chancery, as has been said, the daily record of doings begins in 1544, and though enrolment of final decrees started ten years earlier such enrolment was at the party's pleasure and unquestionably not regular. Yet the chancellor had been issuing judicial decrees to a stream of litigants for at least a century before this date. Worst off of all is Star Chamber whose books disappeared altogether in the Civil War. Except for a small number of entries for the years 1485–1543, transcribed in the reign of Elizabeth,[2] or for the occasional lucky find of an original decree as issued (or the draft for one), we have no primary evidence at all concerning this court's decisions, a sobering thought in the face of the many confident things said about its

[1] Cf. H. E. I. Phillips, 'The last years of the Court of Star Chamber 1630–1641', *Transactions of the Royal Historical Society*, 1938, 103ff.
[2] For these see below, 77.

effectiveness, scope and viciousness.[1] Thus in all these courts it is extremely difficult to discover what finally happened in cases of which often a great deal is otherwise known: in Star Chamber it is impossible, in Chancery rarely possible before the middle of the sixteenth century, in Requests it involves a laborious comparing of entry books and patchy proceedings for which success cannot be guaranteed. Perhaps the biggest difference between the common-law courts and the rest lies in this curious consequence of their record-keeping habits: in cases at common law we rarely know more than the first cause and the final outcome, in cases heard equitably we can usually know a great deal except the final outcome.

All that has been said applies with equal or greater force to the records of inferior jurisdictions, though the Tudor revenue courts are well supplied with both proceedings and order books.[2] But at this point it is necessary to arrest despair. The limitations of these judical records are severe and at times very frustrating, but their possibilities are vastly greater. In the first place, of course, they make possible a very full knowledge of English law and legal administration, but it is even more significant that for all these 450 years we possess massive evidence concerning the doings and fortunes of innumerable people of all social classes—a veritable cross-section of the nation. Men of great account and none, and (even more unusual) many women too, have left memory of their lives in these enormous deposits. Even more than the records of Chancery and Exchequer, those of the law courts make it very unsafe to assume that any given fact of the history of England and her people is certainly lost. It may well be lost, but sufficient possibility of survival exists to compel the necessary and very

---

[1] All conventional notions about Star Chamber derive from the comments of contemporaries and the race-memory of a few political cases heard in the reign of Charles I. For a summary of sounder knowledge see my *Tudor Constitution*, 158ff.

[2] The records of the short-lived Courts of Augmentations and First Fruits are preserved in the Exchequer; see Richardson on Augmentations (above, 51, n.3). For the Court of Wards, see H. E. Bell, *An Introduction to the History and Records of the Court of Wards and Liveries* (Cambridge 1953).

laborious search. All questions concerning property, rights, debts, trespasses and crimes, common opinion and common behaviour, relations between neighbours, commercial enterprise, the fortunes of families and individuals, the daily lives of peasants and artisans and gentlemen, *may* receive some sort of answer in these archives. The state of the records assures that the likelihood and the fullness of the answers vary at different times. Down to about 1350, the evidence is less massive but, being relatively informal, more revealing. Thereafter the real detail—biographical, genealogical, social—is more likely to be found in the archives of the equity courts where it can become very full and exceptionally lively.[1] The problems of public peace are worst documented in the fifteenth and early sixteenth centuries. But at all times much may be discovered to describe the history of this society in real depth.

One last reservation must nevertheless be made. The people who emerge from these records are pre-selected, for we can learn only about those who engaged in private litigation, were sued by the Crown for the securing of its fiscal rights, or fell foul of the criminal law. How serious this undoubted limitation may be it is very hard to say. Obviously, any history which relies heavily on police records is likely to distort reality; obviously, those without property of any kind are unlikely to appear in the evidence of civil cases. Yet (if one may speak from personal impressions) it would seem that for the age under review these points matter less than one might have supposed—much less than they would matter if only court records survived for the twentieth century. The men who appear in the records of crime include not only the criminals, but also those falsely accused; not only murderers but casual rioters and disturbers of the peace; they include suicides and abettors, informers and witnesses. The range is large. As for civil litigation, perhaps the very poor and landless do not turn up at all, though in the eyre and quarter sessions, in Chancery and Requests, the peasantry do manifestly put in frequent appearances. In general, the volume of these records, setting down the

[1] See, e.g. G. R. Elton, *Star Chamber Stories* (London 1958).

doings of a small enough population, suggests vividly that not many people in England totally escaped contact with the courts and therefore preservation in aspic for the information of later generations.

(*d*) STATE PAPERS

In the strictly technical sense, the class of documents known as State Papers are the office archives of the secretaries of state. That office did not exist before the sixteenth century, and indeed the archive (State Paper Office) was not created until the reign of James I when partially successful efforts were made to collect the materials of the previous reign at least. At present, the series called by this name begins in 1509; from 1547 it is divided into domestic and foreign sections, and from 1577 the foreign part is classified under the countries to which the correspondence refers. To the same class belong papers dealing with the Americas, now placed in the Colonial Office archives; these start in 1574. The quantity of the material is, once again, large, and a great deal has been made more accessible through calendars which print abstracts of varying soundness and length.

The quantity increases rapidly as one advances through the sixteenth century. The papers of Henry VIII's reign are relatively primitive; there is no division into foreign and domestic correspondence, and the archives really exist only because certain collections were acquired from individuals (especially the papers of Thomas Cromwell, confiscated at his fall) or later made up out of other deposits (as for instance such reflections of historians' interest in the Reformation as the so-called Suppression Papers and the Theological Tracts, both artificial collections). Even so, there are altogether 304 MS volumes for the reign, well calendared in a production which includes materials from other archives, a practice fortunately not followed by the later calendars.[1] The State Papers Domestic for 1547–1640 fill over 1,100 MS

[1] *Letters and Papers, Foreign and Domestic, of the Reign of Henry VIII*, ed. J. S. Brewer, J. Gairdner, R. H. Brodie (H.M.S.O. 1862–1932): 21 vols in 37 parts.

volumes, calendared in 36 printed ones; some of these last give mere lists. The foreign series is much more massive still: for the forty years before classification by countries there are 176 MS volumes, after which the variety becomes too large to make counting possible. The calendaring of this series (so far 29 volumes) has reached only to 1590. The colonial material is at this time less extensive; this archive got really going after 1660. Poised between the domestic and foreign series are the collections devoted to Ireland (*c.* 260 volumes) and Scotland (151 volumes), both calendared for part of the total; this last class includes 42 volumes concerning the administration of the northern border in the reign of Elizabeth and 23 relating to Mary Queen of Scots during her imprisonment in England.

Even this does not exhaust the mass of this very important material. The Public Record Office itself has been collecting similar papers from other parts of its archives and making artificial classes of State Papers Additional; this underlines that the technical meaning of the class name is much too narrow at this early date in the history of the secretaries of state. For a very long time it proved impossible to prevent retiring secretaries from taking their papers with them, and it is, for instance, purely an accident that Cromwell's papers are in the official archive while most of Burghley's are in the British Museum and most of Robert Cecil's at Hatfield. In origin, purpose and significance all these collections are identical. However, papers still in private hands will here be treated as private papers,[1] though the student should be aware of the fundamental sameness of all these office archives. Apart from Burghley's papers in the Lansdowne collection the British Museum has two collections in which genuine State Papers are found. Both Sir Robert Cotton and Robert Harley, earl of Oxford, were not above acquiring material from the public archives; Cotton, in particular, who in the early seventeenth century created a splendid library which he put freely at the disposal of scholars, seems to have walked out with whatever took his fancy on his frequent visits to the State Paper Office.

[1] Below, 153ff.

It should be added that both these collections as well as the British Museum's Additional Manuscripts preserve material that would otherwise have been lost. By contrast with everything discussed so far, the State Papers are not the records of courts and were very poorly preserved; while the bulk remained in official hands, enough got scattered about to make search elsewhere necessary, and apart from the British Museum, American purchases deposited especially in the Huntington Library (at San Marino, California) should not be overlooked.[1]

However, even if one extends the meaning of the term to everything, wherever it may be found, that in some way arose in the offices of the secretaries of state or their proper predecessors back to 1509, there is still a large part of our period left blank. This is not, however, to say that papers very similar in style and purpose may not survive for earlier ages. A small quantity of writings similar to State Papers Domestic has been discovered here and there in the Chancery and Exchequer files; hardly any seem to survive before about 1440, but since some have turned up more may exist.[2] The Foreign type of State Paper is better represented. There are the Treaty Rolls of the Chancery on which treaties and other diplomatic instruments were enrolled from 1234 onwards.[3] Both Exchequer and Chancery preserve small classes of diplomatic documents to a total of approximately 4,000 pieces covering the period from about 1200 to the reign of Henry VIII; and the artificial class called Ancient Correspondence includes many letters of the State Paper type, nearly all on foreign affairs, running down to about 1500.[4] This shows plainly

[1] This library seems to have only a partial knowledge of what its cellars contain.

[2] Two volumes of State Papers Supplementary (the list published by the List and Index Society, vol. 9) contain material before 1500; some papers of this kind were published in the two volumes of *Letters and Papers of the Reigns of Richard III and Henry VII*, ed. J. Gairdner (Rolls Series, 1861–3).

[3] These rolls were heavily used in Rymer's *Foedera*. Those for 1234–1325 have been published in one volume of transcripts and calendars (H.M.S.O. 1955).

[4] One volume of transcripts of 444 diplomatic documents for the period 1101–1272 has been published (H.M.S.O. 1964); of these only eight precede the year 1200.

enough that in the general sense state papers were nothing new in the sixteenth century but that the administrative reorganisation which produced the secretary of state also resulted in what was effectively a new class of records. It matters that this class quite drastically changes the possibilities of historical knowledge.

What are the State Papers? They contain the correspondence of the chief executive ministers of the Crown and refer both to the internal government of the country and the conduct of foreign policy. Any more precise description quails before their unpredictable variety. In the main they are letters—letters to and from local officers or private persons, interdepartmental letters, letters to and from ambassadors abroad, instructions to commissioners and to special missions, reports to the King, and so forth. In addition, there is, as it were, the supporting material, the working papers of busy departments: treatises and treaties, memoranda and reports, drafts of proposals or of acts of Parliament, lists of matters to be done, evidence collected in police work, depositions, documents concerning the Crown's revenues and possessions, private papers and papers produced by the office's internal administration. There is no aspect of government activity on which the State Papers may not throw light. Very large numbers of individuals appear in them, and since they appear very often in letters written by themselves they at last emerge from obscurity. The State Papers add the dimension of individual personality to our knowledge of English history. As has already been said, we know throughout this period the names, avocations and often the fortunes of a great many people in England, but before the State Papers exist in quantity we know the minds, characters and purposes of only very few. Though judicial records often break through the anonymity from which even the possession of a known name or an assignable place in society cannot save the main bulk of the nation in the middle ages, it is only with the State Papers that we come face to face with large numbers of really live men and women.

Above all, the State Papers make possible a quite different analysis of events. They go behind the scenes, introduce the historian to motive, intrigue, policy-making, the daily actions of people involved in affairs, and often of people hardly so involved. The whole texture of the history that can be written alters. Ideas emerge and ideals; views on politics or religion or art or life in general become available. The machinery of government reveals itself in the sort of detail which the main administrative records conceal behind common form and accomplished purpose. Though it should never be supposed that none of these things may be found before 1500, it must yet be stressed that thereafter, and especially from about 1530 onwards, the historian of England really has at his disposal a mass of materials which transform his approach to the task, draw him away from the analysis of great events and formal institutions into the particular doings of individual men, and enable him to understand what went on on the basis of ascertained fact rather than reasonable conjecture.

Nevertheless, it needs also to be said that the State Papers have serious drawbacks and deficiencies; in some ways they are inferior to the main record series already discussed, and in the past too much of the history of the sixteenth and seventeenth centuries has been written in excessive reliance on them. In the first place, they are entirely unsystematic. Not only is there no knowing what may be lost, but even in their origin system played no part. They are quite as casual as any correspondence, and there can be no telling how representative, how near to completeness, the picture they provide may be. Who writes to a secretary of state or is written to by him cannot be predicted or reduced to rules, and if the glory of this record class is that anything may appear in it the obverse is also true: the papers continually let one down by not including what could reasonably be expected to be there. Added to this is the serious problem of haphazard survival. We know vastly more of the inner history of the 1530's than of the 1520's because Thomas Cromwell's correspondence survives in bulk while of Wolsey's, which must have been massive, most has disappeared. Of the correspondence of Cromwell's colleagues, happier in their personal fate, very little now exists, a fact which no doubt contributes to the apparent dominance of Cromwell during the decade of his ministry. Before the reign of Charles I, all existing State Papers are undoubtedly the remnant preserved by accident—the accident of personality or rats—and it is only after the Restoration that the State Papers assume the characteristics of regular and routine archives which the records of Chancery and Exchequer had acquired as early as the thirteenth century.

Next, it should be remembered that all casual historical material poses technical problems different from those raised by regular record series but no less weighty for that. Apart from the gaps and dead ends, there is the task of getting behind the appearance to the reality, of working out the real purposes of a letter and the motives of the writer, often indeed his identity. The historian may have to face difficulties of dating which do not arise when he is working on continuous rolls dated by the year. The contents of the material may be quite meaningless to him: when the writer, as he often will, alludes to something well known to himself or his correspondent, or when the document consists of private notes, the historian may be left entirely in the dark, without even the help of common form or routine to fill in the blanks.

Both these deficiencies—haphazard preservation and the exceptional obscurities of casual evidence—are very prominent in the first hundred years of the State Paper collections. Dating, in particular, presents many difficulties. Letters were too often dated only by the day and month: before 1550, very few letters give the year. Thereafter, as arabic numerals spread into common use, year-dating becomes more frequent. Since the great offices had long been careful to date their products, this is an odd deficiency, but even a man so devoted to paper work as Thomas Cromwell virtually never dated his letters to the year. Burghley, Walsingham and the other Elizabethan statesmen were much kinder to the historian, for it must be stressed that inability to place a document in its year can have disastrous effects. Error in this respect can completely pervert the true story of events, and failure to assign any convincing date at all can render a document useless, however interesting its content. While internal evidence may often help, the lack of a date on a letter remains an unforgivable idiosyncrasy. In addition, there is always the possibility that the date, when it is given, is wrong.

Still, letters can be sorted and assigned; the situation is much worse when one turns to the other types of documents in the State Papers. Here not only dates but often even authors' names are missing, may have to be conjectured from endorsements or (worse) contents, and often cannot be discovered. When one wants to analyse policy on the basis of memoranda and drafts, this is clearly a serious matter. There are many scraps among the papers which suggest answers to fascinating questions of motive and intent but which are useless because one cannot tell from whom they are, to what they belong, or even to what they may refer. Here another of the historian's tools becomes very important: a knowledge of provenance. One wants to know where the paper was found and preferably how it got there. At the very least, this is likely to tell who received it, and in many cases it can tell more. It is therefore absolutely essential that collections of documents should be preserved in the state in which they originally accumulated, or, if for reasons of convenience they are to be rearranged, that a record of the original arrangement is made. (This is the principle that governs proper archaeological excavation.) Unfortunately, this necessity has not always been recognised, and the Public Record Office has committed many grave sins in its attempts to make its contents accessible. A particularly bad example is provided by the State Papers of Henry VIII's reign, assembled by the editors of its comprehensive calendar from every sort of source and rebound in simple chronological order (often wrong). As a result, for instance, the office papers of Thomas Cromwell, preserved for three centuries in a separate collection, are now broken up and redistributed; and while we may suppose, with good reason, that many memoranda and notes of the time came from that archive, we can no longer be sure. Happily no one has tampered in this way with the State Papers from 1547 onwards, but since the collection was built up later, with a hunt around for whatever could be recovered, no

Tudor State Paper Foreign before about 1580, and no Tudor State Paper Domestic at all, has the character of an organic deposit. This certainly limits their usefulness and renders interpretation in doubtful cases very difficult.

However, the worst deficiency of this body of records remains to be mentioned. In contrast to the medieval Chancery with its enrolment of out-letters, the secretaries of state preserved virtually only incoming correspondence. Out-letters do exist in small numbers and purely by accident, perhaps because the recipient filed one but more commonly because an earlier draft was allowed to survive. Cromwell received thousands of letters of which several thousand are extant; diligent search has discovered only some 360 of those he wrote, which must also have run into thousands.[1] And he was relatively lucky or an exceptional writer of letters; for Stephen Gardiner, busy at the centre of affairs for twenty-five years, only 173 have been found.[2] No one has yet attempted to collect the known letters of Burghley, Walsingham, or the early-Stuart secretaries, but while undoubtedly much more than this would emerge, it would still fall far short of the real total. In any case, these out-letters are mostly collected from scattered and private sources. The record class known as State Papers consists overwhelmingly of in-letters only, and it needs no emphasis to explain the problems of a correspondence of which only one side is known. This is a much worse matter than the fact that this correspondence is necessarily in the main on business, though historians have before this been misled into harsh judgments on generations allegedly so dominated by material concerns that their letters excluded all personal, intellectual or spiritual things.[3] What else would one expect when the extant correspondence belongs either to dealings with government departments or to estate management? The conditions of survival should be considered before evidence is treated in this way.

[1] R. B. Merriman's edition (*Life and Letters of Thomas Cromwell*, Oxford 1902) lists 351; a few more have come to light since.

[2] *The Letters of Stephen Gardiner*, ed. J. A. Muller (Cambridge 1933).

[3] E.g. M. D. Knowles, *The Religious Orders in England*, vol. 3 (Cambridge 1959), 5.

Nothing can be done about the absence of out-letters, but there is one other class of documents, properly called State Papers but not part of the English archives, which offers alternative lines of approach and should be included here. This is the material in foreign archives that bears on the history of England, in the main the reports of ambassadors and other visitors to their own governments. In the nineteenth century, determined efforts were made to search some leading continental depositories (in particular the Venetian records, and the records of the Habsburg empire at Simancas, Brussels and Vienna) for letters of this kind and a good deal was found. It is accessible to the English student in printed calendars of variable quality; many of the transcripts on which these are based seem to have vanished, though the originals are, of course, still to be found in their old place.[1] The value of these papers is great, but again, they should not be used as uncritically as they often have been. Partly because the continental archives in question were better organised than those of England, the series are more complete and, as documents, more reliable. In the main, of course, they contribute to our knowledge of foreign policy and war, but since ambassadors were expected to inform their governments in detail of what went on in the country to which they were assigned, the letters often also give important information on domestic history. Yet an ambassador's information was only as good as his sources, and if he got involved in his host-country's politics his bias could totally distort reality. The effects vary: an account of the 1530's based on the imperial ambassador's violently partisan views and information would be very misleading, while the correspondence of Simon Renard, ambassador and in effect chief adviser to Queen

---

[1] There is one volume of papers from Milan, 1385–1618 (H.M.S.O. 1913). 24 volumes cover the Venetian archives from 1202 to 1639, 15 of them post-Tudor (H.M.S.O. 1864–1933). The Spanish archives, on the other hand, have been published only for the years 1485–1603; a complicated and ill-numbered series of parts and supplements amounts altogether to 24 volumes. The French archives remain curiously untouched, but a volume of ambassadorial correspondence from England for 1537–42 has been published: *Correspondence politique de MM. de Castillon et de Marillac*, ed. J. Kaulek (Paris 1885).

Mary, is both revealing and very much more trustworthy.[1]

The State Papers are not a perfect historical source, any more than any other record is perfect. They pose peculiar problems which, since everybody thinks he can handle letters, have too often been ignored by historians. Evidence of a casual and personal kind always looks easier to interpret than it is, even as formal records tend to look harder to interpret than they are. But the deficiencies and inadequacies of this body of material must not disguise their immense usefulness. They add a new dimension, and on the rare occasions when similar papers exist for the earlier period they cast sudden shafts of light there, too. More than any other archive, the State Papers and their concomitants in private or foreign collections differentiate the historical treatment of the years 1509-1640 from all that went before.

(e) THE COUNCIL

All the records so far discussed were produced by executive branches of the government; they recorded action taken or avoided, and, with the exception of the State Papers, they tell little or nothing about the making of decisions, the debates on policy, and political realities behind action. These matters belong to the central organisation itself, to the King and those who immediately advised him. Kings of England had, naturally, always had advisers, and from the reign of Edward I onwards the evidence is clear that there existed a formal King's Council, a body of men specifically retained to attend upon the monarch and to deal with government business from day to day. Their task was in the main threefold. They advised: that is, they considered the problems facing the Crown and offered solutions. They administered: that is they saw to the ordinary running of the King's government and ordered action by individual officers. And they adjudicated: that is, they dealt with petitions from

[1] See E. H. Harbison, *Rival Ambassadors at the Court of Queen Mary* (Princeton 1940), a book which shows what in this period can be done with diplomatic correspondence. An appendix contains an important discussion of ambassadorial papers.

private persons who brought their troubles before them because they exercised the King's general power to do justice which the creation of regular courts had not exhausted. For the rest of our period such a Council was beyond question always in existence, though it underwent changes in composition and influence. Royal minorities usually produced well organised and active Councils, effectively substituting for the necessarily inactive King; this was particularly true of the years 1377–89 and 1422–37. The Yorkists and Henry VII, on the other hand, placed great reliance on a large Council chosen by themselves and employable in a variety of ways as the executors of the King's own policy. Then, in about 1534–6, Cromwell reorganised the Council in a reform from which emerged the typical Privy Council of Elizabeth and the early Stuarts, a fully organised, usually small, committee of politicians and great office-holders, a truly ministerial body resembling in many ways its later descendant, the modern Cabinet. But while the continuous existence of the Council should not be doubted, its records are very much less continuous and indeed singularly deficient.[1]

The potential records of the Council are of two kinds, proceedings and papers, and the second may be subdivided into papers for the Council and papers produced by the Council. It is at once apparent that only the former could be expected to be regular and systematic, but in truth not even they are. For the better part of its history, the Council either kept no minutes or such as were kept are lost. Only three separate lots now survive. A record was kept in 1392–3, seemingly an experiment which was not continued. More valuable is the register-roll of the Council of Henry VI's minority which now exists for the years 1421–35;[2]

---

[1] For the records of the Council see J. F. Baldwin, *The King's Council in England during the Middle Ages* (Oxford 1913), ch. xiv; E. R. Adair, *The Sources for the History of the Council in the 16th and 17th Centuries* (Historical Association: London 1924); G. R. Elton, 'Why the history of the early-Tudor Council remains unwritten', *Annali della Fondazione Italiana per la Storia Amministrativa*, i (1964) 268ff.

[2] This record started in Henry V's last year, when the King was abroad in France.

since as early as 1449 this seems to have been the only portion in existence, it is likely that the keeping of enrolled minutes ended in 1435. And from August 1540 there exists a continuous series (some years are missing) of the minutes or 'acts' of the Privy Council. Apart from these surviving registers we possess materials which enable us partially to reconstruct some that are missing. For the years before 1420 and again for 1436–44 there survive quite a few of the rough minutes upon which registers, when kept, were based, though it is of course impossible to say what may be lost. Even less satisfactory is the evidence for the Council of the revived monarchy. Nothing at all is known for the Yorkist Council, but it looks as though Henry VII may have instituted the keeping of a record book which, after the reform of 1534–6 and the beginning of the Acts of the Privy Council in 1540, continued as the Star Chamber's books of orders and decrees— the Star Chamber being the formal sitting of the Council as a court. However, these books are lost, and we know of them only because transcripts were made from them in the reign of Elizabeth, transcripts which preserve some of the doings of the Council on a small proportion of the days on which it sat during the years 1487–1543 (there are very few after 1527).[1]

Some of the shortcomings of this material are immediately apparent. For very long stretches of time we have no minute books at all. Even where they exist, they do not cover all the meetings. The fifteenth-century register and its early-Tudor successor record only formal sittings held in the law terms—

---

[1] The 1392–3 register is printed by Baldwin, *op. cit.* 489ff. The 1421–35 register fills vols 3 and 4 of *Proceedings and Ordinances of the Privy Council of England*, ed. N. H. Nicholas (1834–7); vol 7 of this edition is the first book of the Privy Council proper (1540–2). In his remaining volumes Nicholas printed such original minutes and other material as he could find to provide a valuable collection of Council doings for 1386–1421 and 1436–44 which looks much more systematic than it is. From 1542 there is a continuous series of *Acts of the Privy Council of England*, ed. J. R. Dasent and others, whose 45 volumes have so far reached 1631. Of the extant transcripts from the early-Tudor book (at the British Museum and the Huntington Library), those for the reign of Henry VII are printed in *Select Cases in the Council of Henry VII*, ed. C. E. Bayne (Selden Society 1958), 1ff.

about a third part of each year—and while this reflects something important about the Council, it leaves in the dark the many occasions on which councillors indubitably met out of term to advise, administer and adjudicate.[1] The Privy Council proper not only met all the year round but also kept its minutes in and out of term. However, it is by no means clear that every meeting was registered, especially as the clerk was occasionally instructed to leave when specially secret matters were in hand. Still, after 1540 we know of virtually every meeting of the Council, except in the few years whose registers are lost; before that, we know of only a small and haphazard selection from them.

Even where minutes survive, they leave a good deal to be desired. The clerks did not always record that very important point, the names of those present, and the later transcripts are even less consistent in this matter. More serious than occasional lapses are deficiencies created by regular practice. All these records concern themselves exclusively with decisions; they never preserve debate or discussion. And the decisions that interested the clerks were those requiring action. The effect of this is predictable: the Council's work appears in its records very differently proportioned from what undoubtedly it was in fact. There is no evidence of discussion or decision on the major issues of policy: the advisory function of the Council, its work on the problems of the Crown's policy, is entirely omitted from all these minute books. The administrative function—the ordering of executive action locally or at the centre, as well as the receipt of letters concerned with such business—is better represented but still very far from complete. Easily the best documented part of the Council's work is its activity in dispensing justice to petitioners. This is particularly marked before 1540; after that date, the main bulk of judicial business was handled by established Council courts (Star Chamber and Requests), but even so private petitions and appeals fill a disproportionate part of the *Acts of the*

---

[1] The earliest so-called order books of the Court of Requests (above, 58) record out-of-term Council meetings in the reign of Henry VII, but nearly all the business that reached the minutes was judicial.

Privy Council. An unimaginative assessment of the late-medieval Council would thus necessarily suppose that it was mainly a judicial tribunal and had nothing to do with affairs of state or royal policy, and unimaginative historians have duly supposed so. But this is a false conclusion, produced by the peculiarities of record-keeping.

The less systematic evidence of Council papers unfortunately reinforces the weaknesses of the registers. That the Council received a good deal of material, both public and private, on which it took action, is certain, but what has survived is unhappily heavily biased. It would seem that the Privy Council kept some sort of archives, perhaps from the reign of Elizabeth onwards, but in 1619 a fire at Whitehall destroyed all this; almost nothing now survives before 1700 in the class called 'Privy Council Office: Papers'. The medieval Council's papers do survive in one respect: there are many private petitions which the Council judged and annotated, especially for the years before 1340, now classified as parliamentary material but strictly belonging to the business of the Council.[1] Down to about 1530, the proceedings (more adjudicated petitions) in Star Chamber and Requests should be treated as touching the work of the Council and its committees. Council work left deposit elsewhere, too. Since the fifteenth-century Council used the privy seal almost as its own seal, both Chancery and Exchequer preserve a relatively small quantity of what are in effect warrants and instructions from the Council. These naturally concern in the main routine administration, such as orders for payments or for the granting of gifts in land, money or offices. As has already been said, this last business is ultimately recorded on the Patent Rolls, and down to 1485 it was Chancery practice to annotate enrolments with the source of the warrant authorising grants. From these notes a good deal of the Council's activity can be reconstructed in outline.[2]

[1] See below, 84.

[2] See J. R. Lander, 'The Yorkist Council and Administration', *Eng. Hist. Rev.* lxxiii (1958), 27ff, which shows how much can be said about the activities of the Council at a time when no genuine Council records exist at all.

Once the State Papers begin, one can learn much about the Council, both from its own letters, occasionally found here, and from the reports of English politicians and foreign ambassadors who at times speak of what happened at meetings. More such letters may no doubt be found in local or foreign archives, where they were directed, but no serious search for them has yet been undertaken at least in the former. In any case, this is bound to be an entirely haphazard, quite accidental source of historical knowledge.

There is one other record in the production of which the Council played a part and which therefore throws light on its activities. Certainly from the reign of Henry VII onwards, the Crown issued an increasing number of proclamations—orders of a quasi-legislative force most of which, in fact, either simply announced public matters or followed up statutory provisions. An act of 1539, repealed in 1547, demanded that proclamations should be made with the stated consent of the Council, but even before and after those dates it is clear that they were usually the result of conciliar deliberations and decisions, and quite a number mention the Council's assent to their issue. Proclamations were an important enough part of the ordinary administrative activity of the King's government, and a good deal can be learned about their origin, purpose and scope—much less, unfortunately, about their enforcement and effectiveness. Whether we possess all, or even the main part, of what was issued cannot be known; some proclamations certainly issued cannot now be found; but it looks as though at least from the second half of Henry VIII's reign onwards our information is reasonably complete. These materials therefore add satisfactorily to our understanding of the worst documented part of the Council's doings—its function as the centre of government—but they do no more than cast a greyish glow into this obscurity at the heart of things.[1]

[1] The list edited by R. R. Steele, *Tudor and Stuart Proclamations 1485–1714*, vol 1 (Oxford 1910) is being superseded by the edition of the texts made by Paul L. Hughes and James F. Larkin, *Tudor Royal Proclamations* (New Haven) of which vol 1 (1485–1553) is published (1964) and vol 2 (1553–1603) is in the

The result of all this is that what went on at the very centre of government can rarely be known in any detail or completeness; and what can be known is biased towards the routine work rather than the exceptional or exceptionally interesting. The Council as a court, or quasi-court, of justice is quite well documented; the Council as the source of administrative decisions and orders has left less full but still very respectable record; but the Council as an advisory and policy-making body appears very rarely in the evidence. Once again we must note that we can learn much about what was done, much less about the how and why. In this last respect, two stretches of time do better than the rest: the minority of Henry VI and the period from 1540 onwards. But even for them, knowledge remains patchy, uncertain and often conjectural. However, it should be remembered that this problem besets most ages down to the present. At least the medieval Council at times, and the Tudor-Stuart Privy Council throughout, kept some sort of minute book; the later Cabinet had none before 1916.

(*f*) PARLIAMENT

The years from about 1250 to 1640 are the formative years in the history of Parliament. That is to say, between those two dates the primitive beginnings of a representative assembly grafted on to enlarged meetings of the King's Council, called to serve the King's own purposes, developed by stages into that image of the political nation in action, that centre of political activity, with which Parliament thereafter remained identified. In these 400 years two dates approximately indicate moments of crisis, points at which the institution appeared in a new guise or assumed a new function and reality. Round about 1340, the parliamentary

press. This unfortunately leaves out proclamations made by the Council itself, not by the King with the consent of the Council, of which some survive from Elizabeth's reign onwards. For a criticism of the edition see my review article in *Historical Journal*, viii (1965) 266ff. However, the edition has at last made possible serious work on proclamations: for the reign of Henry VIII this is being undertaken by Rudolph Heinze, for that of Elizabeth by F. A. Youngs.

occasions initiated by Henry III and Edward I and tested in the struggles of Edward II's reign crystallised into the characteristic assembly of the King and his great men in Parliament to which the Commons were an essential but extraneous attachment, acting as petitioners and therefore as initiators of action. In the second quarter of the sixteenth century, recent developments from about 1470 onwards, by which Lords and Commons came to be co-ordinate partners with equal functions, were fixed by the use made of Parliament in the Reformation, to produce the 'modern' institution of a politically paramount Parliament. Thanks to the reluctance of Elizabeth and the early Stuarts to accept the political co-operation of the nation in Parliament, the full implications of this transformation were delayed until after the Civil War, but the fundamental changes really occurred in the 1530's. These two points of crisis are reflected accurately enough in the records produced by Parliament.

Like the Council, of which originally it was a kind of by-product, the Parliament did not at first keep proper archives. However, from about 1340 onwards, the Chancery took over the organising of Parliament, and the Chancery was used to record-keeping. The materials produced by Parliament must therefore be sought in the collections of the Chancery, with some help from the Exchequer; until the sixteenth century, there was no assistance from the Parliament itself. The materials resulted from two main aspects of activity: the activity which created each Parliament in the first instance, and the actions engaged in by the Parliament once it existed. The records therefore divide naturally into those concerned with members and those concerned with proceedings.

There is relatively little difficulty in discovering who received individual summons, that is to say, came as a member of what from about 1480 it is proper to call the House of Lords. Until 1542, writs of summons were enrolled on the dorse (back) of the Close Roll, while from 1529 onwards separate enrolments, called parliamentary pawns, were filed in the Chancery. Although there are gaps, the great majority of peers in Parliament are recorded from the middle of the thirteenth century.[1] A collection of proxies given by spiritual peers who either could not or would not attend in person, running from Henry III's reign to the Reformation, gives some information about attendance rather than summons; in the early sixteenth century, the collection includes some documents made out by lay peers.

The members of the Commons present greater difficulty. In theory, the writs of summons sent to the sheriffs were to be returned with the names of the knights and burgesses elected in the shire endorsed on them, and the clerk of the crown in Chancery would then compile from them the official or Crown Office list of the members of that Parliament. The writs and returns survive from 1275, and the Crown Office lists from 1553, but neither series is at all complete. In 1878, a summary of all the information to be obtained from this material was published as a Parliamentary Blue Book, but for our period the list has many gaps, nor can it always be trusted. By-elections complicate the issue, though many Crown Office lists carry amendments consequent upon them. Additional information can sometimes be discovered from writs for payment to members addressed to their constituency, from indentures between returning officers and electors, or from casual mentions in local records. The government-supported History of Parliament Trust is at present engaged in establishing accurate lists and collecting biographical details, but for our period nothing has yet appeared.[2] Though a surprising amount of detail can often be gathered, especially from the reign of Henry VIII onwards, it is likely that we shall never have knowledge of more than perhaps four-fifths of the men who were elected to Parliament.

The proceedings of the English Parliaments, meeting at often infrequent intervals, are sometimes very well recorded and

---

[1] The lists are published: William Dugdale, *A Perfect Copy of the Summons of the Nobility to the Great Councils and Parliaments of this Realm 1265–1685* (London 1685).

[2] The useful compilation edited by J. C. Wedgwood (*Biographical Register of Members of the House of Commons 1439–1509*, London 1936) is marred by much error.

sometimes totally obscure. At first sight it would seem that the apparent master records, the Rolls of Parliament, should give detailed and continuous information. They have been published in six volumes covering the years 1273–1509;[1] in addition those for the years 1512–35 and for the first Parliament of Queen Mary were published in the first volume of the *Lord's Journals*, and some early rolls missed by the original editors have since been put into print.[2] Of course, the material is not complete, but gaps are what one gets used to. It matters more that this apparently continuous series of rolls is nothing of the sort. The editors both early and recent have obscured an important fact by giving a single generic name to all they printed. In actual fact, a genuine series of Chancery enrolments starts only in 1340. The earlier documents, going back to the beginning of Edward I's reign, are a mixture: there are some *ad hoc* rolls, but much of the stuff preserved and printed consists of petitions to the King's Council in Parliament, found loose and unenrolled. The rolls were found in different places, including private possession; much of the material exists in medieval transcripts rather than originals. Essentially it is Council material, even if it accumulated on the occasions of parliamentary meetings. All this well describes the early history of Parliament when most time was spent on the individual petitions of private persons. But it omits, or barely mentions, other business in Parliament which is known from such other sources as the chronicles: the political affairs of the realm and the very important matter of taxation. Information on these issues has to be gathered from casual and unsystematic evidence and can never be remotely complete.[3]

[1] *Rotuli Parliamentorum ut et Petitiones et Placita in Parliamento* (no title page: 1761–83).

[2] *Records of the Parliament holden at Westminster [1305]*, usually called *Memoranda de Parliamento*, ed. F. W. Maitland (Rolls Series 1893); *Rotuli Parliamentorum Anglie hactenus inediti 1279–1373*, ed. H. G. Richardson and G. O. Sayles (Camden 3rd Series, vol. 51; London 1935).

[3] The records are briefly discussed in the edition of Richardson and Sayles mentioned in the previous note, xiii–xxiv. See also B. Wilkinson, 'The Nature of Parliament', *Studies in the Constitutional History of the thirteenth and fourteenth*

Even when the rolls begin in earnest, they do not tell all that much. They are very formal, following a set method. Down to 1483 they consist essentially of a list of petitions presented in Parliament, which usually does no more than summarise the grievance complained of, with the King's reply. That is to say, they do not even record the product of the parliamentary session, the statutes made by the King in response to demands from the Commons and with the advice of the Lords. That information is supplied by the Statute Rolls, eight rolls covering the years 1278–1470; the very patchy series can be supplemented by transcripts of statutes sent to the Chancery for various purposes and still preserved there. Then, from 1483, this matter is transferred to the Rolls of Parliament which become nothing but a record of acts passed; after 1593 these are confined to the public acts, the many private acts being omitted altogether. However, the lack of enrolments is made up for in part by the growing practice, in the sixteenth century, of publishing printed editions of the statutes and more completely by the preservation, from 1497, of the original acts (the documents actually passed through the two Houses) in the Record Office of the House of Lords. This last collection includes not only all public and private acts, but even some bills vetoed by the Crown of which we should otherwise be ignorant.[1]

In any case, in importance the rolls, whether Statute Rolls or Rolls of Parliament, were in the sixteenth century superseded by an entirely new type of record, the Journals of either House. The House of Lords kept a Journal from 1509; the House of Commons followed suit in 1547.[2] In theory, these volumes

centuries (Manchester 1937), 15ff. For a good introductory bibliography of the massive work done on the early Parliament see E. Miller, *The Origin of Parliament* (Hist. Ass., London 1960).

[1] The acts passed are printed in the only edition to be used by scholars: *Statutes of the Realm 1278–1714* (9 vols; Record Commission 1810–28). The acts down to 1640 fill the first four volumes and 178 pages of the fifth.

[2] In the printed edition (for important points the originals at the House of Lords should be consulted), the first four volumes of the *Lords'* and the first two volumes of the *Commons' Journals* cover our period. See A. F. Pollard, 'The

contain entries of each day's business and should give real inside information on the affairs of Parliament. In practice they are less satisfactory than that. Our period contains both the worst and the best of the Journals. There are, as always, gaps; some parts of these materials are inexplicably lost. What survives varies a good deal in purpose. At first both series were very concise, and the Lords' Journal never admitted much detail; it confined itself to a straightforward record of formal occasions (such as the opening of Parliament and the set speeches then made) and of bills presented, read and (sometimes) passed. The Commons' Journal began in much the same fashion, but from the latter part of Elizabeth's reign it suddenly became much fuller, recording speeches and speakers and in general giving a much better account of the House at work. In the whole history of the Journals, only those for the early-Stuart period escape the confines of an essentially formalised record. But while this means that they tell things that might otherwise remain unknown, it also means that they lack the characteristics of a formal document: there is no telling what may have been admitted and what omitted. From about 1572 the Commons' Journal was regarded as a public record, but even after that the idiosyncrasies or deficiencies or even partisanship of the clerk who kept them made them a record needing much critical evaluation.

Deficient the Journals may be, in a variety of ways, but it is obvious that their existence promotes knowledge of parliamentary history in a way quite impossible in the middle ages. Even at their best, the rolls almost always recorded only the end of the process and did not even arrange the business done in chronological order; the Journals display the process itself, day by day. Even more might be known about the Parliaments of the sixteenth and seventeenth centuries if the Palace of Westminster had not burned down in 1833, for the evidence presented in the early nineteenth century to Select Committees leaves no doubt that

Authenticity of the "Lords' Journal" in the Sixteenth Century', *Trans. R. Hist. Soc.* 1915, 17ff; J. E. Neale, 'The Commons' Journals of the Tudor Period', *ibid.* 1920, 166ff.

there then existed genuine if ill-sorted parliamentary archives, containing such invaluable material produced in the course of sessions as draft bills, rejected bills, or papers presented to Parliament. The loss of all this is very serious; the effect of debates on legislation, for instance, which in the absence of well recorded debates could be studied from the corrections on drafts, remains unknown. A little can be learned now and again from corrections on and additions to the original acts,[1] but at least down to 1600 surviving drafts among the State Papers and similar collections are nearly always part of the work of preparing legislation for submission to Parliament and tell nothing of what happened in the Houses.

The official parliamentary material thus gives reasonably complete information on membership, tells a great deal about the work accomplished in Parliament, and for the early seventeenth century provides much information of what went on in the Commons. Apart from this last point, however, it leaves the internal history of Parliament—the manner of proceeding, the clash of interests, the details of debate, the very process of making laws—quite obscure. Yet information on these vital issues can sometimes be obtained from private and entirely accidental sources which, for the sake of completeness, had better be mentioned here. Down to the reign of Henry VIII, the chronicles sometimes help; the usefulness of the Anonimalle Chronicle and of Edward Hall's writings has already been noted,[2] and there are other occasional shafts of light.[3] We possess some treatises on Parliament, from the imaginative and untrustworthy *Modus Tenendi Parliamentum*[4] to the careful handbook prepared by

[1] See, e.g. F. W. Maitland, 'Elizabethan Gleanings', *Historical Essays*, ed. Helen Cam (Cambridge 1957), 211ff; G. R. Elton, 'Henry VIII's Act of Proclamations', *Eng. Hist. Rev.* lxxv (1960), 208ff.

[2] Above, 21.

[3] E.g. a short report from two burgesses survives for 1485 (*Red Book of Colchester*, ed. W. G. Benham, Colchester 1902), and there are occasional reports in English and foreign State Papers.

[4] The *Modus*, a mixture of description and propaganda, was composed in the reign of Edward II: see V. H. Galbraith in *Journal of the Warburg Institute*, 1953, 83ff.

Henry Elsynge, clerk of the Parliaments in the reign of Charles I.[1] From the reign of Elizabeth onwards, new sources transform knowledge altogether. Individual, members began to keep diaries of varying length and accuracy, and a good many of them survive. Some were used by the antiquarian Simonds D'Ewes to produce his *Journals of all the Parliaments during the Reign of Queen Elizabeth* (1682), and for the last four Parliaments of that reign there are Hayward Townsend's journals.[2] Some more, so far unpublished, have been found for earlier sessions.[3] Even more exist for the early-seventeenth century, of which most have now appeared in print.[4] Some late-seventeenth century collections of parliamentary material preserve vital documents of the earlier half which would otherwise be lost.[5]

All this is most valuable stuff: increasingly from 1530 onwards the history of Parliament can be written in detail never to be known before. Once the reign of James I is reached, it seems at times as though nothing could remain obscure, so solid is the array of materials. Yet the historian must throughout remember that the only complete and official records are the least revealing, and that the deeper knowledge comes from unsystematic, unpredictable and often highly personal sources. Sir John Neale was able to tell the history of the Elizabethan Parliaments in a manner quite impossible before private diaries open the door into the House of Commons in session. But private diaries reflect not only the insufficiencies of the diarist who cannot always be

---

[1] Henry Elsynge, *The Manner of Holding Parliaments in England* (best edition: 1675), supplemented by his *Expedicio Billarum Antiquitus*, ed. Catherine C. Sims (Louvain 1954).

[2] See J. E. Neale in *Eng. Hist. Rev.* xxxvi (1921) 96ff.

[3] This additional material is behind J. E. Neale's detailed reconstruction in *Elizabeth I and Her Parliaments* (2 vols; London 1953, 1957).

[4] *Proceedings in Parliament 1610*, ed. Elizabeth R. Foster (2 vols; New Haven 1966); *Commons' Debates 1621*, ed. W. Notestein, F. H. Relf, H. Simpson (7 vols; New Haven 1935); *Debates in the House of Commons in 1625*, ed. S. R. Gardiner (Camden Society, 1873); *The Commons' Debates for 1629*, ed. W. Notestein and F. H. Relf (Minneapolis 1921).

[5] Especially J. Rushworth, *Historical Collections . . . 1618–1629* (7 vols; London 1659-1701); also W. Petyt, *Miscellanea Parliamentaria* (London 1680).

present or always hear what is said; they reflect his judgment as to what is worth preserving and his bias in bringing out the weight of the argument. Such points need to be carefully considered before, for instance, one accepts the picture of constant difficulties, frequent puritan victories, unending arguments on issues of religion and religiously inspired policies, with relative disregard for the bulk of the bills that came to the House, which Neale's volumes present. Most of those diarists—perhaps all—were puritans and radicals.

CHAPTER 3

Official Records: the Church

Because the Church embodied, in the period under review, a system of government side by side with the secular arm, the records produced by its organisation provide yet another source of supply for historical knowledge. However, they pose problems peculiar to themselves. In the first place, they have never been gathered together into one, or even into a few, archives; instead they are to be found scattered across the country. The main part of them survives in those centres of administration which first accumulated them, in the episcopal archives of each diocese; but some quite considerable sections have moved elsewhere, especially the records of monastic institutions, many of which, thanks to the sixteenth-century Dissolution, are found in the royal archives (the Public Record Office) or in private hands.[1] This fact by itself makes it much harder to provide a systematic description. Worse, it explains the most serious problem of these

[1] Mr W. A. Pantin, compiling a table of proxies sent by Benedictine houses to chapters of their Order, used monastic registers which he found either still *in situ* (i.e. in such ex-monastic cathedrals as Durham, Ely, Gloucester, Rochester, Winchester or Worcester), or in the British Museum, the Bodleian Library, the Heralds' College; one turned up in the Duchy of Lancaster records at the P.R.O. (*Documents illustrating the Activities of the General and Provincial Chapters of the English Black Monks* [Camden 3rd Series], Vol. 3, 197–8.)

BIBLIOGRAPHY. The only reasonably complete survey of English ecclesiastical record depositories was made, in 1951, by the Pilgrim Trust; though the results were never printed, a typescript 'Survey of Ecclesiastical Archives' was deposited in the major English libraries. This covers the materials still in the hands of the Church; others have been moved to local record offices (see F. E. Emmison, *Archives and Local History*, London 1966). Some Church records have been printed, either by societies specifically established for the purpose or by local historical societies, and the introductions to such volumes often offer

records: they survive quite unpredictably and very patchily, at least down to the seventeenth century. For our period, ecclesiastical materials are indeed plentiful, but the extant papers represent an often small proportion of what once existed, and there is no telling beforehand what may still survive or what may have disappeared in a given diocese. All that can here be done is to describe the kinds of records which the government of the Church could and did produce, with some indication of what may still survive and where it exists.

The Church's archives differ from those of the Crown in one other particular: they did not employ the roll but, following the example of the Papacy, used the book-type register called a codex. The register—a bound volume made up at intervals from the folded sheets on which entries were recorded—is the characteristic form of the ecclesiastical record. Codices are probably better at surviving vicissitudes than rolls, but they are less flexible in their make-up and require a pretty rigid schedule of contents if the keeping of records is not to get impenetrably confused. The archives of the English Church provide examples both of the orderly (but therefore rather formal) register and of the haphazard volume containing unpredictable varieties of entries. Most of them belong to the former category.

The bulk of the records to be considered here was produced by the central processes of English Church government—by the administrative and judicial activities of bishops and archdeacons. They shall be described first, and ancillary materials of various kinds will follow after.

The records of episcopal administration fall into three cate-

---

the best help to understanding them; the best guide to these productions (avowedly not exhaustive) is E. L. C. Mullins, *Texts and Calendars: an analytical guide to serial publication* (London 1958), which is very well indexed. A start on understanding these materials may be made through J. S. Purvis, *An Introduction to Ecclesiastical Records* (London 1953). An excellent and thorough discussion of ecclesiastical government and records, though admittedly confined to part of the English Church, is found in I. J. Churchill, *Canterbury Administration* (2 vols; London 1933).

gories: registers, visitation papers, and court papers. Of these the first are the most complete, the most systematic, and the most important. In effect, they preserve the history of the bishop's rule of his see. Into them were copied such of his letters—both those sent out and those received—as he or his clerks thought worthy of preservation; and in them were listed his official actions, in particular ordinations of clergy and institutions to livings in his diocese. The earliest extant are sometimes in roll form, but the episcopal chanceries soon adopted the book instead. None at all survive before 1200, but thereafter they get plentiful. In theory there should be a single register for every bishop, but a great many are, of course, missing, while in the greater dioceses and especially the archbishoprics a prolonged incumbency might necessitate splitting different sections of the register into separate volumes. Quite a number have been published; more, no doubt, are in preparation; but very many (especially nearly all post-medieval ones) remain untouched. The beginning historian should know that if he will agree to edit an episcopal register he will learn a lot and also be more than commonly useful; it is, however, unlikely that by this means alone he will grow famous.

The most important registers are, naturally, those for the archiepiscopal administrations at Canterbury and York.[1] The former are almost continuous from 1207, and the latter still more complete from 1215; except for Parker's register at Canterbury (1559–75) none at all have been published for the post-Reformation period. Other relatively well served dioceses are Durham (published with gaps from 1314 to 1575) and Lincoln (published for most of the thirteenth century and for the years 1571–84).[2] Little has so far been done for such important sees as London and Winchester, and no register for Ely, Exeter or

---

[1] E. F. Jacob, *The Medieval Registers of Canterbury and York* (York: St Anthony's Hall Publications no. 4, 1953). His lists of printed registers must be corrected by Mullins' *Texts and Calendars*, itself already behind the times.

[2] To the list in Mullins must be added the register of Oliver Sutton, 1280–99, ed. R. M. Hill (Lincoln Record Society, vols 43, 48).

Gloucester seems to have attracted editors. However, sufficient registers are in print, and plenty more exist in diocesan archives, to justify the opinion that for the bulk of English ecclesiastical administration in the years 1200–1640 there exists the chief source, the record book of the bishop's activities. For one particularly important archbishop, Stephen Langton, a quasi-register has been constructed by collecting, from a great variety of archives, his surviving deeds, letters and other papers.[1]

A register's contents fall essentially into two parts. There are, less significantly, the bishop's dealings with his diocesan clergy: ordinations, institutions and collations to livings, appointments to vicarages (deputies for absentee incumbents), grants of dispensation for pluralities and non-residence, and such like. Some archives contain supporting material confirming or enlarging knowledge of these sorts of matters: at York, a class of 'benefice papers' fills gaps in the register, while Lincoln possesses some 'clergy lists' or directories of beneficed clergy drawn up on occasion. Supporting evidence is supplied from about 1400 onwards by the records of matriculation and graduation kept by the Universities. If the registers had all been kept well, it would thus be possible to reconstruct the total history of England's clergy in those four and a half centuries—their names, dates, educational achievements and careers. In practice this is less easy. Not only are there very large gaps, especially in the University records, but the difficulties in distinguishing individuals often identical in name, or individuals whose description changes without notice, are so large that even for the parish clergy, describable by the livings they held, anything resembling a good list is virtually unobtainable. Monks, friars and nuns are no better served, except at the Dissolution when inmates of religious houses can in most instances be at least listed. The great mass of unbeneficed clergy in the main escape the record altogether, or (since their ordination at least will probably be recorded) anything like useful knowledge. It has proved possible to compose repertories for so

[1] *Acta Stephani Langton, Cantuariensis Archiepiscopi 1207–1228*, ed. Kathleen Major (Canterbury and York Society 1950).

well-documented a body as the London clergy,[1] and diocesan officials and cathedral chapters can, by and large, be identified.[2] Beyond that one can only say that while many individuals may be known, many more remain obscure or lost, nor is there any way of predicting into which category a man will fall. The searcher may or may not find what he wants. The mass and frustrating difficulty of the available material have certainly postponed attempts to discover the answers to such questions, but they also guarantee that there is a lot more yet to discover. One class of clergy for whom careful biographical dictionaries, varying in quality, have been composed, are the members of the Universities.[3]

More interesting is the first part of the usual register, the bishop's business correspondence. Here one will find copies of his out-letters, of grants made by him, of deeds and indentures, but also transcripts of letters received from popes, kings, archbishops and lesser men. That is to say, the register records his *acta* and incoming directions to act. If any of this material survives elsewhere, it is either by accident (in originals) or in the in-letter files of the bishop's correspondence; it is naturally most likely to be found in the one archival source which meant to preserve it, in the register. On the other hand, medieval business methods being what they were, there is nothing complete or systematic about the average register. What was entered depended on choice, even whim. An efficient administration kept a thorough record; an indifferent bishop or incompetent chancellor resulted in a thin and uninformative register. Indispensable to a study of

[1] R. Newcourt, *Repertorium ecclesiasticum parochiale Londinense* (2 vols, London 1708–10).

[2] John Le Neve, *Fasti Ecclesiae Anglicanae*. A new edition of the 1300–1541 section of this eighteenth-century compilation was produced, in twelve volumes, by the London Institute of Historical Research (1962–7).

[3] A. B. Emden, *A Biographical Register of the University of Oxford to A.D. 1500* (3 vols, Oxford 1957–9) and J. Foster, *Alumni Oxonienses 1500–1714* (4 vols, Oxford 1891–2). For Cambridge Emden has covered the middle ages (*A Biographical Register of the University of Cambridge to 1500*, Cambridge 1963); thereafter see J. and J. A. Venn, *Alumni Cantabrigienses: Part I, to 1751* (3 vols, Cambridge 1922–7).

the medieval Church in all its aspects and often very useful in the accidental knowledge revealed, the registers do not guarantee the answer to any question one may reasonably ask of them. It may be there, or it may not. Some registers preserve unexpected and, as it were, unrelated material. Thus they can contain accounts of current events or transcribe the records of visitations. Among the Canterbury registers there is, 'improperly', a volume of wills proved.[1] But this is not only exceptional; it is disconcerting. The register is not the proper place for such records: it should deal with the administration of the see, leaving court matters to other archives. The intrusion of such freak entries underlines the frequent irregularity of these documents; however nice it may be to learn of all sorts of matters but vaguely dependent on the diocesan activity, it is chastening to be reminded that the ostensible purpose, the record of the bishop's real work, may be very incomplete.

Registers roughly similar in kinds were kept by monastic institutions, though, of course, religious houses had nothing to do with the government of a territorial division of the Church or with the ordaining and instituting of parish clergy. But the official business and correspondence of a sufficiently public institution, and its duty to provide vicars for livings in which it had acquired the rectorial rights, found record in volumes properly described by this name. Few seem to have survived, but two —one an original now at Oxford, the other a later copy now at the British Museum—enabled Cardinal Gasquet to produce two volumes illustrating the fortunes of the Premonstratensian Order in the fourteenth and fifteenth centuries.[2] No doubt other similar volumes exist, but not a single monastic register seems ever to have been properly edited.

The registers form a partially systematic record of administration. Records of visitations are in themselves more systematic, but their importance is lessened by the fact that, at least for the

[1] See *Register of Henry Chichele*, ed. E. F. Jacob (1943), vol. 1, cxv.

[2] *Collectanea Anglo-Premonstratensia*, ed. F. A. Gasquet (Camden 3rd Series, vols 6 and 10; London 1904–6).

middle ages, they survive very patchily. Visitations of course, took place at intervals only, but it would seem that only quite a small number of those that did occur have left traces behind, and most of those that did touched religious houses, not parishes and their clergy. Visitations were the means by which the bishop or the archdeacon, or some other superior, informed himself of the state of his charge. The procedure was quite rigorous and stereotyped.[1] After a formal opening, the visitor examined each member of the house privately, in the presence of a notary who kept a record of the matters disclosed to the visitor (*detecta*) and of the visitor's subsequent findings (*comperta*). Both sets of information were then openly declared to the whole convent, after which the visitor issued verbal injunctions, later followed by written injunctions, designed to remedy anything found amiss. A visitation of the parish clergy was necessarily more complicated and less well organised, and moreover it was usually conducted by the archdeacon whose records are less well preserved than the bishop's; but except that the lay churchwardens were also examined in each parish concerning the condition of the church and the behaviour of the local clergy, it followed much the same method.

In the *detecta*, *comperta*, and injunctions, visitations should therefore have produced plentiful record material, and if the diocesan officials had acted as regularly as was laid down by canon law, we should possess pretty complete evidence of the state of the Church and clergy at frequent intervals. The facts of practice are different. In the later middle ages, few bishops attended regularly to this laborious duty, and while the decades of the early Reformation produced some fresh pressure,[2] visitations became rare and altogether haphazard after the reign of Elizabeth. Furthermore, in the later middle ages most monastic orders were exempt from the authority of the diocesan bishop,

[1] There is a good description in the introduction to *Visitations of Religious Houses in the Diocese of Lincoln*, ed. A. Hamilton-Thompson (Canterbury and York Society 1915), vol. I, pp. ix–xiii.

[2] Hooper, as bishop of Gloucester, carried out a well-known visitation which recorded the deplorable state of that diocese (J. Gairdner in *English Historical Review*, xix, 1904, 98ff).

and though they were visited at times by representatives of their order evidence of these occasions is even less likely to have survived. Lastly, the records of all visitations have come down to us in a state of confusion and loss; they have suffered not only from needless neglect, as do all records, but also from the understandable reluctance of cathedral officials to burden their small muniment rooms with papers of a purely historical interest. In the great diocese of York, the extant visitation papers begin only in the reign of Elizabeth I,[1] and in that of Lincoln the monitions (instructions to the clergy to be ready for the visitor) begin in 1500, the churchwardens' presentations in 1570. Typically, the two archdeaconries of that vast diocese whose records have migrated to the episcopal see preserve very little for our period, though the years 1533–1638 are covered by twenty-one valuable visitation books for the archdeaconry of Lincoln which have not, so far as I know, been exploited by historians of the Church.[2] This state of the record is quite normal, and York and Lincoln seem in fact to possess more than most diocesan archives. What knowledge we have of visitations before the sixteenth century comes in the main from episcopal registers; while it is certainly incomplete, there is no telling how incomplete it may be.

Questions concerning the state and behaviour of the clergy can sometimes be answered from accidental evidence. Thus the Puritans of the late-sixteenth and early-seventeenth centuries occasionally collected material to prove their point that the established clergy were falling down on the job, and similar detail may be found in literary sources, in sermons and pamphlets.[3] It ought

[1] J. S. Purvis, *The Archives of the York Diocesan Registry* (York: St Anthony's Hall publications, no. 2, 1952), 9.

[2] Kathleen Major, *A Handlist of the Records of the Bishop of Lincoln and of the Archdeacons of Lincoln and Stow* (Lincoln 1953). The three volumes of extracts from *Visitations in the Diocese of Lincoln 1517–1531*, ed. A. Hamilton-Thompson (Lincoln Record Society, 1940–7) have been allowed to dominate views unduly. The records of the other archdeaconries are still in their original location; no lists have been published, and they might be worth investigating.

[3] The best-known example of this kind of thing is the Puritan survey of the clergy in *A Part of a Register* (Middelburgh 1593).

to be unnecessary to draw attention to the insufficiencies of evidence produced by avowed enemies with a patent propaganda interest to serve, but much history of the Elizabethan Church has been confidently written out of such material, without any application of stringent criticism.[1] In particular, this evidence lacks the safeguards inherent in records produced systematically by a known administrative process. However, even genuine visitation papers should not be so readily accepted as they often are. Certainly the visitor's *comperta* form a check on the possible malice or prejudice concealed in the *detecta*, and his injunctions should reveal fairly accurately what to the observer on the spot seemed genuinely in need of correction. But, for one thing, the injunctions did not and could not deal with everything found at a visitation. In so far as the visitor uncovered general errors or weaknesses, he pronounced his remedies by enjoining amendment. Thus if he found a monastery generally in a state of hostility to its abbot or failing to perform the services of religion, or if he found the fabric of a church in decay or a parson at war with his parish, he could state the truth and call for better things in his injunctions. If, on the other hand, the matters revealed touched specific delicts of particular persons—breaches of the law, especially the sexual offences much stressed at visitations— the visitation was but the first step in establishing the truth and enforcing the law of the Church. Historians have often taken it too readily for granted that the stories of fornication, nuns' children, homosexuality, and other breaches of the moral law (frequenting of taverns, for example, or the playing of bowls) prove the truth about the condition of the clergy. When priests by committing these offences allegedly rendered themselves punishable in the Church courts, the result of a visitation should have been trial in the bishop's or archdeacon's court, and in every such case it is, by rights, necessary to follow the matter further in

[1] E.g. Christopher Hill's valuable *Economic Problems of the Church from Archbishop Whitgift to the Long Parliament* (Oxford 1956) relies very uncritically on the *ex parte* statements of witnesses known to have been hostile. Their statements may have been true, but they have not here been tested against ascertainable fact.

the records of these tribunals. These records do often exist, but that is not to say that the task is easy or even, quite often, possible at all.

The largest part, in fact, of the extant product of the medieval and early-modern Church lies in the archives of its many courts, and yet even so more is unquestionably lost than preserved. What does survive is often unsorted and hard of access—there is room for much work here—and even when available far from easy to use.

The medieval Church, in England as elsewhere, was organised around a hierarchy of courts, linked by rights of appeal from lower to higher and culminating in the overriding authority of the papal court at Rome. Except that it replaced this last by *ad hoc* royal commissions, the Reformation made no difference to either structure or competence or activity. In practice, the most important courts (from the litigants' and offenders' points of view) were those held by the archdeacon and by the bishop. The former presided over a single court of first instance; he was the main disciplinarian of the Church in the front-line of the battle, a fact which accounts for the popularity in the debates of the schools of the question 'whether an archdeacon can be saved'. The bishops, and especially the two archbishops, held both courts of first instance (consistory courts) and of appeal (sometimes called audience). One of the researcher's greatest problems is posed by the existence of courts which both for first instance cases and for appeals cut across the usual geographical divisions. Thus in every bishopric and archbishopric there were 'peculiars', parishes exempt from the usual superior jurisdiction and subject to special courts; while the archbishop's Court of Arches (records at Lambeth Palace) and the statutory Court of Delegates (records at the Public Record Office) gathered in appeal jurisdiction from all over the place. Cases have often to be followed into unpredictable locations.[1]

[1] The best general account of medieval Church courts is B. L. Woodcock, *Medieval Ecclesiastical Courts in the Diocese of Canterbury* (Oxford 1952); see also Holdsworth, *History of English Law* (ed. of 1956), i.64*–77*, 598–614, and in

The materials produced by these courts depended in part on the manner in which the case was started. In 'instance' cases, a private party initiated the action; in '*ex officio*' cases the judge himself began the business, either on behalf of the court ('*ex officio mero*') or on behalf of a third party, usually an inferior official ('*ex officio promoto*'). Cases arising out of visitations belong to the '*ex officio mero*' category: that is, no special procedure was necessary to bring the matter to the notice of the court, the discoveries of the visitation being treated as equivalent to a formal accusation. In instance cases, the action began with an information in writing delivered to the registrar of the court which requested that the defendant be called to answer (citation). Once a case had commenced, procedure was essentially the same for both types and very like that used in the King's equity courts, which, in fact, had borrowed their methods from the Church courts. The parties exchanged written statements; proof was obtained by examining witnesses; and the stages of the process, as well as the final decision, were registered in act books. By contrast with the equity courts, those of the Church at all stages used oaths to bind the parties to future truthfulness and involved the judges far more as active pursuers of the facts; also, of course, the law administered was different—down to 1538 the canon law of the universal Church, and thereafter a mixture of inherited canon law, modifying civil law, and personal preferences.[1]

This procedure thus produced two main categories of records, the cause papers (or documents in the case) and the act books.

general Miss Churchill's book (see 94). Useful detail is found in R. Peters, *Oculus Episcopi* (Manchester 1963) and E. R. Brinkworth, *The Archdeacon's Court* (London 1942); on the consistory court see C. Morris, 'A Consistory Court in the Middle Ages', *Journal of Ecclestical History*, xiv. 150ff. The only entry book of a court in print was published by M. Bowker, *An Episcopal Court Book for the Diocese of Lincoln 1514–20* (Lincoln Record Society, vol. 61, 1967), with a valuable introduction.

[1] The law of the Church of England has never been authoritatively reformed or stated, despite frequent expressions of interest and occasional attempts. In practice the courts seem to have accepted the revision of 1604, though it lacked parliamentary endorsement and therefore legal force.

The latter should give a full account of every process, though in summary and standardised form, while the former should amplify this by providing the full details of the case, the arguments of the parties, and the testimony of witnesses; and if either category survived in anything like completeness this would, no doubt, be a fair description. In practice, however, cause papers are rarely found and very many act books are missing. Archdeacons' records are particularly rare, and a run of act books like that from the archdeaconry of St Albans which in nineteen volumes covers the years 1574–1627 continuously is quite exceptional, and very valuable for that reason.[1] But bishops' courts do not fare much better. Even the diocese of Canterbury provides books only from 1372 onwards;[2] in the well provided archives of Lincoln there is no court book before 1446, while cause papers, in great variety, begin only in the middle of the sixteenth century.[3] In general, it would appear to be true that the records get very much more complete after the Reformation and especially from the seventeenth century onwards, which means that fullness of information and relevance to historical studies have got reversed: we can know most about these courts when they have ceased to play any significant part in English society. Nevertheless, the total quantity, even for the period covered by this survey, is large enough. To quote Woodcock: 'All modern scholars will be dead before a thousandth part of the *acta* of English ecclesiastical courts can be printed, so vast is their bulk'.[4] In actual fact, only one has so far been printed;[5] the remainder the historian must seek out in the depositories themselves, and except for the occasional survey and the preliminary list provided by the Pilgrim Trust (see p. 93) he can have little idea of what he may find.

Inaccessibility is one reason for the neglect these records have received; their difficulty is another. The act books of Church

[1] Peters, *Oculus Episcopi*, 107.

[2] Woodcock, *Medieval Ecclesiastical Courts*, 140–1.

[3] Kathleen Major, *A Handlist of the Records of the Bishop of Lincoln* (Lincoln 1953).

[4] Woodcock, *Medieval Ecclesiastical Courts*, 140.

[5] Above, 102, n. 1.

courts are among the more strikingly repulsive of all the relics of the past—written in cramped and hurried hands, in very abbreviated and technical Latin, often preserved (if that is the right word) in fairly noisome conditions, ill-sorted and mostly unlisted, unindexed and sometimes broken in pieces. Cause papers, where they exist, are likely to be found in total confusion and with no guide to their contents. It is a great pity that the Church did not pay better attention to its records at a time when it had the money and leisure to do so; the heroic efforts of the present are handicapped by serious lack of both. Only young scholars, still enthusiastic, physically strong, and possessed of a sound digestion, are advised to tackle these materials. On the other hand, they offer a most promising field to research because they illumine the history of Church and people in ways that no other source can. They take one to the realities. This is because of the wide range of cases that came before these courts, and because that range touched the human being so very near his personal centre.

In the first place, the courts constituted the chief instrument for ordering the Church and the clergy themselves. They enforced the law, both moral and positive, upon men in orders, protected buildings and equipment, and saw to the observance of the faith. Thus the records should reveal much concerning both the standards of the clergy and the problems of heresy, to take matters in which historians have been too ready to rely on remarks made by onlookers in books and pamphlets, instead of seeking the facts. At the very least, the court records greatly amplify what may be learned from bishops' registers, for these record only a selection of the matters dealt with by the authorities. Secondly, the courts attended to disputes which arose between the clergy and the laity over the former's rights, more particularly their claims to tithe. And lastly, they had to be used by the laity themselves in some matters of vital private concern—moral delinquency, matrimonial affairs, and last wills and testaments, all of which led to massive litigation. The information available on this wide range of issues, if it were ever properly extracted and evaluated, would add great detail, precision and depth to our knowledge of the lives of people, both lay and spiritual, at all levels of society. It might for instance confirm the generalised picture, derived from opponents' denunciations, which historians have formed of the state of the Church on the eve of the Reformation or in the face of the Puritan attack, but what little has so far been done suggests that serious study would at least modify, very probably largely subvert, these somewhat glib notions, The life of the village, and even its beliefs and attitudes, which on occasion make themselves known in the records of the State, are likely to present themselves much more fully in the obscure, difficult, patchy records of the Church. Once again one must say that while the condition of the manuscripts makes certain that no total, systematic study is possible, it is equally clear that no single detail or circumstance can confidently be asserted to be lost until the matter has been investigated.[1]

One class of ecclesiastical court records deserves a word to itself. Until 1857, all testaments had to be proved in a Church court: in the archdeacon's or bishop's, if the property involved all lay in one diocese, in the archbishop's 'prerogative' probate court if it extended into more than one diocese. As between Canterbury and York, the probate of wills remained to the end of our period an essentially unresolved dispute. This activity produced a huge deposit of records, especially at the prerogative court of Canterbury, consisting of wills and accompanying papers, and the wills themselves were, in this court at least, transcribed into legible and well indexed registers. Until recently, all this stuff was kept at Somerset House in London, but everything except the registers is in process of being transferred to the Public Record Office which hopes in time to be able to sort it properly and make it accessible. A name index of this collection, covering the years from 1383 to outside our period, was published, in

[1] The sort of thing that can be done is variously suggested by A. Hamilton Thompson, *The English Clergy and their Organisation in the Later Middle Ages* (Oxford 1947); F. D. Price, 'The Abuses of Excommunication and the Decline of Ecclesiastical Discipline under Queen Elizabeth', *Eng. Hist. Rev.* lvii (1942), 106ff; M. Bowker, *The Secular Clergy in the Diocese of Lincoln 1495–1520* (Cambridge 1968).

several volumes, in the Index Library of the British Record Society which has also dealt with a number of episcopal probate registries.[1] The importance of wills, especially when accompanied by administrative documents like inventories of possessions, needs no stressing. For the history of individuals, families and their possessions they are much better evidence than official inquisitions; they throw light on fluctuations in the standard of living and on social mobility; their contents may testify to literacy and learning; in their pious formulae, they can even yield indications of changing religious climates and the beliefs of obscure men and women. So little is known about Shakespeare that not surprisingly the rather conventional opening words of his will have become a main point of study for those who want to claim him for this or that variety of the Christian faith. The value of a more serious use of wills has been demonstrated by W. K. Jordan who also usefully discusses the technical problems which they present to the researcher.[2] Even though little exists before the fifteenth century, the available mass is enormous, and very little of it is in print. Wills are not, by and large, inconvenient of access, can usually be read, and ought to be used more often.

Episcopal records were the product of the regular organisation of the Church; beside them we must put the deposit of the more intermittent work of institutions intended to rule the Church from above. Throughout the middle ages, the Church had its monarch, the pope; however often he might prove unable to exercise direct rule, more frequently he was only too efficient as ruler of his distant charge. The pope as monarch both administered the English Church (drew revenues from it and gave executive orders) and provided justice to litigants. Of both activities there is plentiful evidence in the papal archives in the Vatican, but these are neither readily opened nor made accessible by published lists or indexes. Attempts have been made to ex-

---

[1] See Mullins, *Texts and Calendars*, 104ff (incomplete). Testaments have sometimes been published, here and there, by local record societies: see the index to Mullins.

[2] W. K. Jordan, *Philanthropy in England 1480–1660* (London 1959), esp. 22ff.

tract from the papal registers matters relevant to English history; these have been calendared in one volume of petitions to the pope (1342–1429)[1] and, so far, fifteen volumes of papal letters to England (1198–1492),[2] but there need be no doubt that much more can be found. The whole financial and economic position of the English provinces receives much illumination from material found at Rome,[3] and new things concerning its political and spiritual fortunes are at intervals discovered there.

By rights, the replacement of the pope by the King in the 1530's should make such studies easier, and in so far as ecclesiastical matters (legislation, administration, taxation) were transferred to the royal bureaucracy this is true. However, the royal supremacy over the Church was also embodied in ecclesiastical institutions, and here the position is less satisfactory. As vicegerent in spirituals, Thomas Cromwell undoubtedly organised some sort of court in the years 1536–40, but of this body's possibly slight activities no record has yet been discovered.[4] After 1559, the royal government over the Church was exercised through frequently renewed ecclesiastical commissions which acquired institutional identity as the two courts of High Commission for the provinces of Canterbury and York respectively. Here again fate has been unkind to the historian: the records of the larger and more important court for Canterbury were destroyed in the storm which in the first session of the Long Parliament swept the institution away. In writing its history, R. G. Usher in the main relied on piecemeal, haphazard evidence in the royal archives,[5] and though rather more is known by now the real material is

[1] H.M.S.O. 1896.

[2] H.M.S.O. 1893–1960.

[3] See W. E. Lunt, *Financial Relations of the Papacy with England to 1327* and *1327–1534* (2 vols, Cambridge, Mass. 1939, 1962) which utilises both English and Vatican archives.

[4] In this respect as in others it resembles the court held by Wolsey as papal legate equipped with authority over both the English provinces. I am, however, informed by Dr R. S. Schofield that the materials recently transferred from Somerset House to the Public Record Office may contain some evidence of Cromwell's vicegerency.

[5] R. G. Usher, *The Rise and Fall of the High Commission* (Oxford 1913), 361ff.

gone for ever. On the other hand, that produced by the northern High Commission has recently been found, in quantity, in the York archives, and its exploitation has begun. The High Commission used the procedure of the ordinary Church courts and in much of its business simply duplicated them, but it also concerned itself more exclusively with weighty matters, especially with the enforcement of the Elizabethan settlement upon Puritan and other dissenters; and the northern records show, by illuminating the history of Puritanism in the smaller, less populous and more backward part of the country, what we have lost for the history of the main part.[1]

The other general organ of the Church, embodying a representative as against a monarchical principle, consisted of Councils, sometimes for the whole realm and often organised by papal legates, and the more normal Convocations, one for each province. These were assemblies with an upper house of bishops and abbots and a lower house of elected representatives of the lower clergy. They met at irregular and sometimes long intervals to settle disputes, make provincial regulations, and grant taxes to King or pope.[2] Unlike the Parliament, which the Convocations resembled and often accompanied, these ecclesiastical meetings never in our period achieved an independent series of memorials; there was nothing like the King's Chancery available to attend to the keeping of records. However, the products of those meetings were usually communicated to all the bishops in letters from the archbishop and have therefore left record in many registers; and in the later middle ages Canterbury archiepiscopal registers sometimes contain actual accounts of proceedings.[3] The materials

[1] See R. A. Marchant, *The Puritans and the Church Courts in the Diocese of York 1560–1642* (London 1960). The book rests on all the surviving records of the northern Church courts (pp. 220–1) among which those of the High Commission take pride of place.

[2] D. B. Weske, *Convocation of the Clergy* (London 1937). For a list down o 1536 see *Handbook of British Chronology*, ed. F. M. Powicke and E. B. Fryde (2nd ed., 1961), 546ff.

[3] This became standard practice from the archiepiscopate of Simon Islip, 1349–66 (see *Register of Henry Chichele*, ed. E. F. Jacob, 1943, vol. I, cxv).

left behind by Councils and Convocations cannot therefore be sought in any one place; the task of assembling them from the actual archives into which they were transcribed calls for the intervention of an editor whose task is invariably formidable.[1] Yet heroes in this mould have come forward. The eighteenth-century antiquary, David Wilkins, single-handedly searched registers to produce four volumes of materials of ecclesiatical assemblies covering eight centuries.[2] Pioneering work of this kind is bound to be deficient, and a commission of scholars has for many years been at work producing a new collection of such materials, properly edited. How much more immense than even Wilkins' achievement the product will ultimately be is shown by the fact that the only two volumes so far published devote over 1,400 pages to the years 1205-1313 alone.[3] This collection includes summons to meetings, often from papal legates who assembled representatives from all the provinces, orders and statutes issued, and complaints received—like the statement of grievances of 1264 which begins: 'The realm of England is grieved because the lord pope is not content with the subsidy called peter's pence but extorts from the whole English clergy a heavier contribution, and tries to extort one heavier yet.' For the political and constitutional history of the English Church, and also at times of the secular power, these materials are of vital concern.[4]

From the very top to the very bottom: the records of one ecclesiastical organisation remain to be discussed, namely those of the parish. The lives of parson and parishioners are widely

[1] Thus it has been shown that there are sixty-four MSS containing material relevant to the statutes issued by two thirteenth-century archbishops (C. R. Cheney, in *Journal of Eccl. History*, xii [1961], 33f).

[2] D. Wilkins, *Concilia Magnae Britanniae et Hiberniae* (4 vols, London 1737). The years 1200-1640 are covered in vol. 1, 505-vol. 4, 553.

[3] *Councils and Synods, with other Documents relating to the English Church*, vol. 2, ed. F. M. Powicke and C. R. Cheney (Oxford 1964).

[4] A primitive piece of collecting and editing has produced *The Records of the Northern Convocation*, ed. W. D. Macray (Surtees Society, no. 113; 1907). This covers the years 1279-1714; after 1545 it is based on a specialised record, the surviving Act Books of the York Convocation. Nothing like this appears to exist for Canterbury at so early a date.

illumined by the materials already considered, especially those of visitations and courts, so much so that a collection from such material—none of it produced by the parish—has been entitled *Tudor Parish Documents*.[1] But while there we may read of the parish church ('the chancel is not whited nor paved in such decent sort as it ought to be'), behaviour there (a man is excommunicated for forcibly putting another 'out of his stall before prayer time on the Sabbath day'), or the inadequacies of the clergy ('their curate doth not instruct the youth of their parish every Sunday and holy day'; 'the said curate doth not celebrate and read the divine service plainly and distinctly'), they touch the parish from outside and, as it were, by accident. The parish itself, in fact, produced very few documents and these of two kinds: registers, and the accounts of churchwardens and overseers.[2]

Parish registers are in a unique position among English records in that we know exactly how they came to be instituted: they were ordered to be kept by Thomas Cromwell's *Injunctions* of 1538. Every incumbent was there enjoined to keep a record of christenings, burials and marriages in his parish. The purpose, almost certainly, was to provide a statistical basis for government action, a record of the people of England, but not unnaturally the usual suspicion arose that the government intended to use its knowledge in order to tax, and the injunction was not at first generally observed. However, in 1598 the clergy were once more instructed to the same effect and permitted to copy earlier registers especially back to 1558, if there were any, into parchment books, for better preservation; and from the second half of the sixteenth century onwards a surprising number of parishes do in fact possess registers of this kind. An older list for Canterbury diocese shows some surviving back to 1538, but a general proliferation from about 1570.[3] It is said that registers dating back to 1538 exist for about one-eighth of all of England's parishes,

[1] Ed. J. S. Purvis (Cambridge 1948).

[2] A. Hamilton Thompson, *Parish History and Records* (London 1919).

[3] C. E. Woodruff, *An Inventory of the Parish Registers and other Records in the Diocese of Canterbury* (Canterbury 1922).

but most of them are later copies.[1] No really complete list has yet been published, though one is being prepared by the Society of Genealogists. It would appear that hitherto unknown registers from the sixteenth and seventeenth centuries can still be found in obscure corners in country churches.[2]

The value of parish registers is immense but limited. That is to say, they are so specialised in purpose that they contribute to almost nothing except a study of population—size, age, distribution, mobility, family structure—but for that single purpose they are not only indispensable but enormously revealing. If anything like a reasonable quantity can be obtained, and it looks as though this will happen, they will provide a systematic basis for this very fundamental aspect of social history from the later sixteenth century onwards. The task is difficult, and anything like amateur confidence in tackling it could be disastrous, for these registers pose some hidden problems. They were kept very differently in different places—with different degrees of precision and even on different principles of selection. A register of christenings is not the same thing as register of births. Even before the Church of England gave up its claim to comprehend all subjects of the Crown, some nonconforming members of the society could escape the parson's attention. Technical questions like these stand quite apart from the inevitable gaps in the series which a technical training in mathematical statistics can sometimes overcome. Nor do the registers offer more than a tabular form of history; the people recorded there remain units that get baptised, married and buried, and have assignable relatives, but beyond that they lack identity. However, the scientific study of population not only depends on parish registers but can with confidence be based on what survives.

[1] Emmison, *Archives*, 50f.

[2] For published registers see the publications of the Parish Register Society (80 vols) and the various productions for individual counties—e.g. 47 volumes for Shropshire, 107 volumes for Lancashire, or 127 volumes for Yorkshire. The index to Mullins, *Texts and Calendars*, lists some scattered publications. A word of warning: old registers are not only being found but also being destroyed by heedless incumbents.

The accounts of churchwardens (responsible for the financial problems of the parish church, vestments, church furniture and the like) and overseers of the poor (responsible from 1597 for the collection and distribution of the poor rate) survive much more patchily but—the former at least—start rather earlier. According to Mr Emmison, only one in a hundred parishes possesses pre-Reformation accounts, though the number doubles for the reign of Elizabeth.[1] The sixty parishes listed by Woodruff yield six accounts before 1500 and another fifteen in the sixteenth century, in the diocese of Canterbury alone. The earliest so far found appears to be at St Michael's Church in Bath where seventy-seven rolls cover the years 1349-1575.[2] Many other parishes provide occasional medieval evidence, but in Cox's list for the sixteenth and seventeenth centuries (about 260 items) only six start before 1640. This is a source which becomes systematic and complete only after our period ends. The overseers' records are in much the same condition. Where they exist they provide evidence of the actual working of the poor law—whether and how the statutory relief was applied—evidence that cannot be got either from the pious intentions of the lawmakers or even from the testimony of justices' sessions that poor rates were levied. Overseers' accounts are among the more surprisingly unused categories of English records, in part at least because almost none have been printed.[3] Yet there is a special value in all these parish records: they take one below the level of the politically articulate part of society. Though the many court records, of Church or State, do this too, they see the poor and the commons very much from above—from the point of view of government and law-enforcement—while the parish records see them, so to speak from inside. But their evidence is very restricted in its applica-

[1] *Archives*, 50ff.

[2] J. C. Cox, *Churchwardens' Accounts from the fourteenth century to the close of the seventeenth century* (London 1913), chs 2-3.

[3] For an example see E. M. Leonard, *The Early History of English Poor Relief* (London 1900), 327-30; so valuable a study as T. G. Barnes, *Somerset 1625-1640* (London 1961) seems to have done without overseers' accounts or indeed any parish documents.

tion and rather impersonal, quite apart from being extremely patchy and incomplete. It is, perhaps, no wonder that these materials have in the main attracted the attention of the genealogist, the antiquary, and the local amateur. Yet they have important things to say about the very base of society and await systematic exploitation.

In general, then, the records of the Church make possible a great deal of knowledge within well defined limits. They tell much about the organisation, government and general running of the Church, and the judicial material, like all court records, preserves massive evidence of many people's lives. Before the last quarter of the fourteenth century, episcopal and monastic registers compose almost all the material there is, but this causes less distress than it might because of the often unpredictable variety of their entries. From the fifteenth century onwards, the records of courts vary the diet, and after the Reformation the deposits left by the Church increase rapidly to enormous size. Post-Reformation Church records have scarcely been touched so far by the historian. The history of the reformed Church of England, even more than that of its medieval predecessor, has been mainly written out of secular materials and far too often simply out of opinions expressed (as a rule) by opponents and critics. This is the more understandable because these records are widely scattered, are full of technical difficulties, and throw light on little except government—government in repose and government in action. If we want to know about the spiritual side of the Church, about the Church as an instrument of salvation and a servant of God, about people's beliefs and faith and the problems of the soul, we shall rarely find even a hint in the records of the Church. The occasional persecution of an heretic is almost the only thing to bring such matters into the archives, but it does so in a peculiar and limiting way because the organisation is concerned only with discovering and punishing offences, not with the human and spiritual realities behind the often standardised charges of deviation. After the Reformation, the records of visitations, Church courts, and churchwardens provide quite frequent evidence of the impact of the new order, but again rather at one remove. We learn about the attempts to make the clergy conform to whatever the official ruling of the day was; we hear of attempts to create a more learned or better behaved ministry; we can trace the vicissitudes of Reformation politics in the fortunes of vestments and altar candles.[1] But what it all meant in terms of faith and worship, of obedience and resistance, is something that at best we can imaginatively divine from these records.

[1] See J. E. Oxley, *The Reformation in Essex* (Manchester 1965) which uses six churchwardens' accounts to help out the evidence of quarter sessions and archdeacon's records.

CHAPTER 4

Official Records: Lesser Authorities

Although in the theory of the law all authority in England emanated from the king and all government was his, to exercise in person or by delegation, in practice the majority of Englishmen before 1640 felt most frequently and knew best the attentions of lesser agencies. To them, the officers of boroughs and manors—the two main peripheral units of secular government—certainly represented government more consistently than did those of Chancery or Exchequer, of King's Bench or Common Pleas, even of the sheriff or justice of the peace. The powers exercised by these lowly courts and agents might all be derived from the Crown, but, from our present point of view, the chief significance of that fact lay in the Crown's ability to investigate them by enquiries of *quo warranto*: by what right do you—lord of a manor, or mayor and corporation—claim to hold these rights? *Quo warranto* proceedings, initiated by a statute of Edward I and thereafter frequently employed until their use by Charles II to rig his Parliaments brought them into disrepute, give much valuable information on the origin and extent of local government, its powers and deficiencies but they properly belong to the records of the central government. The records of local government are the products of those inferior jurisdictions themselves. They are naturally found scattered in many places. Those of chartered boroughs are as a rule still in the muniment rooms of townhalls and the like; those of manorial administration may be in private hands, in county record offices, in the libraries of colleges and the like, or—massively—at the Public Record Office. The two categories are best taken in turn.

Borough records are essentially of four possible kinds: charters, court records, minute and letter books, and accounts. Of these, the first again really belong to another originating agency.

Boroughs based their rights of self-government on charters which enfranchised them from the control of a feudal lord, and the larger part of these charters came from the Crown. However, lesser lords, too, owned towns to which, often slowly and sometimes very late, they granted rights of incorporation and government, and while the royal charters may be found enrolled in the archives of the King's Chancery, private charters survive only in the archives of the receiving boroughs, with the exception of those that have found their way accidentally into such places as the British Museum. Even though the charters are not, therefore, 'organically' the product of borough administration, they are best looked for in borough archives. Fortunately the work has been done, and the published catalogues are comprehensive.[1]

The other three categories explain themselves. Once a borough existed, and whatever the precise arrangements for its government might be, it possessed the usual medieval instruments of government, that is courts of law; it was ruled by committees which might record their transactions and keep copies of instructions received or letters sent out; and it collected a revenue for purposes of local administration which needed to be accounted for. There might be other miscellaneous deposits in its archives, but those three kinds sum up the bulk of it. What really matters is the extent to which such potential record-material either ever existed or now survives, for it is on this question that the value of these materials for the writing of history really turns. And here one encounters the greatest variety as well as every kind of frustration.

In the first place, borough records now extant start at a great many different dates. In 1932, a committee set up by the House of Commons to organise the study and publication of the lives of all members of the English Parliament, since its inception, produced a return of records available in archives of boroughs 'which returned burgesses to Parliament before 1547'.[2] Parlia-

[1] A. Ballard and J. Tait, *British Borough Charters 1047–1307* (2 vols; Cambridge 1913, 1923); M. Weinbaum, *British Borough Charters 1307–1660* (Cambridge 1943).

[2] House of Commons, *Accounts and Papers* 1931–2, vol. 10, 663ff. Why 1547 is not clear: the membership of the unreformed House was settled, after a

mentary boroughs, especially before that date, are by no means equal to chartered boroughs; still, they composed the substantial part of England's medieval towns, and no other comparable list yet exists. From it, it appears that only four towns had records going back before 1300: Hereford, London, Totnes, and Wallingford. The fourteenth century yielded sixteen, including such important centres as Norwich, Bristol and Salisbury. Nine more start in the next half-century (including Southampton, Coventry and Winchester), and another twelve—among which York at last appears—before 1500. But twenty had to wait for the sixteenth century, and four did not manage to preserve anything even for a time as late as this. The accidents of survival no doubt account for much of this diversity; not only were records often ill-treated or neglected but much was unquestionably destroyed in occasional risings, rebellions and riots. The peasants' rebellion of 1381 is known to have removed much historical material; the northern risings of the sixteenth century contributed their part to the policy of unplanned weeding; decentralised muniments are among the most perishable of commodities. The tale is not yet ended: the Commons' committee were informed by the mayor of Bodmin that his town's records had been thrown away a few years before because they had become rotten. As it is, the relative internal peace which England has enjoyed since 1154 has enabled more to survive the centuries than one might have expected, and in many instances the enormous gaps and deficiencies can confidently be ascribed to the authorities' failure ever to keep decent, regular, or complete records of their doings.

The remarkable diversity, and the kind of thing one can find, may best be illustrated by looking at a few selected, specially important, but reasonably representative towns. Reading possesses a 'diary of the corporation' or minute book, from 1431.[1] This is quite late, but it is detailed and informative. Shrewsbury, on the other hand, starts early but tells less: admissions to burgess-

considerable increase in the sixteenth century, in the reign of James I, and the committee should have gone up to 1625.

[1] Published for 1431–1640: ed. J. M. Building (3 vols; Reading 1892–6).

ship are recorded from 1209 (and the rolls give the names of parents and children: demographers, please note), the accounts of the bailiffs begin in 1256 and the rolls of their court in 1272.[1] In general, such rolls are older than other town records: Gloucester preserves account and burgess rolls from the early and late-fourteenth century respectively, but has no minute books of council before 1486.[2] A town well supplied with muniments is that important Midland centre, Coventry, but almost nothing pre-dates 1400: court books begin in 1421,[3] rolls of recognisances in 1392,[4] the chamberlains' account books in 1499, the municipal treasury books in 1561.[5] The 4,580 miscellaneous deeds go back to the reign of Henry III, but that sort of document strictly belongs to the category of private papers, discussed in the next chapter.

Two important towns of medieval England provide an instructive contrast: Exeter and Southampton. Both have massive municipal archives, but the second also has an active Record Society, so that much valuable information is in print, whereas the first has done nothing to make its records better known or available to anyone except the researcher on the spot. And yet it possesses rolls of the mayor's court back to 1263 and of the provost's court from 1328; other rolls, mostly of accounts, start in the early fourteenth century. Characteristically, the chamber (the town's governing body) did not begin to keep minute books until 1508.[6] Southampton's records, though not really so good, are much better known.[7] It helps that early town officers here believed in collecting books of precedents and evidences which

[1] Historical Manuscripts Commission, *15th Report*, Appendix X, 1ff.

[2] W. H. Stevenson, *Calendar of the Records of the Corporation of Gloucester* (Gloucester 1893).

[3] Published as *The Coventry Leet Book* in 4 volumes covering 1421–1622, ed. M. D. Harris (Early English Text Society 1907–13).

[4] Published for 1392–1416, ed. Alice Beardswood (Dugdale Society 1939).

[5] Hist. MSS Comm., *15th Report*, Appendix X, 101ff.

[6] Hist. MSS Comm., *Report on the Records of the City of Exeter* (H.M.S.O. 1916).

[7] Listed in Hist. MSS Comm., *11th Report*, Appendix III (1887); the corporation has also published a useful guide, *Southampton Records* (1964).

have preserved much material: thus the Oak Book is a register of ordinances collected about 1300, the Black Book transcribes ordinances, letters, conveyances, leases and other things for the years 1390 to 1620, and the town clerk's Book of Remembrances notes fines, accounts and descriptions of events from about 1300 to 1600.[1] On the other hand, current materials start much later than at Exeter: records of the court leet in 1550, the Assembly Books (minutes of the governing body) in 1602, the stewards' account books in 1428. These series, of which parts have appeared in the Southampton Record Society's publications, are incomplete and this description is even more so, though it will give a sufficient indication of the sort of thing to be found there. Both Exeter and Southampton were important ports and both preserve records relevant to this fact, though these records are, in a sense, more specifically emanations of the central than of the local government: customers' accounts at Exeter from 1300, port books (recording the traffic in the harbour) from 1427 at Southampton.

As against this variety in the south may be set the case of York where seemingly only one series survives, but this is more complete and more full of mixed information than anything to be found at Exeter or Southampton. York corporation was among the first to keep a minute book, continuous from 1474 (when it is called the Corporation House Book); but this was preceded by an earlier memoranda book which started in 1376.[2] This is a very miscellaneous record of the city's affairs, full of fascinating detail. The first and last entries so far published are so apposite to this present enquiry that they deserve quoting at length:

(2 March 1475). 'Forasmuch as the testimony and due declaration of truth been not only full pleasant to our Lord God but also been full necessary and behoveful to be made in and for the avoiding of all

[1] All these are published by the Southampton Record Society, three volumes to each book of records.

[2] *York Memoranda Book Part I (1376–1419)*, Surtees Society, vol. 120 (1912); *York Civic Records*, vols 1–8, ed. A. Raine (Yorkshire Archaeological Society, Record Series, vols 98, 103, 106, 108, 110, 112, 115, 119)—covering, so far, 1474–1588.

manner ambiguities, debates, undue titles and injurious claims,' a search of the records is ordered in a land dispute.

(13 August 1588). A letter to the Privy Council. The Corporation refuse to grant the office of town clerk in reversion because 'the said office is an office of great charge, attendance and trust by reason that all the records, charters and remembrances touching the liberties and inheritances of the said city remain in the custody of the town clerk'.

But there are now no other main series, or if there are no note of them appears to be in print.

Of all the towns of England, one has always stood apart, and the bulk of its surviving records distinguishes London quite as much as do its size and importance. They are also probably better ordered, more accessible and better catalogued than the records of any other city.[1] Though they are all kept at the Guildhall, they are clearly distinguished into two groups which are separately housed. The Corporation of London Record Office looks after the official records of the city government; the Guildhall Library takes care of other city material, more casually collected. Since what is in question here are the products of municipal government, the first is much the more important to us.

Apart from the collection of charters, dating back to 1155, and various collections and precedent books (the earliest compiled in 1274), the most important medieval record of London consists of the so-called Letter Books of the Court of Aldermen and Common Council. There are fifty of them, spanning the years 1275–1689, and the gaps are few. Though there are some letters in them, the name is derived from their classification, which is by letters, running from A to Z and AA to ZZ, with a few extra. The books are really the entry books of proceedings in the two main ruling committees of the city; or rather, they contain these important minutes down to the fifteenth century when separate Repertories for the Aldermen (1493) and Journals for the Common Council (1416) take over. Once these matters

[1] P. E. Jones and R. Smith, *A Guide to the Records in the Corporation of London Record Office and the Guildhall Library Muniment Room* (London 1951).

had been removed, the Letter Books came to be concerned with petty affairs, and the later volumes deal mostly with orphanage matters; the published calendar therefore—and rightly—does not extend beyond 1500.[1] The Repertories and Journals, unpublished and so far little used, have to be consulted in manuscript. This continuous record of the city's administration is not, however, supported by much else. A stray record of out-letters survives for 1350–70;[2] but there are, unfortunately, virtually no financial records before 1550 and few thereafter. As usual, legal records are better preserved. The oldest of the London courts, the Court of Hustings, has evidence of its (mostly civil) litigation back to 1250; the most important court, that of the lord mayor sitting in his sole capacity, is recorded from about 1300.[3] The so-called plea and memoranda rolls were produced by the Court of the Mayor and Aldermen sitting jointly; 102 in number, they cover the years 1323–1485 and have nearly all been published in summary form.[4] Down to the middle of the fourteenth century they are not, in fact, properly legal records at all but rather similar in content to the Letter Books; especially they register many royal writs. Thereafter they preserve the activities of a straightforward court of law whose business seems at first to have included many breaches of the peace but came soon to specialise in suits for debt.

The deficiencies of the corporation records for the medieval period are not much helped out by the holdings of the Guildhall Library. Here one finds some parish and ward material, for in-

[1] *Calendar of the Letter Books of the City of London*, ed. R. R. Sharpe (11 vols; London 1899–1912).

[2] *Calendar of Letters from the Mayor and Corporation of the City of London c. A.D. 1350–1370*, ed. R. R. Sharpe (London 1885). There are two rolls, with a gap for the years 1360–3; the letters are nearly all addressed to other towns, ranging from Bristol to Florence, and in the main request assistance or compensation for citizens of London.

[3] *Calendar of Early Mayor's Court Rolls 1298–1307*, ed. A. H. Thomas (Cambridge 1924). Mr Thomas's introduction gives a good brief account of the several overlapping London courts and jurisdictions.

[4] *Calendar of Plea and Memoranda Rolls*, ed. A. H. Thomas and P. E. Jones (6 vols; Cambridge 1926–61).

stance elections of ward representatives to the Common Council, and the archives of some city companies, hardly any of which precede the sixteenth century.[1] The records of even London are therefore less complete and informative than one might have hoped of a city so full of its history and so conscious of it. In fact, that the history of medieval London can be written has been triumphantly proved, but the historian who undertook that task relied far more on the central archives of the Crown than on the materials found in the city itself.[2]

None the less, there are, taking them all in all, plenty of municipal records in England, though they become really full only in the sixteenth century and massive after our period ends. How useful are they, and what do they tell? It can be said in general that they will disappoint the seeker for information on national history; they are heavily local. Of course, there are exceptions. The London Letter Books, for instance, contain an account of the coronation of Richard III, and the York registers notoriously record at that time a delighted reception of the new king which compares sadly with an equally enthusiastic tribute two years later to his victorious successor. But in view of the fact that national affairs—the affairs of kings and bishops, earls and knights and peasants—impinged all the time on all towns, such deposits astonish by their rarity. England's boroughs, to judge by their records, were intensely insular, concerned only with their own affairs and oblivious to the world around them.

Of course, this is not true, and it is especially untrue of London whose capitalists were playing a leading part in government finance by the early fifteenth century, whose gates opened on a road leading straight to the King's courts at Westminster, and within whose walls were the officers of the King's Chancery as well as the King's main fortress and prisons. The fact is that the records give the impression of insularity because they were bound

---

[1] The most important companies still retain their own records (below, 162) and are not too willing to let researchers into their secrets.

[2] Gwyn A. Williams, *Medieval London: from Commune to Capital* (London 1963), 341ff.

to do so: they are the results of internal administration and pre-serve the doings of men engaged in running the affairs of merchant communities. That these same men could be employed about other things was of no interest to the occasions which produced these records. Thus we find ordinances concerning trade and in-dustry, registers of recognisances testifying to credit transactions and borrowing, council minutes dealing with commercial prob-lems and the representatives of commercial interests, court rolls full of disputes over goods and debts. In addition, these bodies had to keep the town clean and govern an often violent community, so that there is plentiful evidence concerning street-paving and nuisances as well as minor criminal justice and the problems of the peace. 'Larger' matters are not totally absent—for instance, borough records naturally contain information on elections to the King's Parliaments—but, to say it again, there is far less than the historian might like.

The materials of town archives are therefore fundamentally of use only to the historian of those towns, which is not to deny that local history of the right kind is vitally important to a real understanding of the history of England. There are thousands of names, and some can acquire the outward semblance of men. In some places it is possible to reconstruct registers of burgesses; much demographic information can be painfully extracted; almost everywhere (wherever records survive) economic and social history finds crucial evidence. But the level of approach must be local: the records are locally produced, locally informed, and locally significant. This is by no means a form of condem-nation, which in view of the fact that all men are in some sense local would be absurd, but a proper definition of the purpose with which the historian must come to these, in the main, still unexploited sources, and of the answers which he can reasonably expect to find.

In any case, parochialism has its compensations. Where except in a civic record would one find the sad story of one William, rector of St Margaret's Lothbury in the city of London? Charged in the lord mayor's court in the year 1300 with importing four putrid wolves sent in a cask from abroad, he explained that he needed them to prepare a remedy for a disease called 'le Lou'. Under examination he admitted that he himself did not suffer from this disease, and also that he was neither a physician nor a surgeon and therefore had no call to dabble in medicine. The mayor committed him to the sheriffs' custody and called a meeting of all the medical men living in the city. This expert body, having searched their books and their minds, came to the conclusion that they knew of no illness for which the flesh of wolves was a cure (a remarkably restrained decision, when one considers the medieval pharmacopoeia), and William was handed over to his archdeacon to be punished for his insanitary presumption.[1]

If the records of towns are parochial, those of manors are likely to be more so, though it should be stressed that some manors were not only larger in area but much more populous than many towns. The origins, character and development of the manor have given historians many problems to discuss, but these need not concern us here. In the theory of the law, all England was divided into units of various sizes, not necessarily all in one piece but sometimes scattered across several villages, which cohered because they belonged to one lord and looked to his court. Since the manor is best treated as a legal entity, the only satisfactory definition one can give of it describes it as a body of rights possessed by one individual over a given quantity of lands and people. In other words, it was the lowest unit of landed proprietorship at the level of lordship or rule, a fact which distinguishes it from other administrative districts with which it overlapped, as for instance the parish (the lowest unit of the Church's organisation for the cure of souls) or the vill (the lowest unit of primitive popular self-government). But because landed proprietorship and the problems of real estate formed the main preoccupation of both medieval law and medieval society, the manor came to be the most pervasive unit even of local administration; land nearly always passed from hand to hand as manors or parcels of manors, but also men below the possessing

[1] *Calendar of Early Mayor's Court Rolls*, 51.

classes came to think of themselves as manorial tenants rather than members of a village community. The manorial court relegated its rivals to neglect, taking over the social functions of the village gathering and acquiring, by grant or custom, those police powers which the Crown had inherited from the ancient popular sessions of hundred and vill. Though manorial records are not the only material produced by the work of government at this local level in the countryside, they are so very much the most important that it will here suffice to look at them.

In fact, the manor strictly speaking produced only one kind of 'official' record, the court rolls in which the work of the manorial courts was set down. They survive in quantity, and in very many places. Thousands of manors, mostly in private hands, producing (in theory) an annual court roll for over 400 years, naturally turned out a mass of material and left it wherever a manorial lord kept his estate papers. In the course of time, these documents have gravitated to two main repositories: the Public Record Office and county record offices. The former contains rolls relating to Crown lands of all kinds, including, for instance, the extensive possessions of the Duchy of Lancaster, and, thanks to the Dissolution, also the rolls of many medieval monasteries. The total would seem to be in the region of 10,000 or more.[1] County record offices possess collections that came to them haphazardly and by a species of accident. It is known that many rolls have been destroyed; they were often kept in overcrowded solicitors' offices, and especially the drive for scrap material in the last war proved disastrous to ancient estate papers, court rolls amongst them. Since the war, most counties have been making energetic efforts to get owners to deposit their papers, so that what time, neglect and stupidity have not destroyed should be preserved in some order and become available to scholars. At present no lists exist of the material, but it is clearly very massive and at the same time thoroughly incomplete. Generally speaking, few court rolls survive from before the middle of the thirteenth

[1] Public Record Office, *Lists and Indexes*, vol. 6, a catalogue of court rolls comprising 377 pages with at least 30 entries to the page.

century, but thereafter they become quite plentiful; the well organised Essex Record Office at Chelmsford possesses a big collection dating back to 1271.[1] More, no doubt, are still in private hands. Some sixty years ago, information on these was collected by the Manorial Society, now defunct or at least silent, whose lists show that the earliest then known dated from 1246,[2] that few were then traced before 1400, and that many series did not even start until after the Restoration.[3] Those lists, however, are useful only as an indication of the size of the problem and as a start to the search. Many of the rolls recorded in them have since migrated to county record offices, others have vanished, and a good many not known at the time have since been found.[4]

The value and usefulness of court rolls are great but varied and variable. The documents are at their most useful when they consist of continuous series for given manors, but few series are as continuous as all that before the seventeenth century. The contents are miscellaneous. Court rolls are simply the record of business transacted in the manor court, held by the lord's steward for all the tenants of the manor, free and unfree, with the help of a jury or 'homage' of the manor whose size could vary from six to the whole tenantry. The homage were the sole judges of fact in any given dispute; in them was vested the knowledge of the law administered, the so-called custom of the manor, which was to be discovered by relying on agreed memory helped out at need by a search of earlier rolls. The business dealt with fell into two main categories, and from the sixteenth century onwards the classifying interference of professional lawyers and the pro-

[1] F. G. Emmison, *Guide to the Essex Record Office*, vol. 2 (Chelmsford 1948), 2ff.

[2] It was found by F. W. Maitland and now belongs to King's College, Cambridge.

[3] *Manorial Society's Monographs: lists of manor court rolls in private hands* (3 vols; London 1907–10).

[4] There are some useful near-series in the archives of St George's Chapel at Windsor (*The MSS of St George's Chapel, Windsor Castle*, ed. T. N. Dalton: Windsor 1957).

liferation of handbooks for lords and stewards produced an institutional division for those two functions. It came to be held that a manorial lord's jurisdiction comprised a court leet ('with view of frankpledge') and a court baron. The court leet elected the manorial officers (reeves, bailiffs, woodwards, etc.) and dealt with petty misdemeanours, breaches of the peace, disputes over the boundaries of holdings, nuisances, and such like; its existence allegedly depended on an explicit grant from the Crown since the powers exercised touched matters originally triable in the King's hundred and shire courts. The court baron, on the other hand, may be called the manorial lord's court for civil cases; its business concerned in the main changes in tenancy, claims of inheritance, the regulation of the manor's agricultural arrangements in open fields and commons.[1] Legal theory considered it to be the lord's natural perquisite, a right vested in him by virtue of his lordship and not derived from the King. Before about 1500, however, these distinctions are not reflected in the evidence: one manorial court, producing a single court roll, did both civil and penal business, and the entries run indiscriminately down the roll.

A manor is not a very large place, when all is said and done; its people and tenants are counted in tens, not hundreds, and the rolls are small—usually about two feet long when unrolled. The entries, too, are brief. The two of the greatest importance touch offences for which a fine or amercement fell due to the lord, and the transfer of a holding to a new tenant—both good reasons for careful record keeping. This last would concisely state the terms upon which the land was held: the claimant and his claim, the annual rent or labour services, the lump sum paid by way of an entry fine, and some reasonably accurate description of the bit of land involved. A tenant might obtain a copy of this entry as a form of title deed; he was then said to hold 'by copy of court roll' and became a copyholder. The terms of his

[1] Sometimes laywers distinguished between a court baron for free tenants and a court customary for unfree, but it is certain that in practice both sorts of tenants usually attended the same court even when villeinage was still a real thing.

copyhold, however, depended entirely on the manorial custom which lay behind the words of the roll and which varied greatly from manor to manor. The rolls provide a rapid corrective to any tendency to treat the agrarian society of medieval and early-modern England as in some way stereotyped. When to the matters mentioned are added the fairly regular record of manorial officers and the occasional notes about farming practice, the value of the rolls is essentially defined. They provide a main backbone in any analysis of the two related aspects of this rural society: the rights, claims and economic practices of the lord, and the lives, duties and rights of the peasantry. In addition, since they offer much evidence of names and family relationships, they can be used for population studies, but their variety and scattered location, and especially the many gaps in series, make systematic exploitation difficult and at times impossible.

What these rolls may tell is best shown by an example. The court rolls of a Bedfordshire manor have been published for the last years of the thirteenth century, and on the first few pages the following entries, interspersed with others of a like kind (here omitted) are found in straightforward and uncategorised sequence:[1]

Order to attach Gregory Moule for that he married one of the lord's bondswomen without licence.

Richard Attestile, Christina Attestile, attached for that they were found coming out of the lord's corn. In mercy,[2] 6*d*. Pledge,[3] Simon Edeline.

. . . Lord Peter de Loreng demised and granted to John, elder son of Richard of Wootton, for his service and for 2*s*. by way of entry fine, 3 acres of land of the field of Wingfield [the exact description of the land, half-acre by half-acre, follows].

[1] *Court Rolls of Chalgrave Manor 1278–1313*, ed. M. K. Dale (Bedfordshire Historical Record Society, vol. 28, 1950), 2–6. The editor has usefully provided a translation, but I have taken the liberty of slightly amending her English text by the Latin.

[2] I.e. fined.

[3] Guarantor of payment.

Roger of Tilsworth distrained to be at the next court to answer for that his winnowers hoed badly and cut the lord's corn.

All the customary tenants of the lord paid fine for tallage, 20s. . . .

The whole court says that Juliana le Berre . . . has unjustly carried away four sheaves of oats . . . Therefore the bailiff is ordered to attach her.

Gilbert le Hare came [into court] and sought the land held by William Ive, his father. And is received as tenant of that land, doing therefor to the lord his services due and accustomed. And has paid 23s. 4d. fine to the lord for entry into that land.

Enforcement of good order, the protection of the lord's rights, the registering of changes in tenancy mingle in characteristic fashion; the last note, recording the admission of a new tenant and his entry fine, would have been the basis of a copyhold.

That, however, even contemporaries made some distinction of weight in the business dealt with by the manor courts appears from another form of record. It would seem that in many places the rough and clumsy court rolls were, on occasion, excerpted or abstracted into more permanent documents bound in book form —court books. Thus there are hardly any court rolls extant for the abbey of St Albans, one of the great manorial lords of southern England, and while the peasants' destruction of muniments during their rebellion may account for the dearth of materials before 1381, practice must account for the fact that later years do no better. For all the many manors of the house, rolls for only twenty-nine years have been found between 1348 and the Dissolution (1539). On the other hand, registers of the court book type give a pretty full account of things from the earlier thirteenth century onwards.[1] But, essentially, of only one kind

[1] A. E. Levett, 'Courts and Court Rolls of St Albans Abbey', *Transactions of the Royal Historical Society* (1924), 52ff; 'Studies in the Manorial Organisation of St Albans Abbey', *Studies in Manorial History* (Oxford 1938), 79ff. The present location of these books shows how much search is necessary in gathering these manorial materials: British Museum, Cambridge University Library, Sidney Sussex College (Cambridge), Hertfordshire County Record Office, Bodleian Library, several private hands.

of business: transactions in land. The ephemeral and petty affairs of the village vanish; what happened to the one reality—real estate—was carefully transcribed for the information of later generations and the establishment of rights. Court books, as distinct from the rolls from which they derive, are really registers of grants, admissions to tenancy, transfers of holdings, enquiries and occasionally disputes.[1]

The court rolls, the official papers produced by manorial administration, thus form a necessary first instrument in any serious study of the lives of far and away the largest part of the people and of the major sector of the economy. They stand behind any book on these subjects, whether it be the detailed investigation of a single manor[2] or an attempt to analyse the features of the whole agrarian economy.[3] However, as the foot-notes and bibliographies of such works show at a glance, by themselves court rolls do not take the historian very far. Archivally, as 'official records', they do stand by themselves, but—more than any other category so far discussed—they really belong to a complex of materials most of which has no 'official' origin. The historian of rural England, and much else besides, must search among the sources produced by the private concerns of private individuals.

[1] See *Chertsey Abbey Court Rolls Abstract*, ed. Elsie Toms (Surrey Record Society, vol. 21; 1954). This is a calendar of an MS volume (British Museum Lansdowne MS 434) which, despite the title given to it by the editor, is itself an abstract from the rolls.

[2] E.g. Lord Leconfield, *Sutton and Duncton Manors* (London 1956).

[3] E.g. E. Kerridge, *The Agricultural Revolution* (London 1967).

CHAPTER 5

Private Materials

The distinction between official material and private is not easy to make but it is real nevertheless. The latter may be defined as documents produced by individuals or organisations that are not in any way representative of government, lay or spiritual, but—especially in the period under review—many seemingly private organisations closely resembled those of government and had governmental functions. Thus it is hard to know what distinguishes the territorial domain of, say, the Percies from that held by the duke of Lancaster or the prince-bishop of Durham, except that the last two came to be absorbed into the Crown's competence whereas the former did not. Yet this point, irrelevant in a way to historical understanding, has archival consequences and therefore offers a criterion valid here. Those documents which in the end properly belonged to the royal archives may be defined as official, while similar materials from the past of families that never came to be absorbed by the Crown remain private. Even this archival distinction is not perfect because (as we shall see) records of an indisputably private kind sometimes quite rightly and naturally survive among the Crown's records without thereby becoming official. Nor has it been possible in this book to keep all truly private materials from being listed together with the truly public stuff to which they belong: witness the private parliamentary diaries discussed above.[1] Yet, all this allowed for, and firmly reminding ourselves that what are in question are not only character and content but also at times origin and location, we must insist on the distinction and turn to the historical materials produced by persons not engaged in the government of State or Church.

The records of the past have ever been exposed to the hazards

[1] P. 88.

of survival, and here private records are likely to have fared worse than public. Public documents have two advantages: the needs of a continuous administrative machine, and especially of courts of law, to create an official memory for themselves, and the relative continuity of location. It is true that the present-day contents of the Public Record Office were collected, after 1839, from several government depositories, and it is also true that some of those depositories were then in a shocking state. However, by comparison, private archives face much more uncertain conditions. The King's government never lapsed between 1200 and 1640; families die out, properties are dispersed, private muniment rooms are rare and private record-keeping has little continuity. It can be taken for granted that proportionately more is lost of what was produced by non-governmental agencies, that regular series are hard to find, that survival is entirely haphazard. To the historian, and especially for this present purpose, only what still exists really matters, but it is worth remembering that the predominance of the public record in the period 1200–1640 owes something at least to its greater power to survive. This is not, however, to make out that the private material is ever likely to have rivalled the public in bulk, only to suggest that its present, rather fragmentary state is not quite real: private lives and their daily ordering were not as primitive as the extant materials suggest. In any case, there is plenty of the stuff still around. Once again, these materials are scattered and unsystematic, and there can be no hope of giving a full account of them here. All one can do is to analyse their types, describe samples, indicate their uses, and especially discover the facts of chronological differentiation. The types to be discussed are three: estate documents, letters, and business archives.

(a) ESTATE DOCUMENTS

Property produces records, and throughout these centuries property virtually equalled land. Landowners of all kinds, from the greatest duke to the peasant (let him be called owner for once) with his village holding, needed evidence of their wealth in order to retain, exploit and transfer it. Above all, they needed proof of possession, that is to say title deeds. Deeds—documents which recorded grants, sales, leases, agreements, and settlements of disputes—form the basis of a landed society; those issued by the Crown have already been discussed, but vast numbers also survive recording the activities of lesser men. They are found either in originals or in copies, either singly in the form in which they were first produced or transcribed into some sort of register.

Original deeds exist in various archives, as for instance family or town muniments (like the Coventry deeds mentioned above)[1] or, nowadays, in the county record offices into which so much private material is being directed. They are far too scattered to be listed here: even in so ancient an archive as that of the archbishop of Canterbury they have not been kept in one place since the thirteenth century, being found even then variously at Lambeth Palace, at the priory of Christ Church Canterbury (later the deanery of the cathedral), and at Rochester—outside the archbishop's own diocese.[2] But the biggest single collection is in the Public Record Office, in and outside the artificial class called Ancient Deeds. These extend from the twelfth century to the reign of Elizabeth ('Modern Deeds' take over in 1603 and add to the mass of material), and an incomplete list of them fills six volumes.[3] The totals are staggering. Some 12,000 were found among the records of the Chancery and about 35,500 among those of the Exchequer; the old Court of Augmentations provided some 13,000, the Duchy of Lancaster 4,000, and the jurisdiction of Chester and Wales a mere 600. These documents, over 60,000 in all, are, it must be emphasised, almost all private documents, not records of Crown action. They are found in their present place for one of two reasons. Sometimes whole private archives

[1] P. 122.

[2] F. R. Du Boulay, *The Lordship of Canterbury* (London 1966), 5f.

[3] Published H.M.S.O. 1890–1915. The Ancient Deeds were collected from three archives: Exchequer, Augmentations, Chancery. But even there they did not catch everything, and other collections add to the total without being listed in these volumes.

were transferred to the government collection, especially when the Court of Augmentations gathered the muniments of dissolved monasteries for the better information of the new owner (the King) or when the Duchy fell to the Crown in 1399. But the bulk of this material would seem to have reached its present resting place because it was entered into court by way of evidence or exculpation in a suit. At any rate, there it is: 60,000 pieces of parchment and paper. Most of them are conveyances, that is instruments recording the movement of lands by grant or sale among private individuals, but there are also other types of estate papers such as agreements, bonds and recognisances, or acquittances for payment. If to this mass is added what may be found elsewhere, for instance in the casual collection of deeds at the British Museum whose 'additional charters' run into tens of thousands in number and are mostly private, it will be seen that originals alone give an astonishing amount of information about land transactions in these 450 years.

Nevertheless, the evidence of copies is even more impressive. Two types of registers need attention. In the first place, there are the entry books of charters and deeds kept by property owners to protect themselves against the loss of originals, the books known as cartularies.[1] Some 1,268 written in England and Wales before 1485 have so far been found, of which 159 commemorate lay estates while the rest (1,109) belong to the records of religious houses and episcopal sees. More may turn up: about 100, reported to have existed after 1540, have so far proved untraceable. These volumes, too, are nowadays widely scattered, though some, especially those concerning cathedral property, are still found in their original place. The Dissolution of the Monasteries once again saw to the dispersal of this material; cartularies have been frequently sold and can end up in any library, public or private, on either side of the Atlantic. However, some two-thirds of what survives is now in public collections, and half of that in the British Museum.

[1] G. R. C. Davis, *Medieval Cartularies of Great Britain: a short catalogue* (London 1958).

Cartularies transcribe the deeds affecting a given estate's property; compared with bundles of originals, they have the advantage of a preliminary sorting by circumstance and the scribe, so that they are both more coherent and likely to contain more important stuff than a box of old deeds. The date of a cartulary, obviously, is not the date of the earliest but of the latest document in it, and the contents often go right back, even before the Conquest. Some thirty of those listed by Mr Davis were composed before 1200, but most of those now extant belong to the thirteenth and fourteenth centuries; some were continued after the first collection was transcribed. No lay cartulary is known before the thirteenth century. Even when they confine themselves to deeds, the contents are reasonably miscellaneous; some cartularies include alien intrusions, such as accounts or letters or even cooking recipes. But the overwhelming bulk of the contents are documents from which the owners could prove possession and rights. Some of the grants recorded are naturally royal, but a great mass of private deeds—grants and concessions by bishops, abbots, lay lords, the business transactions of the worldly and the benefactions of the pious—compose the main part of these volumes. They pose one spectacular problem. Unlike originals and unlike royal enrolments, they were the work of interested parties and they therefore raise the spectre of forgery as no other class of documents so far discussed does. Indeed, it is a well-known fact that many possessors used cartularies to fill in gaps in their legal title to land, sometimes innocently, in the sure knowledge that some property had been granted so long ago that the missing deed could be explained, but sometimes with the usual fell purpose of the forger. However, forged charters are a problem for the historian of an earlier time than ours; it is reasonably clear that no one bothered to forge post-1200 deeds which were usually well kept and too recent to deceive opponents in court.

One cartulary needs special mention. It belonged to Peterborough Abbey and was written up in the early fourteenth century. But what appears in it are not the abbey's dealings as a landowner; instead we find charters and deeds executed in the course of the thirteenth century by the peasants on some of the abbey's manors.[1] Contrary to all that one was ever taught about the medieval peasant and villein, here is proof that men so well down the social scale could use written and sealed instruments to conduct their transactions in usually very small parcels of land. Though some freemen appear as buyers and sellers, the greater part of the men involved were technically bondmen. The importance of this discovery for the understanding of medieval society is obvious, even if the first effect has been to undermine clear notions without offering anything very clear in their place. What matters here is that these Northamptonshire peasants cannot have been absolutely alone in their freedom and willingness to employ such sophisticated methods. Other peasant charters must surely have existed, even if none were ever registered in a cartulary. A search of the surviving original deeds would seem to be indicated: just how exclusively upper-class are the Ancient Deeds?

The second main register of private deeds is, as has already been briefly mentioned, the back or dorse of the Close Roll kept by the King's Chancery. The material found here is pretty mixed, but in our period most of it touches the activities of private persons dealing amongst themselves and seeking the security which enrolment in Chancery could provide.[2] A statute of 1382 stimulated this activity by empowering people who had lost muniments in the peasants' rising of the previous year to seek remedy from King and Council: if they could convince the authorities of the justice of their claim, the reconstituted ashes of the deed would be preserved on the Close Roll. An attempt of 1535 to extend the principle unfortunately failed. In an act of that year it was enjoined that all private conveyances by bargain and sale (the commonest method of transferring land) were to be

[1] *Carte Nativorum*, ed. M. M. Postan and C. N. L. Brooke (Northamptonshire Record Society 1960). The edition contains an important introduction.

[2] The Close Roll ended in 1903. In more recent centuries, the documents enrolled there often had a quasi-public character (enclosure awards, settlement of parish boundaries), whereas medieval and Tudor materials were overwhelmingly private.

registered either at Westminster or with the relevant shire's clerk of the peace. This attempt to create a complete land-register and prevent the frauds and accidents which the well-disguised complications of land-holding and property sales made so common, was defeated by lawyers' devices designed to preserve the secrecy which, by ensuring litigation, was so useful to the legal profession, and by hiding transactions was so convenient to the less scrupulous landowners, though it has proved very frustrating to, among others, the historian. England therefore still lacks the proper land register which Thomas Cromwell planned.

Apart from originals and registered copies of deeds, there is a third group of documents, quite as large as the others, which does not quite fit into either category. While, like them, recording private land transactions, they were not produced or executed by private individuals but by a court; yet, though neither orders of the court nor originals put in there, they are also not copies made for mere registration. This is the famous and mysterious class known as final concords or, for short, fines, the product of a highly characteristic legal fiction practised in the Court of Common Pleas. The fine was the end-product of a collusive action at law, and the process by which it was obtained was known as levying a fine. Since freehold property could not be passed or settled without expensive licences from feudal lords and similar legal impediments, landowners eager to treat their freehold as disposable property developed by the late twelfth century at the latest a means for evading these restraints which yet had the reassuring blessing of the King's court. This means consisted of a pretended action in which (at its simplest) the plaintiff (querent) demanded the performance of a fictitious covenant from the defendant (deforciant); alternatively—though this method led to genuine fraud and attempts were made to control it—he sued for the recovery (restitution) of lands which he had never possessed against a deforciant who in actual fact was selling them to him or assisting him in some way to get free disposal (settlement upon a son, ousting an inconvenient lessee, etc.) over them. In any case, the parties at once sought the court's permission to come to the amicable agreement (*finalis concordia*) which had been intended from the first. This agreement was then embodied in a tripartite indenture of which the parties each took one part, while the third—called the 'foot' from its position at the bottom of the parchment before it was cut into three—remained on file in the Court.

This simple device proved extremely popular—for its security against fraud and theft with the parties, for its profitability in fees with the Court of Common Pleas. In consequence, there is a large class of documents at the Public Record Office, the bottom parts of finals concords or 'feet of fines', which provide further massive evidence for the sale, acquisition, redistribution, or family settlement of land. Numbers run into thousands. Some local record societies have printed transcripts or calendars of feet of fines relevant to their counties, a fact which underlines the importance of this material for family and estate history.[1] Feet of fines are particularly notable because they help to redress the balance of the other collections of deeds. Mainly because religious houses were the best preservers of charters, the most careful compilers of cartularies, and the most undying of owners, the evidence of deeds concentrates quite heavily on ecclesiastical estates; but feet of fines throw much light on the doings of lay owners as well.

All these deeds, of one kind and another, provide quantities of detailed information on the ownership of land. They illumine the history of individual estates, manors, and parts of manors: the accumulation and dispersal of landed property, as well as the fortunes of individuals, families and ecclesiastical institutions. Their details may include information on rights and burdens resting on land, on the price of land, on changes in population density, on the colonising activity of this agrarian economy.

---

[1] See Mullins, *Texts and Calendars*, s.v. 'feet of fines' and under particular counties. E.g. the Yorkshire Archaeological Society has published English calendars of feet of fines for Yorkshire for the years 1218–72, 1327–77, and 1485–1625.

And they do all this for virtually the whole range of landed property in England, which is not, of course, to say for every bit of it. Nor do they form a complete picture because land transactions—gifts, sales, leases, and so forth—occur at unpredictable and irregular times: the properties step forth at intervals to be inspected. And even of the properties actually mentioned many make rare appearances. Once again, not everything is there but one cannot know what may be until one has looked: everything has a chance of being there. However, the chief deficiency of this deed evidence is that it describes the transfer of land rather than its use. For what was done to exploit this potential wealth we must turn to other kinds of estate documents.

Information on the running of estates is, of course, to be found in letters to and from estate officers. Such material is scattered through archives containing letters in general; these are discussed in the next section. It is also found here and there in such documents as bishops' registers, already discussed. What is exceedingly rare is a collection specifically devoted to letters concerning the administration of estates; though more perhaps exist, I know of only two of this kind. Oddly enough, these two belong to the remains of two brothers, Edward the Black Prince and John of Gaunt, duke of Lancaster, the most famous of Edward III's several sons. Both have left behind registers which in the main deal with the administration of their extensive estates.[1] The Black Prince's is the bigger and covers a longer period of time—twenty years (1346–65) against John of Gaunt's four (1379–83). Edward's possessions were the greater and more diversified, so much so that from 1351 his officers divided the register into business touching England, Chester and Cornwall respectively; there was probably another for his continental lands, which is lost. His register is also more single-mindedly the product of estate-management. A not untypical entry is that of 2 February 1352 which, noting that the lawns at Rostomel (Cornwall) are

[1] *Register of the Black Prince* (4 vols; H.M.S.O. 1930–3); *John of Gaunt's Register*, ed. E. C. Lodge and R. Somerville (2 vols; Camden 3rd Series, vols 56–7; 1937).

reported to be overgrown with moss, orders the steward to lease them out as profitably as he can for as long a time as he thinks it will take to get them back into good heart.[1]

The duke of Lancaster's register is, in fact, more a general record of his business affairs; estate matters, mostly of a formal kind, share it with other concerns. His out-letters—in these four short years 865 are registered—do, however, mostly concern themselves with his lands. There are also twenty-one presentations to livings, thirty-three indentures of service, thirteen obligations (bonds), sixteen receipts, sixty-two grants and gifts, thirty-nine leases, six sales of wardships, ninety-one commissions and appointments of officers, seven licences to grant land in mortmain (to the Church), nine pardons and releases, twelve letters of homage, fourteen letters of protection, fourteen safe-conducts, and a quantity of miscellanea. In short, the register reflects the problems of a great territorial lord who was not only a landowner but also head of a social organism—a king in miniature —but whose strength rested on his wealth, whose wealth grew from land, and whose first concern therefore had to be to management of those lands.

Such careful record-keeping required, and was only required for, a complex organisation, but every landlord had to know something about the use and profit of his lands. The materials which were produced by that need fall into two groups: detailed descriptions, and accounts of income and expenditure. Both are well represented for our period. Descriptions carry various names. Extents (or terriers) are documents which list the holdings and tenants, normally of a manor, give their duties (in labour services or money rents due), and may describe the crops grown and animals kept. Surveys—a term which grew current in the sixteenth century when one first encounters professional surveyors —usually add a detailed topographical description of the fields and give adjacent occupiers; they are quite frequently accompanied by maps. Rentals tend to be briefer, confining themselves to a list of tenants, the acreage held by each, and the rent payable. Then

[1] *Register of the Black Prince*, vol. 2, 27.

there are custumals, documents which detail the units of tenure on an estate and the customs governing lord's and tenants' rights and duties; that is, they try to define the custom of the manor—the terms upon which land was held there, and therefore the law of the manorial court—for future use. The virtue of such documents is obvious enough: they offer a clear understanding of how the land was laid out, how it was supposed to be used, and what it was supposed to yield to the lord, so that they can give an unusually systematic, if intermittent, picture of rural conditions, population, agricultural practices and the like.

There are plenty of such surveys extant, and once again the collection at the Public Record Office, deposited there because lands once in private hands had ultimately come to the Crown, must take pride of place. The result is a total of about 8,500 extending from the reign of Edward I to the middle of the seventeenth century and covering just about every county in the kingdom.[1] They include the surveys made for Parliament of royalist lands confiscated after the Civil War, a source of much information for the generation or so before the war. But extents, surveys and rentals may be found anywhere where medieval or early-modern materials are preserved. The Essex Record Office has a large collection for its own shire.[2] The earliest Canterbury rental belongs to 1220; an extensive survey carried out by Archbishop Pecham in 1283-5 and based on sworn returns, gives a very clear description of the Canterbury estates at just about the height of medieval agrarian prosperity.[3] The extents and rentals of St Albans Abbey are now lodged partly at the British Museum and partly at the Hertfordshire County Record Office; they include surveys of the years 1331-2 that are so detailed and extensive that they have very plausibly been identified as the remnant of a full and systematic survey of the abbey's possessions.[4] Altogether, it is unsafe to say that any piece of landed

[1] Public Record Office, *Lists and Indexes*, vol. 25.

[2] Emmison, *Guide*, vol. 2, 7ff.

[3] Du Boulay, *Lordship of Canterbury*, 11.

[4] A. E. Levett, *Studies in Manorial History* (Oxford 1938), 79ff.

property will not yield a single descriptive document in this period, and some important ones can be studied in a spaced succession of surveys; but the material, naturally, remains patchy, incomplete, unpredictably distributed over space and time, and many questions will find no answer.

The chief deficiency of such surveys lies in the fact that they give information on what was due, not on what actually came in. Here the so-called ministers' accounts, the last and biggest class of private estate documents, come into their own. Ministers' accounts are accounts rendered by the various officers engaged in estate-management to their superior and ultimately to the lord. They range from the accounts of manorial bailiffs[1] or persons charged with particular sales of timber and produce, to the comprehensive accounts for a whole estate produced by receivers-general. Occasionally they are preserved in the form of a consolidated account rendered before the head-officers, but most of them are individual accounts, offered by each accountant on his own behalf in support for his claim to a final acquittance. Of the former kind, the best known are the so-called pipe rolls of the bishopric of Winchester, of which two have been printed, covering the years 1208–11 altogether.[2] Individual accounts are again found anywhere but particularly at the Public Record Office, which has several thousand.[3] Many are among the family papers of the great families, some calendared by the Historical Manuscripts Commission, some (for instance those of the Cecil possessions) so far inaccessible in print. Thus the Sidney papers at Penshurst include deeds, court rolls and accounts going back to the early fifteenth century, the Hastings papers cover properties back to the mid-thirteenth century, and so forth. Those preserved at the Public Record Office naturally deal in the first place with Crown lands, and while forfeitures and escheats brought into the

[1] The Essex Record Office possesses bailiffs' accounts for 1325–1500 (*Guide* vol. 2, 8).

[2] *The Pipe Roll of the Bishopric of Winchester 1208–9*, ed. under the supervision of H. Hall (London 1903); *The Pipe Roll of the Bishopric of Winchester 1210–11*, ed. N. R. Holt (Manchester 1964).

[3] See *Guide to the Public Records* (London 1963), vol. 1, 185, 191.

royal archives the papers of the private estates acquired, it does not appear that the annual accounts of bailiffs and stewards from before the Crown got the lands were also transferred. Miss Levett, for instance, found almost none there for the abbey of St Albans.[1] Nevertheless, the collection includes some monastic accounts, as well as some other private matters; and in any case, from the point of view of what ministers' accounts reveal (the affairs of landed property) the Crown lands, the biggest single possession in the realm, must always be taken into account, too. The income of 'alien priories' (monastic houses dependent on superior houses abroad) was usually confiscated during periods of war in the thirteenth and fourteenth centuries, so that their affairs got into the depository: and bishops' temporalities were administered for the benefit of the Crown at any time that the see was vacant. Nevertheless, strictly private estate papers must be looked for in local record offices and private muniment rooms, and many will indeed be found there.

The information to be derived from these accounts is varied and important. A good impression can be gained by looking at the accounts of Wellingborough manor, a possession of Crowland Abbey, which are now in the hands of Queen's College, Cambridge, and have been well edited.[2] In form these accounts are quite typical. Each is divided into a cash account and a stock account. The first gives receipts (rents, aids [a manorial tax], fines, perquisites of the manorial court, sale of produce, miscellaneous) and expenses (paid over to the lord; paid out by the lord's orders; purchase of stock, grain and tools; upkeep of equipment and buildings; harvest expenses in wages and equipment; regular wages; allowances for exemption from dues; expenses of threshing and winnowing). This was supposed to balance, the real profit (if any) being disguised as money paid over to the lord, but there might be an outstanding profit still to be paid over or a

---

[1] Levett, *op. cit.* 75ff.

[2] *Wellingborough Manorial Accounts A.D. 1258–1323*, ed. F. M. Page (Northamptonshire Record Society 1936). For other published accounts see Mullins, *Texts and Calendars*, s.v. 'Ministers' accounts'.

deficit which would appear next year, confusingly, as arrears—
further income still due to be paid. The stock account gives
minute details of beasts and grains, detailing wheat and rye and
oats (with particulars as to production, consumption, sale, reservation for seed) and giving precise figures of hens and cocks,
geese and ganders, ewes and wethers, cows and oxen and bulls:
what was found at the beginning of the year, what sold or lost
and what acquired, and what the stock was at the end. The
Wellingborough accounts say nothing of villagers' labour
services, though a survey of 1320 shows that these survived on
the manor, but then one would not expect them to. The steward
—and his lord—were concerned with cash and stock, with the
cost of running the estate and with its financial health; that is
what the account was about. How the farming was done formed
no concern of this type of document. But while ministers'
accounts, no more than any other type of record, do not tell
all the story, they do give very precise and detailed information on what they were supposed to tell and are quite invaluable in reconstructing the history of estate management,
agricultural fortunes in general, and the wealth of the landed
classes.

A particular type of account remains to be mentioned: household accounts in which, among other things, the fate of the estate's
produce in commodities and cash may be tracked further. These
are relatively rare—very rare before the sixteenth century and
not common thereafter. Something may be learned about the
economy of monastic institutions from the accounts of cellarers
and other obedientiaries (officers) which at the Dissolution got
into the hands of the Crown, but these are certainly only a very
small remnant of what once existed. Early household accounts
are usually not very informative.[1] A fifteenth-century household
book allows a deep look into the daily life of a gentleman's house,
with its daily visitors at table, its stock in pantry and kitchen, its
purchases of 100 oysters for 2*d*. and 100 smoked herrings for

---

[1] E.g. *A Roll of the Household Expenses of Richard de Swinfield, Bishop of
Hereford* (*1289 and 1290*), ed. T. Webb (2 vols; Camden Old Series, 1854–5).

1*s.* 6*d.*[1] Accounts and similar papers for the time of the ninth earl of Northumberland (1564–1632) describe the man's affairs in every detail, from his losses at cards to his tailor's bills, from the furnishing of his house to the food on his table.[2] Fairly full summaries of the household accounts of the Manners, earls of Rutland, for the years 1522–1640 have been published.[3] Undoubtedly there are more such materials around, but it should be noted that they almost always concern the households of the nobility—exceptionally large and exceptionally expensive—while those even of the middling gentry remain obscure. However, one of the best documented households is that of a man who never made it into the peerage, Sir William Petre's establishment at Ingatestone in Essex; a remarkable collection of estate and domestic papers have made possible a description of this man's life and mode of life which in weighty detail well exceeds the intrinsic interest of his personality.[4] Royal households, of course, are the best known and best documented,[5] but private ones need not always be obscure. Of course, this is very occasional material.

With this range and quantity of estate documentation at his

---

[1] *The Household Book of Dame Alice de Bryene 1412–13*, ed. M. K. Dale and V. R. Redstone (Suffolk Institute of Archaeological and Natural History, 1931).

[2] *The Household Papers of Henry Percy, ninth early of Northumberland*, ed. G. R. Batho (Camden 3rd Series, vol. 93; 1962).

[3] Hist. MSS Comm., *Rutland MSS*, vol. 4, 260–530.

[4] F. E. Emmison, *Tudor Secretary* (London 1961).

[5] The households of kings and members of the royal family belong in one sense in the public, in another in the private domain. They are well documented in the public records, especially of the Exchequer and of two household departments (lord steward's and lord chamberlain's). For materials in print see *A Collection of Ordinances . . .* (Society of Antiquaries, 1792); *The Household of Edward IV*, ed. A. R. Myers (Manchester 1959); *The Privy Purse Expenses of Elizabeth of York*, ed. N. H. Nicolas (London 1830); *The Privy Purse Expenses of King Henry VIII*, ed. N. H. Nicolas (London 1827); *The Privy Purse Expenses of the Princess Mary*, ed. F. Madden (London 1831). And see T. F. Tout, *Chapters in Medieval Administrative History* (6 vols; Manchester 1928–37); G. R. Elton, *The Tudor Revolution in Government* (Cambridge 1953); E. K. Chambers, *The Elizabethan Stage* (Oxford 1923), vol. 1.

disposal, and remembering cognate materials mentioned in earlier chapters, the historian can certainly hope to answer almost any question concerning the activities of the landed classes from lords to peasants; and since these formed the overwhelming majority of the nation he can hope to produce an historical sociology of the whole country in considerable detail, for all the various and very different regions, and for most of the decades involved. Much, indeed, has been done. Individual estates have been described and studied in depth, some of them monastic,[1] some episcopal,[2] some lay.[3] The lives of villages and villagers have been dissected to varying degrees of scientific refinement.[4] Studies of the manorial economy abound, mostly in articles, but sometimes also in books.[5] More general descriptions, based on the full range of materials, have been attempted.[6] The time is thought ripe for the production of a multi-volume *Agrarian History of England and Wales,* based on detailed research in the sources.[7] These are only some indications of what has been done—and they can barely hint how much more of this same sort, deeply revealing as well as truly interesting, remains to be done, and remains capable of being done. For it all the widely scattered, piecemeal, difficult but rewarding private estate papers (including those of the King as landowner) are the chief source. For once, and for the whole range of the period, it is possible to get away

[1] E.g. F. M. Page, *The Estates of Crowland Abbey* (Cambridge 1934); A. E. Levett, *Studies in Manorial History,* 69ff (estates of St Albans).

[2] E.g. E. Miller, *The Abbey and Bishopric of Ely* (Cambridge 1951); F. R. Du Boulay, *The Lordship of Canterbury*; P. M. Hembry, *The Bishops of Bath and Wells 1540-1640* (London 1967).

[3] J. M. W. Bean, *The Estates of the Percy Family 1416-1537* (Oxford 1958).

[4] H. S. Bennett, *Life on an English Manor* (Cambridge 1948); G. C. Homans, *English Villagers of the Thirteenth Century* (Cambridge, Mass. 1942); D. A. Harvey, *A Medieval Oxfordshire Village: Cuxham 1240-1400* (Oxford 1965).

[5] E.g. E. Kosminsky, *Studies in the Agrarian History of England in the Thirteenth Century* (Oxford 1956).

[6] R. H. Hilton, *A Medieval Society: the West Midlands at the end of the thirteenth century* (London 1966).

[7] General editor, H. P. R. Finberg; vol. 4 (1500-1640), ed. J. Thirsk, has appeared (Cambridge 1967).

from the dominance of the public record and the prevalence of central government studies.

Yet we must be careful not to suppose that in this field, any more than in any other aspect of the period under review, all questions that we should like to ask will find an answer. These papers do not solve every problem. Even on such fundamental issues as the manner in which the land was actually farmed much uncertainty still prevails and looks likely to endure.[1] The records are biased towards ecclesiastical land-owners, and among them towards monasteries; only in the sixteenth century do lay estates become as well known as spiritual ones, and even then the main bulk of the evidence belongs to the greatest estates, those of the peerage. But for this group they are so massive that they make possible a broad-fronted attack on all the socio-economic questions touching it, though (perhaps happily for the continuation of historians' arguments) they remain difficult, full of gaps unsatisfactorily filled by statistical calculations, and debatable in their import.[2] Above all, estate papers by themselves offer virtually nothing on individuals or personalities. Names, family relationships, possessions and rights are freely mentioned, but there is no individual reality to most of these people, even among the upper classes. Administrative documents have that necessary character that they hide the individual. However, the matter alters when one turns to letters.

(*b*) LETTERS

Letters have, no doubt, always been written by and to all literate persons, but their preservation is another matter. In fact, one finds

[1] See the controversy on the open-field system between J. Thirsk and J. Z. Titow, *Past and Present*, 29, 3ff; 32, 86f; 33, 142ff. Though mainly concerned with the origin of the open field, the contestants make plain how obscure the matter is even for our period. And see the sometimes very differing interpretations put on essentially the same material by the contributors to the *Agrarian History* and by Dr Kerridge (above, 134, n. 3).

[2] Lawrence Stone, *The Crisis of the Aristocracy 1558–1641* (Oxford 1965); and see, e.g. the criticism of Mr Stone's arguments and conclusions in G. Aylmer's review, *Past and Present*, 32 (1965), 113ff.

letters of one kind and another all over the place, in this and that collection, loose or bound in volumes or copied into letter-books, and some closer definition of the documents to be discussed here is clearly necessary. In the first place, what distinguished letters as private rather than public documents? The State Papers, for instance, or the Ancient Correspondence, contain mostly letters from private persons, and though most are addressed to official recipients some considerable part of them are purely private in content, too. At the same time, seemingly private collections often contain very official papers. Thus the distinction here applied must for once be not so much by subject matter as by place of deposit—an archival rather than an historical distinction. Yet secondly, while in the main we must concern ourselves with collections that have naturally and organically grown up, we must not forget the artificial bodies of documents created when an editor gathers the correspondence of a given man.

The first principle means that, while attention should be drawn to the existence of private letters in public archives, they do not concern us; the second points to such volumes as the letters of the thirteenth-century bishop Robert Grosseteste, of the sixteenth-century bishops Richard Fox and Stephen Gardiner, or of the sixteenth-century lord chancellor Thomas More.[1] For Grosseteste, 131 letters were found in various collections and episcopal registers; Fox's letters were taken from registers, municipal archives, Oxford College muniments, and the State Papers; the State Papers are also the main source for Gardiner's; More's correspondence is widely scattered, mostly in copies and sometimes in print. Collections such as these suffer from some obvious disadvantages. They were made because the man in question seemed important and leave out materials that may be as significant but do not belong to the lives of significant men.

---

[1] *Roberti Grosseteste episcopi quondam Lincolniensis Epistolae*, ed. H. R. Luard (Roll Series, 1861); *The Letters of Richard Fox 1486–1527*, ed. P. S. and H. M. Allen (Oxford 1928); *The Letters of Stephen Gardiner*, ed. J. A. Muller (Cambridge 1933); *The Correspondence of Sir Thomas More*, ed. Elizabeth F. Rogers (Princeton 1947).

Since they come from archives that have been created by quite other purposes, the surviving letters are not only a very partial remnant but one biased towards the formal and official. If Grosseteste ever wrote truly personal letters, they do not now seem to be extant, and even in More's correspondence only the very private letters written in his last imprisonment, preserved by natural piety, really reveal the man. These same shortcomings afflict other letters found in documents not principally designed for the purpose of preserving letters, the sort of documents from which the artificial collections have been made. There are letters in chronicles, and a curious letter of personal apology from the earl of Northumberland is found in John of Gaunt's register.[1] Gaunt, beyond question, received many private letters and no doubt wrote many too, but his register was not the place for them and they are lost. All this gathering together of such materials is useful in providing evidence for the historian, and useful here in reminding ourselves that only the accident of preservation and survival puts the date of the first specific letter archive so relatively late, but it cannot disguise the facts that private collections do start late and that they at once alter the nature of the historian's knowledge.

They start, in fact, in the fifteenth century, with the magnificent body of documents known as the Paston Letters—1,083 items which include a few public documents (such as the proclamation of 1485 against Henry Tudor, earl of Richmond) and some private legal instruments, but are in the main the letters, to and fro, of a Norfolk gentle family over some ninety years.[2] Although they are not all any longer in one place—time and the witlessness of owners have somewhat dispersed them—they were originally preserved as a single family archive. Much smaller in size is the correspondence of a Yorkshire family, the Plumptons, copied into a letter-book in the reign of James I but including material back to the reign of Edward IV. The book is now at the Bodleian

[1] *John of Gaunt's Register*, vol 2, 410f.
[2] The best edition is by J. Gairdner, *Paston Letters A.D. 1422–1509* (6 vols; London 1904). Most of the originals are now at the British Museum.

Library: a selection from it has been published.[1] The private archives of Thomas Cromwell and Arthur Lord Lisle, deputy at Calais in the 1530's, were confiscated and are now in the official State Papers, but the latter in particular, and the former in part, do not differ in essence from these earlier collections and some later ones. Our principle, which here is the right one, excludes Cromwell's correspondence from the class of private letters, while it must include the correspondence of William Cecil, though the two are remarkably alike in every respect except size (Burghley lived much longer), because the latter never reached the public archives. Cecil's papers are in two places: the smaller part is in the family archives at Hatfield House, while the larger forms part of the Lansdowne Collection in the British Museum. Another large part of the Lansdowne MSS is composed of the papers, official as well as private (but another private collection), of Sir Julius Caesar (1558–1636), master of requests and a judge of the Admiralty Court. Because these two great bodies of papers were acquired by an eighteenth-century collector and ultimately sold to the British Museum, they appear in a public depository but belong to the present section.

Even more accidental are other British Museum possessions, especially the Cottonian and Harleian manuscripts which contain among other things many volumes of sixteenth- and seventeenth-century letters and papers collected by these avid gatherers of manuscripts on no archival or historical principle, but just on the basis of interest and availability. The correspondence especially of the greater figures of the Tudor period has been much pillaged by collectors and is therefore to be sought in a number of depositories. A particular complication was introduced when American wealth took over from English, with the result that some sizeable bodies of private papers are now not even in the country of origin; thus the Huntington Library at San Marino, California, has among its extensive and ill-catalogued possessions the letters of Sir Francis Hastings, puritan and politician in the reigns of

[1] *Plumpton Correspondence*, ed. T. Stapledon (Camden 1st Series, 1839).

Elizabeth and James I.[1] Collections of letters still occasionally
turn up, and some of them get published, like the interesting
papers of an early-Tudor Yorkshire family or the singularly
unrevealing letter-book of a humanist monk-scholar on the eve
of the Reformation.[2]

However, the main part of private letters seems to have
remained in private possession or been transferred entire to local
record offices; and the reports of the Historical Manuscripts
Commission, founded in the middle of the last century precisely
to discover and list such materials, form the best guide to them.
Unfortunately the productions of the Commission themselves—
well over a hundred volumes by now—are not easily surveyable;
they vary a good deal in quality, the early ones in particular being
little more than inadequate lists; and it is hard to say how many of
them belong to our period.[3] At any rate, that a large number,
perhaps a majority, contain no material before 1640 is clear.
Nevertheless, there is plenty of relevant material, too, in these
massive volumes, and by way of illustration a few specially important collections shall be considered.

Easily the most remarkable production of the Commission's
labours are the *Calendars of the Hatfield or Salisbury MSS*. These are
the archives of the Cecil family, and so far nineteen volumes have
appeared. The first contains a few items reaching back into the
reign of Henry VI, but in fact there is virtually nothing before
1547. Then, with William Cecil entering upon his career, the
collection gains in weight, and even though the better part of his
own papers have ended, as was said, in the Lansdowne collection,
some two-and-a-half volumes of the Calendar are filled with

---

[1] I owe this information to Dr Claire Cross who is preparing an edition of
the Hastings letters.

[2] *Clifford Letters of the Sixteenth Century*, ed. A. G. Dickens (Surtees Society
vol. 172; 1962); *The Letter Book of Robert Joseph*, ed. H. Aveling and W. A.
Pantin (Oxford Historical Society, new series, vol. 19; 1967).

[3] The best list, to its date of publication, is in Mullins, *Texts and Calendars*,
61ff. There are also comprehensive topographical and name indexes in three
volumes each; these refer the reader to the indexes of particular volumes. A
chronological list of contents would be welcome.

abstracts of letters and documents growing out of his public and private life. The quantity, however, becomes really enormous only round about 1590, from which date the papers are essentially the archives of William's son, Robert, the first earl of Salisbury. Three volumes take us to 1590; the remaining sixteen manage to get only to 1607 (so far). For the last decade of Elizabeth's reign and the first of James's, these Salisbury papers clearly constitute a major source, even rivalling the State Papers to which, in effect, they are an equivalent complement. The Calendar itself is good, with very full abstracts, so that (perhaps unfortunately) it is rare for historians to resort to the originals.

No other collection for our period can compete with that at Hatfield, but even lesser bodies of material are sizeable. The possessions of the marquess of Bath, at Longleat (Wiltshire), have so far been very inadequately reported on. Of the three volumes published, only the second contains material for the sixteenth and seventeenth centuries, but still unpublished remain several important collections which got to Longleat as the Thynnes intermarried with other families. Some of the leading Tudor families are represented here: the Devereux, earls of Essex, the Seymours, earls of Hertford, the Thynnes themselves. A big enough collection helps at last to illumine the first important Seymour (Edward, duke of Somerset, lord protector under Edward VI) who has hitherto been hard to make much of; a calendar is in the press. The Rutland papers, on the other hand, have been thoroughly sifted; among them is the correspondence of the Vernon family back to 1450, as well as, of course, the Manners' archives forward to the Civil War.

There is an interesting mixture of stuff at Penshurst, among the muniments of Lord De L'Isle and Dudley, of which the bulk are Sidney papers. In particular this includes the massive correspondence of Sir Henry Sidney, a leading Elizabethan administrator, and his son Robert, later earl of Leicester, courtier, soldier and country gentleman: the calendared documents fill three volumes. Sir Henry for years presided over the Council in the Marches of Wales, and his papers are the best source of information we have for an institution whose own archives have virtually all vanished; he also ruled Ireland, and the history of Elizabethan Ireland relies heavily on the Sidney papers. Sir Robert, after retiring from court, kept up a vigorous correspondence which thoroughly illumines the court life and politics of James I. Also at Penshurst are the family papers of the Cromwells of Tatteshall, a fifteenth-century family which produced a leading politician of the reign of Henry VI; they have nothing to do with the other Cromwells. The Hastings collection, with only some eighty pages of correspondence in the calendar (though much estate material) would be more disappointing if we did not know of the family papers now in California. All these collections, and others, include also other things than letters, though letters must be our concern here; some of the estate documents have already been mentioned. The Hatfield Calendar has so far confined itself to letters only; the great mass of other papers remains accessible in manuscript and on the spot only.

Letters and papers of this kind offer an entirely different order of knowledge from that obtainable from the more formal documents discussed so far. As the State Papers are to the records of the King's government, so are these collections of private correspondence to the deeds and court rolls of the landed classes' formal administration of their properties. In the main, the letters deal with business. That this is not because no one at that time thought of anything but business is proved not only by common sense but also by the occasional presence of purely private and highly personal letters. Husbands write to wives and wives to husbands, mothers to daughters and suitors to young women— and the subjects discussed are not confined to house and garden, dowries and marriage portions. The Paston and Stonor[1] letters contain some well-known examples of this sort of thing. But casual letters, love letters, and letters of no further import suffer the accidents of all evidence more readily than letters dealing

[1] The family archives of the Stonor family, mostly of the fifteenth century, are preserved among the Public Record Office's Ancient Correspondence; two volumes were edited by C. L. Kingsford (Camden 3rd series, vols 29, 30; 1919).

with purchases of land, the extraction of profit from property, law suits, or political involvement on a local or national stage. Business letters survive. The business dealt with may be personal or not. The archivally private letters of eminent statesmen—secretaries of state, for instance, like the two Cecils—are in effect as much concerned with the affairs of the realm as with those of family or individual, and all these collections have much to say about 'general' history. These are the papers of a ruling class, and rule it did. That, within the limits set by subject matter and the formalities of language, they also throw light on personality, mind and motive need not be stressed again: in all this they share the special qualities of the State Papers whose coverage of history, people and lives they enormously extend.

But, of course, there are deficiencies. As always, collections of letters are unsystematic; the accident of preservation can completely distort the state of information, and much greater care than is often applied must be exercised in using this material. Thus the pure and most fortunate accident of the Paston letters—an accident in that they were first kept and an accident in that they still exist—coming at a time when official documents are exceptionally inadequate, may well have done harm to the conventional historiography of the fifteenth century. That picture of turmoil and decay owes a good deal to these letters. The Pastons were deeply involved in the Norfolk politics of the century and especially in the fortunes of the house of Howard; willy-nilly, they played the tight-rope game of survival in a cutthroat society for all they were worth. Perhaps the picture of constant intrigue, of seeking ever fresh 'good lordship' and avoiding the consequences of a patron's misfortunes, is indeed typical of their layer of society, the middling gentry, in that age. Yet Norfolk is known to have been a peculiar county, equipped with an unusual number of ambitious gentle families and not clearly dominated, as other counties certainly were, by one or two identifiable interests to which lesser men subordinated themselves, with much gain in stability. It is at least possible that the lack of enduring loyalties and the bitter in-fighting that so graphically emerge from the correspondence were less typical than particular. This is just one example of the way in which interpretation can be bedevilled by the presence of a large and fascinating collection of documents lacking in systematic origin or coverage.

The best cure for these problems naturally lies in finding a variety of materials, so that the common elements may be distinguished from the particular or purely personal. And here it should be noted that the historian of this period faces a peculiar fact. Down to the fifteenth century there are no private collections of papers, and few private papers even scattered around; for those years he lacks, in the main, any evidence which would take him into the personal lives of individuals, though, of course, there are some exceptions to this rule. For the years from about 1420 to 1550 he has some collections, some of them large and all invaluable, but the more invaluable because still so relatively rare. The middle of the sixteenth century, with a suddenness unusual in the problems of records and archives, marks a dramatic change. Collections of private letters and papers suddenly appear all over the place, springing up like mushrooms after rain: we are on the eve of that great change in the study of history when the ascendancy of the public record at last goes down before the flood of less formal, more diverse material. The effect which this sudden increase of informal, non-royal source material has on the writing of history should by now be obvious. The reign of Henry VIII is really the first period in English history when we can get beyond the possible discovery of any fact or event to a closer understanding of the why and wherefore; the reign of Elizabeth so far accelerates the process that we can suddenly hope to reconstruct events both large and small almost day by day and come to grips with people of all sorts and conditions as they step forth from the grave to explain themselves, to reveal motive and emotion, to show up the interaction of personalities. The historian, if he wants to, can at least turn biographer. By comparison with later ages the material is still thin and the possibility of this kind of knowledge limited; compared with what came before, the addition of private letters to the historian's equipment works a revolution in the history he can write.

(c) BUSINESS ARCHIVES

The papers of business houses and entrepreneurs form a specialised section of private record material which from the later seventeenth century onwards becomes massive and important. In our period it is rare, but not so unknown as not to deserve separate mention. At the level at which they were likely to reach permanent record-keeping, business activities in the middle ages and the sixteenth century were usually in the hands of institutions—companies of one kind and another—which should have encouraged the preservation of such material. However, a search ends in disappointment. The Staplers, who from Calais controlled England's wool exports for 200 years, seem to have left no archives of their own behind. Some of the trading companies which began to be formed from the middle of the sixteenth century onwards did better, only to find fate unkind. Thus the Russia Company's records perished in the Great Fire of London, and its history must be written from sources found in many places but mostly among the public records.[1] The same is true of the Levant Company, though for a different reason which, from the historian's point of view, is more fortunate: because the authority first granted to it in 1583 was resumed by the Crown in 1825, most of its archives found their way into the State Papers.[2] Right at the end of our period begin the records of the East India Company, preserved, but not for this time in quantity, in the India Office Library.[3]

The most promising company records of the period are those of the London Livery Companies. Some of them are now deposited in the Guildhall Library, but more (and the more valu-

[1] T. S. Willan, *The Early History of the Russia Company 1553–1603* (Manchester 1956), v.

[2] See the bibliography of MSS in A. C. Wood, *A History of the Levant Company* (Oxford 1935), ix–xii.

[3] W. Foster, *A Guide to the India Office Records 1600–1858* (London 1919), 2f, 11.

able) are still in the Companies' possession and not easily seen. The bibliography appended to George Unwin's *Gilds and Companies of London* gives some idea of what exists, though, mixed up with the real stuff, that list includes a preponderance of archive material not produced by the companies as well as published histories and suchlike secondary material.[1] The manuscript material in great part belongs to the municipal records of London, already discussed. Nevertheless, there are some real business archives there, mostly of ordinances and regulations but also some accounts and minutes of governing bodies. The Grocers preserve both sorts of records from 1463;[2] the Mercers have archives from much earlier;[3] many companies would seem at least to have registers of members. The Mercers' records are particularly important because this Company gave birth to and for a long time remained the formal organisation of the London Merchant Adventurers. The minutes of its ruling body—its 'Acts of Court'—thus throw light on the most active trading company of the late-fifteenth and early-sixteenth centuries, and for this crucial period they have been published.[4]

This is not a great deal, and it tells little enough of the great commercial and industrial activity of medieval England. The historian interested in such matters is forced to resort to other sources, those of the Crown and those of the towns. Customs and other accounts in the national archives, port books in places like Southampton or Lynn or Hull: these tend to be his main stand-by. The central archives are also really the only source for the history of international finance; papers concerning the transactions of such Italian houses as Bardi and Peruzzi appear among the Chancery Miscellanea, and the accounts of English possessions on the continent are effectively the sole evidence for

[1] 3rd edition (London 1908), 2ff.

[2] *Studies in English Trade in the Fifteenth Century*, ed. E. Power and M. M. Postan (London 1933), 412.

[3] *Acts of Court of the Mercers' Company 1453–1527*, ed. L. Lyell (Cambridge 1936), vii: the Acts run continuously from 1453, while the wardens' accounts begin in 1391, with a stray earlier record for 1347.

[4] See preceding note.

the exchange trade in wine and wool which flourished between England and France through much of the middle ages. The cloth trade of the Merchant Adventurers in the sixteenth century left its traces not in the Mercers' books but in the King's customs accounts and in the Netherlands archives.[1] This last fact is worth noting: continental materials, in the main so far uninvestigated, may throw light on English commercial history. But none of this is business archives in the proper sense; none of it is the product of individuals or companies engaged in business and keeping their own records.

So far as I know at present—judging by what has appeared in print—there are only three collections of specific business papers now in existence for our period. The first is the Cely correspondence, the papers of a family of merchants of the Staple in the last quarter of the fifteenth century. This is a collection of genuine firm's papers—letters and accounts and subsidiary material—which thoroughly describes the dealings and business affairs of a pretty representative merchant of his day. Or at least he was representative of the declining specialists in the trade in raw wool; but the papers do in fact illumine more of the normal practices and ventures than such a restrictive definition might suggest.[2]

Secondly, there is the Johnson correspondence, the letters exchanged between John and Otwell Johnson who were merchants of the Staple and wool exporters some half-century later than the Celys, in the reigns of Henry VIII and Edward VI. The firm went bankrupt in 1553, and its papers were consequently confiscated by the Privy Council. They are now among the public archives, but as a special collection. About 1,000 letters survive from what was originally perhaps twenty times as much, and the years

[1] *Brunnen tot de geschiedenis var den handel met Engeland, Schotland en Ierland 1485-1585*, ed. H. J. Smit (2 vols; The Hague 1942, 1950).

[2] The archive is now in the Public Record Office (Chancery Miscellanea). A selection has been published (Camden 3rd Series, vol. 1; 1900), but a better and fuller edition is in hand (see P. Grierson in *Miscellanea Mediaevalia in Memoriam Jan Frederik Niermeyer*, Groningen 1967, 379ff). The papers formed the basis of Eileen Power's description of a merchant in *Medieval People* (10th ed: London 1963), 120ff.

covered are 1542–52.[1] This is certainly a find, for the papers make possible a really detailed analysis of business methods, conditions and fortunes. Unfortunately the period covered is so very short, and unfortunately, too, the Johnsons were rather specialised traders.

Thirdly, there is the archive of Lionel Cranfield, merchant, speculator and ultimately (till his downfall) lord treasurer to James I. These are in private hands, among the Sackville papers preserved at Knole. They form an enormous collection which covers the years 1551 to Cranfield's death in 1645. Commercial and business material mingles with personal and political, but it forms a major part of the whole, from 1597 onwards, and the second volume of the Calendar published by the Historical Manuscripts Commission deals exclusively with business affairs. Here one finds massive information on the activities of a man who ranged widely in his interests, but even so there is some specialisa-ation, for Cranfield was essentially a merchant adventurer trading in cloth to Germany and northern Europe. However, he also speculated in the import of grain from the Baltic and in foreign exchange. His papers have naturally attracted historians, and there are now two excellent studies based mainly on them: one which employs the material rather sovereignly as the basis of a general description of European trade,[2] and another which sticks more closely and in deeply revealing detail to the particular doings and fortunes of Jacobean England's most successful entrepreneur.[3]

Business archives are therefore rare and skimpy; what there is,

[1] They are included among State Papers Supplementary (*Guide to the Public Records*, vol. 2, 9). The papers were used by Barbara Winchester who on the strength of them produced a rather sloppy book, *Tudor Family Portrait* (London 1955) which in its foreword gives a very inadequate account of the material.

[2] R. H. Tawney, *Business and Politics under James I* (Cambridge 1958).

[3] Menna Prestwich, *Cranfield: Politics and Profits under the Early Stuarts* (Oxford 1966). Mrs Prestwich includes a note on the Cranfield papers (xix). The story of Cranfield's temporary associate, Arthur Ingram, has been told in part from private collections and in greater part from public materials, but among the first must be included the family papers at Temple Newsam which, in small measure, constitute a business archive (A. F. Upton, *Sir Arthur Ingram*, Oxford 1961).

moreover, deals with overseas trade and offers little on details of industrial production or internal trade. And while central and municipal archives can provide some help here, they too tell much more of the export trade than of anything else. The important questions of what was in fact produced for the home market, what that market was like, who served it and how, and what the relationship between home and overseas trading amounted to, will, for this period, always remain obscure. We are, after all, still only at the start of the flood of private material, and it needs private, not official, records to tell of such things.

CHAPTER 6

The Law

The importance of the law, its administration and its practitioners in medieval and early-modern society has already been mentioned. The quantity of the surviving material in itself testifies to it, though, of course, the historian will do well to remember that such proofs work both ways: it is possible that matters of law loom so large because they have left record behind. However, such scepticism is unjustified: the all-important role that rights and duties, to be tested and established in the courts, then played in most men's lives should not be doubted.

The bulk of the sources for the study of the law and its accompanying features belongs to the official records of the Crown, to the material produced by the law-courts; it has already been listed but should not be forgotten here. The rolls and papers of King's Bench, Chancery and all the rest are essential to the study of the law which was, after all, mainly created by agencies of government either through legislation or through judicial decisions, and it is therefore worth recall that very little of the history of English law so far produced takes extensive account of these materials.

However, while an enormous quantity of research remains to be done here, that research cannot confine itself to the records of administration. The neglect of the bulky, difficult and ill-ordered products of the courts has been made possible by the existence

BIBLIOGRAPHY. W. S. Holdsworth, *Sources and Literature of English Law* (Oxford 1925) provides a good first introduction to the range of materials. The same author's *History of English Law* (14 vols, London 1904– 59) discusses sources here and there; as a guide to the history of law and government it is unavoidable, though frequently wrong. That great classic, F. Pollock and F. W. Maitland, *The History of English Law before the Time of Edward I* (2 vols, Cambridge 1895) is not only

of materials produced, as it were, unofficially. These materials are the direct consequence of the fact that the English common law was served by a profession, the only non-clerical profession known in medieval Europe. From the fourteenth century onwards, English legal practitioners, from the judges downwards, composed a body of trained laymen, experts in a single enterprise, equipped with schools (the London Inns of Court), textbooks, books of practice, and a steady flow of professional information. Other systems of law were served by clerics, sometimes nominal but often aspirants to a career in the hierarchy, and taught at the Universities by means, in the main, of commentaries on standard codes. The records of the common law are really unique. In this they reflect the exceptional condition of this legal profession, a condition which has led to much pride and some very insulated thinking. Although the records of the common law must here be discussed by themselves, students of English law would do well to escape from the inward-looking, self-satisfied attitude which has afflicted England's lawyers as far back as the memory of man goes; they might remember that even in the story of English law the really great names—Bracton, Coke, Maitland—were those of men who knew things and laws beyond the common law and could consider it without falling into the trance of the acolyte.

As early as the reign of Edward III, therefore, the common lawyers had all the hallmarks of a profession, except one: they did not at first record themselves very well. The Inns of Court existed for some time before the beginning of their surviving records, and the reconstruction of their history before the sixteenth century is very difficult. Neither membership nor institutional

---

fundamental to a study of the subject but also demonstrates what can be done with the materials available. For background reading, Alan Harding, *Social History of English Law* (Harmondsworth 1966) is strongly recommended. Samples from the sources are published in the volumes of the Selden Society (SS: see 34). Anyone working in this area needs a good dictionary of the old law; the best is that compiled in the eighteenth century by Giles Jacob (several editions).

action is regularly documented before then.[1] Thereafter things improve. The 'Black Books' of Lincoln's Inn, surviving from 1422, record the activities of its governing body and, fortunately, also enough about its membership for a register of admissions to have been extracted from them.[2] The Middle Temple preserves the minutes of its so-called parliament from 1501, though there are serious gaps in the sixteenth century, and from these minutes admissions lists have been compiled.[3] The Inner Temple possesses the acts of its parliament from 1505 and admissions books from 1547.[4] Originally the least distinguished of these bodies, Gray's Inn did not begin to keep records of its doings until 1569, but admissions registers begin in 1521 and are less marred by gaps than usual.[5] In addition to the materials produced by their own activities, these institutions possess in their archives a motley gathering of manuscripts, including the private papers and collections made by eminent members with antiquarian interests,[6] but this, though often important for general history, is not organic material and throws no light on the institution. Other cognate bodies—Serjeants' Inn and the lesser schools known as Inns of Chancery—have nothing before 1640.

[1] D. S. Bland, *A Bibliography of the Inns of Court and Chancery* (SS 1965).

[2] *Records of the Honourable Society of Lincoln's Inn*, vol. 1: 'Admissions from A.D. 1420 to A.D. 1799' (London 1896).

[3] *Middle Temple Records: Minutes of Parliament*, ed. C. W. Hopwood (3 vols, London 1904); vols 1 and 2 cover the years 1501–1649. *Register of Admissions to the Honourable Society of the Middle Temple from the Fifteenth Century to the Year 1944*, ed. H. A. C. Sturgess (3 vols, London [1949]); vol. 1 covers 1501–1781. See also the *Middle Temple Bench Book*, 2nd ed. by J. Bruce Williamson (London 1937) which collects names for treasurers, readers and masters of the bench back to *c.* 1460.

[4] *A Calendar of Inner Temple Records*, ed. F. A. Inderwick (5 vols, London 1896). Vols 1 and 2 cover the years 1505–1660; vol. 1 contains a rather amateurish essay on the records. The note at the beginning of the registers printed in *Students Admitted to the Inner Temple 1547–1660* (London [1877]) suggests that no registers ever existed before that date.

[5] *Register of Admissions to Gray's Inn 1521–1889*, ed. J. Foster (London 1889).

[6] E.g. the Inner Temple possesses the papers of William Petit (seventeenth century) which include originals gathered by him and transcripts of legal and constitutional documents for some of which the originals are lost.

Thus a fundamental problem of this field of history resists investigation. From such literary sources as handbooks we know all about the structure of the profession—its hierarchy of apprentice, utter barrister, serjeant—but before the middle of the sixteenth century we can put little flesh on these bones. Names of practitioners can be recovered piecemeal from such sources as plea rolls or Year Books, and the names of the judges are found on the patent roll, but before about 1530 the biography of the profession as a whole can never be written with confidence. Things are worse still on the fringes: what we can know about the eminent men who practised in the courts is massive compared with our knowledge of the probably large numbers who acquired sufficient learning to work as attorneys or conveyancers, lowly men advising and drafting for clients, but rarely able to escape complete obscurity. In the equity courts of the sixteenth century, the names of attorneys acting in a case as well as of the counsel retained to plead were supposed to be written on the plaintiff's bill and defendant's answer, and laborious work could establish a useful list from such evidence. But there can be no equivalent to the lists of the modern Law Society or Bar Association; total numbers of lawyers even cannot be provided, and personal details are available for a minority only. It is probable, for instance, and supported by contemporary comment, that the size of the profession increased markedly from about 1550 onwards, but no one has yet succeeded in documenting this important fact statistically. The history of England's lawyers must in the main be written from materials not produced by themselves—from official documents and private papers—and can therefore never be complete. Even so, there is a skeleton of 'organic' documentation, while the extraneous materials offer plenty of evidence, however scattered and haphazard they may be. The fact that we still have far more large assertions and inherited convictions about the lives of lawyers and their part in society and politics than we have attempts at really studying such questions is not entirely to be explained by the state of the evidence.

However, the existence of the profession is certain enough, and even if it did not leave behind full evidence of its membership or organisation (the earlier history of the Inns of Court remains one of the great gaps in English history), it was bound to provide another kind of evidence. A profession trains its recruits in set ways and supplies its members with the instruments of their labours. England's medieval lawyers were no exception: they took steps to disseminate knowledge of the law in writings which can properly be called the products of professional activity. There were three kinds of these: the records of teaching at the Inns, the reports of cases tried in the courts, and manuals of practice.

Teaching at the Inns concentrated on readings and moots, that is to say, lectures by senior men and mock trials.[1] Evidence of both these activities survives from the fifteenth century onwards, but not, of course, in any systematic way; manuscripts are found at places as various as the British Museum, Lincoln's Inn, the libraries of the University of Cambridge or the Harvard Law School. Since no moot is yet in print, I cannot say what this material looks like and what light it may shed, but the value of readings can be assessed. They were delivered by senior barristers on a duty roster laid down by the Inn—usually two lecturers gave courses in the spring and autumn respectively—and they followed standard form. The lecturer took as his theme one of the major restatements of the law made in an earlier royal statute (usually one of the statutes of Edward I, but other acts might be used) and elaborated the law that had grown upon the statute by decisions in individual cases. In that way he taught his audience

---

[1] For this see *Readings and Moots at the Inns of Court in the 15th Century*, ed. S. E. Thorne, vol. 1 (SS 1954). This contains a preface on materials and the transcripts of five readings, with parts of eleven more. Vol. 2 (not yet out) is to print some moots as well as a general account of legal education. An additional reading in print is Robert Constable, *Prerogative Regis*, ed. S. E. Thorne (New Haven 1949), but the long-announced publication of further readings by D. M. Brodie and Bertha Putnam which, Professor Thorne tells us, would complete the extant material before the reign of Henry VIII, seems never to have taken place. Similar readings no doubt exist for later years, but none have so far been edited or even listed.

the present state of the law on central problems of litigation without ever burdening their minds with such things as first principles, though of course, like any lecturer, he could also by the choice of his precedents and *dicta* influence the future developments of the law. The lecture notes which survive are naturally void of the personal; all that these documents illumine is expert opinion of the law and, to some extent, the training of the young. Like moots, in which the student learned the essence of his craft by pleading and arguing an imaginary case before substitute judges, readings were designed to equip him with the arguments for his case, with the best and most recent authority on points likely to arise in disputes, and with the authoritative interpretation of earlier codifications of some area of the law.

English law, being case law and made by judges relying on the precedents put before them by counsel, was for ever in a flux; dependent of necessity on ever-renewed explanations of specific points, it fought shy of all system and even of the fundamental principles beloved by jurisprudence; to the advantages of relative flexibility and some closeness to real life, it added the drawbacks of mindlessness, potential whimsicality, and occasional arbitrariness. But in particular it added difficulties in teaching since the state of the law could be defined only in terms of an accumulation of precedents, a particularly difficult thing for the beginner to assimilate. And like the student, the teacher and the practitioner, too, needed means of preserving and collecting these precedents. From the reign of Edward I onwards they were served in this respect by the remarkable production called the Year Books, gradually replaced in the later sixteenth century by another form of collection called Reports.

The Year Books are a peculiar, even a unique, record. In form a collection of notes on cases which the note-taker had attended as an uninvolved onlooker, they offer a great deal of information not only on the law but on many aspects of life.[1] To quote

[1] The best discussion is W. C. Bolland, *A Manual of Year Book Studies* (Cambridge 1925), though the book, like so much lawyer's history, is marred by a certain pawkiness and open-mouthed wonder at the marvels of the past. See also W. H. Dunham's introduction to his edition of *Casus Placitorum* (SS 1952).

Maitland: 'The Year books come to us from life. Some day they will return to life again at the touch of a great historian.'[1] It will need a man experienced in many things to fulfil this task, and so far only Maitland himself, too busy to attend to it, could have met the demand. For this source in its contents and appearance poses as many problems as it solves. The surviving manuscripts were nearly all copied from original notes, with the usual corruption of texts resulting from that fact. The originals, scribbled down in court, must themselves have been very difficult to read or make sense of. The note-takers—junior lawyers attending in court as part of their training—took down what seemed important to them, and this unfortunately did not include, as a rule, the precise details of a case. Actual dates occur virtually never, parties and matters in dispute (if mentioned at all) are likely to be given in impenetrably obscure form, and—most peculiar of all—the entry very rarely records the outcome of a case. It was the reporter's interest that determined what went in, and his interest was very specialised, miles distant from the historian's. He mainly wished to preserve the arguments of counsel and judges over tricky points of law or novel matters, for these were the things which in both matter and manner he had to learn if he was to be a successful practitioner himself. The special abilities of the experts engaged by litigants were not called for in the explanation of the disputed facts or in the ultimate fate of a case but in the stage of a case which took place in open court—the sorting out of the true legal position, the jockeying for ascendancy, the stage known as 'the argument' (often concerned with the technical details of writs, process, and plea). The aspiring pleader therefore needed to know how leading members of the profession had handled things, as well as what points of law they had successfully relied on. The Year Books consequently do not record so much the precedents (court decisions) upon which a system of case-law must rest as the argument about the true precedents and the technicalities of process from which the unrecorded decision emerged. On top of everything else, they are written in law French (very occasionally

[1] F. W. Maitland, *Year Book Series* (SS), vol. I, xx.

there are Latin entries), full of common form, abbreviations, and etceteras.

Nevertheless, the difficulties of the record do not abolish its immense usefulness. First of all, there are very many Year Books. Of the thirty-four years of Edward I's reign, twenty are covered, and from 1307 to 1602 one survives for nearly every year.[1] Originally, of course, compiled in manuscript, they early attracted printers because their fundamental importance to trainee and practising lawyers made them a very profitable proposition. A great many down to 1536 were printed variously in the fifteenth and sixteenth centuries, in those black letter editions which have to be used for lack of anything else but are often about as difficult and problematic as the manuscripts themselves. Attempts have been made to render their use easier. The Rolls Series printed editions for eight years of Edward I and twelve years of Edward III; though better than the black letter versions, they cannot really be called good. Very much better is the Selden Society's Year Book Series, initiated by Maitland, whose first volume contains the most important analysis of this material and the language in which it was written that we have. But this series has so far achieved only the first twelve years of Edward II (1307–18) and one volume each for Henry VI and Edward IV. The Year Books for three years of Richard II (1387–9) were published by the Ames Foundation of Harvard University. The interest in Year Book studies is at present at a low ebb, and these series seem stagnant. Both the Selden Society and Ames Foundation editions print the original version, properly edited, with a useful English translation.

A vast mass of material thus remains untouched, available either in the barely useful sixteenth-century printings or in manuscript. No one has ever used the unprinted Year Books compiled after 1536 whose existence was in fact so little known until recent years that Maitland could point to the alleged cessation of Year Book production in that year as a vital clue in his argument

[1] Jennifer Nicholson, 'Register of MSS of Year Books extant' (typescript published for the SS by Historical Manuscripts Commission, 1956).

concerning the perils which allegedly afflicted the common law in the reign of Henry VIII.[1]

The first importance of the Year Books lies in the fact that they take us beyond the mere record of the case into its details. However incomplete these details may be, they are vastly more than is to be found in the formalities of the official record of the court. The two do, indeed, complement each other, and a good editor will trace his Year Book cases on the roll, thus enabling the historian to add dates, names and outcome to the particulars jotted down by the note-taker. The sort of detail to be found may be illustrated. In 1302 someone took an interest in the problem of local custom as against the growing dominance of the generally applied common law:[2]

> Presented etc. that J., a bailiff, took bribes from men indicted of theft to get them dismissed in peace; impleaded how etc., said he would acquit himself by the country [be tried by a jury] excepting his accusers. The twelve said that it was and is usage in the said wapentake that if a man be condemned for a trifling theft . . . the bailiff of the place may take a penny from him to have him go in peace.—The Judge: that custom is void, because it is to the detriment of the Crown . . .

More typical are extracts from arguments in the case, like the following:

> [1308–9]. One A. brought his writ of debt against Robert of N. and demanded a hundred shillings, and put forward a deed which witnessed this.
>
> *Laufer* [counsel for defendant]. By this deed you cannot bind us or demand anything, for we were in prison on the day [of the making of the deed]. We demand judgment.
>
> *Bereford, J.* [trial judge]. In whose prison, and by whom imprisoned, and at whose suit?

[1] F. W. Maitland, 'English Law and the Renaissance', *Historical Essays* (ed. H. M. Cam, Cambridge 1957), 143. The statement has become orthodoxy but is wrong.

[2] *Year Book 30 Edward I* (Rolls Series), 532f.

Laufer. In the King's prison, and at the suit of this same A.

Hunt [counsel for plaintiff]. We sued against him at the common law, by which law he was convicted, so that for the trespass that he had done to us he was adjudged to prison, and, to satisfy us for the trespass, he made this bond for the said debt. And we pray judgment whether he shall not be bound, since you cannot say that we are lord of the gaol or the gaoler.

Laufer. At your suit we were put in prison, and while therein were badly treated until we had made this bond, and when it was made we were forthwith delivered. Therefore we demand judgment whether this deed ought to bind us. Moreover, in such a case the law requires that you should take sureties for [the prisoner] until he be delivered, and when delivered—but not while he is in prison—he can bind himself. Judgment.

Bereford, J. You shall say whether, as he has said [your client], was imprisoned by suit and process of law.

Laufer. It cannot be denied that we were [thus] imprisoned; and the Justices were on the point of departure, and for doubt that we might die in prison we made that bond. And we demand judgment.

Stanton, J. [another judge]. Forasmuch as you cannot deny that you were imprisoned by judgment for the trespass that you did to him, therefore the Court awards that he [the plaintiff] recover etc.[1]

Counsel's wrigglings are very patent. Even more characteristic was the following exchange in a case in which a writ had been brought against a man alleging that he had refused to return some charters which plaintiff had left with him in safekeeping. The writ of summons called him 'John Curson, son and heir of John Curson'. His counsel claimed judgment because 'the said defendant is son and heir of William Curson, not son and heir of John Curson'. One of the judges, the great Littleton, reproved counsel: 'You cannot traverse [plead victory on a technical error] both statements, that is to say, that he is not son and heir,' and counsel obligingly amended his words to the effect 'that he is son and heir of William Curson and not son of John Curson'. This must have

[1] Selden Society, *Year Book Series*, vol. 2, 156.

been instructive to the apprentice pleader. Another of the judges now went into a technical rigmarole alleging that counsel could not have judgment on this technical error in the writ, seeing that in the charge preferred the question of whose son and heir defendant was was not material. He elaborated cases in which the plea might succeed and for good measure threw in that 'if a writ were brought against one by a name like J. son of R. of S. this writ is worthless because it has not the surname before *filius*'. Counsel objected that if the plea were not allowed the defendant would at some other time be unable to assert that he was not John Curson's son, to which a third judge retorted that 'a man will not be estopped from that to which he cannot have traverse', with lengthy illustrations to the point. Since the judges disagreed, the argument whether the plea existed and the defendant's description was material to the issue went on for pages.[1]

The main use of such material is certainly for the history of the law, but that is not its only value. Many aspects of life in that lost society find remembrance there. The Year Books are among the few records which break through the obscurity that usually shrouds personality before the arrival of personal papers in the fifteenth century. Thus there is hardly anyone, the king excepted, in the reigns of Edward I or Edward II whom one seems to know more intimately than that eminent lawyer, William de Bereford, ultimately chief justice of Common Pleas. Clearly he was that familiar type on the bench, a man of wit, and fortunately he was so popular with the profession that his jokes got as well recorded as his opinions. It was he who told the parties in a case: 'As the girl said to the young man who asked if she was a maid: just you try it. And so do you try it, and if the action be not settled blame me.'[2] The books sometimes preserve the exclamations and expletives of an argument, occasionally describe counsel by the nicknames current among students, bring actual speech out of

[1] Selden Society, *Year Book of Edward IV* (SS, vol. 47), 104ff.
[2] Quoted by Maitland, *Year Book Series*, vol. 1, xvi. I have chosen this among several of Bereford's quips cited there because Maitland, a trifle surprisingly, preferred to leave it alone untranslated.

oblivion. Even though their subject matter is so technical and so necessarily confined, they exceptionally preserve, as Maitland said, the essence of life—of lives long dead—in a way which no other medieval record does. Of course, since they were the product of individual and unorganised enterprise, they are quite unsystematic and highly selective, liable to embody error and confusion: they can be the despair of the student. But their very origin has saved them from being reduced to the formality which embalms life, and historians in general would be well advised to remember them. No doubt historians of law have a first claim, but others should invade that unsought and undefended monopoly.

From early in the sixteenth century a different sort of record began to be compiled for the use of the profession. The Reports are a much more sophisticated thing than the Year Books, and their ultimate triumph brought both gain and loss. In particular they were intended to bring gain to the compiler. Nobody knows who collected the Year Book cases; their anonymity reflects a lack of concern with personal promotion. The reporters published —using the printing press—over their own names. Men like Keilway and Dyer thus acquired a standing in their profession hitherto reserved for the better-known judges. When the reporters were also great lawyers their authority became overwhelming; for centuries the weight of Plowden and particularly Coke lay upon the law.

The first thing to distinguish the Reports from the Year Books is the fact that the former were not annual and therefore not cumulative. Of course, each new enterprise built up on its predecessor's collection, but in itself it was thought of as, in a sense, definitive: not a rag-bag of the more interesting cases currently argued but a body of leading cases of special significance and meant to clarify the law on some given point. Secondly, the Reports were much more single-mindedly concerned with establishing the law. As a rule they analysed the issues in a case and gave the court's decision, rather than concentrated on the arguments of counsel. In this they both reflected and confirmed the growing authority of the judges, no longer so much arbiters between the real leaders of the profession, the great serjeants, but self-conscious makers of the law. The Reports were an altogether more professional production, designed to instruct rather than present materials for study. The historian of the law will find them easier to use and more straightforwardly informative, but from the point of view of historical evidence in general they are less useful than the Year Books. It is rare for them to offer the incidental insights into life which the medieval compilations so often preserved, and they give far less of the real live speech. Of course, one can miss these facets of Year Book evidence the more easily because other sources (letters, Star Chamber bills, literature in general) supply so much more for them from the sixteenth century onwards. Nevertheless, while the use of the Year Books should be urged upon all historians of the English middle ages, it cannot be said that the neglect with which most scholars treat such works as Dyer's, Plowden's, or Coke's *Reports* leads to anything more serious than the occasional avoidable ignorance.

At the same time, while the Reports certainly embody some purposes different from those which produced the Year Books, it will not do to regard them as strikingly new in intent. They show the law's reliance on authority, but in this itself there was nothing novel. Of all the developed systems of law, the English common law is probably the least intellectual, the most pragmatically higgledy-piggledy, and English lawyers seem always to have been trained to absorb the guidance of the 'authorities' rather than attempt independent and reasoned appreciations themselves. In both their formation and their practice, therefore, the most obvious need has always been for compendia, for works collecting the facts of the law and especially of legal procedure (until the seventeenth century the only systematic part of the law) to which the practising lawyers could refer. X on Torts, or Y on Contract, have predecessors reaching into the thirteenth century.

In particular, the essential foundation of medieval procedure, the original writs (the writs initiating actions), early attracted the makers of textbooks: the 'Register of Writs', a collection of specimens and precedents, achieved its final form under Edward I and thereafter proved rather restrictive to new developments. Abstracts and summaries were also made, especially in Sir Anthony Fitzherbert's *Natura Brevium* (1534); Simon Thelsall's *Digest of Original Writs and Things Concerning Them* (1579) provided quite an orderly summary of court procedure. The mysteries of pleading attracted textbook writers (mainly in the sixteenth century) whose products, precedent books called 'books of entries', succeed quite well in making the subject more mysterious still. Branches of the law began to be written up—one might say, more systematically, if it were remembered, as a glance at these productions will show, that system can be a relative term. A legal order so devoted to the problems of landed property naturally produced good works on title and conveyancing, of which Littleton's treatise (*c.* 1481) was the best early one and John Parkyns's *Profitable Book* of 1524, last republished in 1827, the most long-lived. It has historical meaning that the criminal law did not attract writers till the sixteenth century, when Staunford (*Pleas of the Crown*, 1560) and Ferdinando Pulton (*De Pace Regis et Regni*, 1609) turned their attention to this hitherto despised area and imported some of the technical refinement required to give it respectability in the eyes of the profession. Above all, the needs of the usually amateur administrator of the law in the localities had to be catered for, and so they were, from the thirteenth- and fourteenth-century treatises on the Court Baron[1] to the many little books useful to justices of the peace which culminated in William Lambarde's *Eirenarcha* (1584).[2] To the historian, himself as a rule an amateur of the law, these books are useful because they help him understand the details of the technical evidence, but they vary greatly in quality and accuracy. In a legal system so fluid in its detail and so often dependent on individual whim, the generalisations of the textbook writers quite often do not touch actual practice except here and there. This is especially true of treatises on certain courts, even when written by seeming experts. Thus

[1] Ed. F. W. Maitland and W. P. Baildon (SS, vol. 4, 1890).

[2] See Bertha H. Putnam, *Early Treatises on the Practice of the Justices of the Peace in the 15th and 16th Centuries* (Oxford 1924).

The Practice of the Exchequer Court, ascribed to Thomas Fanshawe, the Elizabethan Queen's remembrancer, but probably written by Peter Osborn, his colleague as lord treasurer's remembrancer, and first published in 1658, or William Hudson's well-known treatise on the Star Chamber,[1] should not be believed where they contradict the evidence of the record.

It is no surprise to find that a body of professionals who accord authority to textbooks should in fact cherish a class of works described technically as 'books of authority'. These are the works of the *great* textbook writers, men of towering intellect who came near to producing system even in the common law and, in fact, under the guise of description provided reinterpretation. On the fringes of this select group stand lesser summarisers like the fourteenth-century Britton and 'Fleta'. 'Fleta', a compilation produced in the reign of Edward I and accorded excessive respect simply because it was useful, is, in fact, rather nice.[2] On the face of it an account of the King's courts, their practice and their law, it takes every opportunity to stray and becomes a kind of general handbook, faintly reminiscent of Mrs Beeton.[3] The author has to mention the assize of bread and ale, but he also instructs the clerk responsible in what his proper profits are. Local courts lead him into estate and domestic management; he speaks of the surveying and valuing of land, remarks that 'the month of April, the time, that is, when all things are opening, will be a fit and propitious time for fallowing', or that 'if any of the breeding sows shall continue to be fertile, they should not be allowed to farrow in winter', and instructs the dairy-maid in honesty and frugality. His whole 'chapter' on the cook reads: 'It is the cook's duty to render account each day to the steward for every course at table.' Perhaps one may see a sign of progress in the fact that 200 years

[1] This work exists in several MS copies of which I possess one; it has never been printed in full, but the partial edition by Francis Hargrave, *Collectanea Juridica* (1792), vol. 2, 1–240, has its uses.

[2] See the edition by H. G. Richardson and G. O. Sayles (SS, 1953). The first volume, in which the editors will discuss their text, has not yet appeared.

[3] Has anyone ever pursued the thought that 'Fleta' may have been written by a man-and-wife team?

later Fitzherbert separated his *Boke of Husbandrye* from his *Natura Brevium.*

Two of the 'books of authority', however, stand out in our period, neatly bracketing it between two vast and exhaustive descriptions of the law which really amount to a total and creative treatment of it. The first is the great treatise of Henry de Bracton, a judge in the reign of Henry III, who in a busy and quite short life found time to apply an organising mind to the recent rapid and massive developments in procedure and practice, to produce his *De Legibus et Consuetudinibus Anglie* which in the currently best edition by G. E. Woodbine (New Haven, 1915–42) fills three hefty volumes of text.[1] Bracton's greatness has never been doubted, and rightly so. He rested his work on a thorough acquaintance with the rolls whose haphazard accumulation he searched for decisive cases[2] and reduced to order by means of the systematic cast of mind with which acquaintance with the law of Rome, reviving in his day in the Italian schools, had equipped him.[3] Though the law changed and developed continuously, Bracton's remained the only truly comprehensive statement of it, and therefore its foundation.

Some 400 years after Bracton's day, the same task was undertaken by the equally monumental Edward Coke whose four volumes of *The Institutes of the Laws of England,* resting not only on long experience but also in great part on his own thirteen volumes of *Reports,* achieve what he set out to do: a total review of English law and law courts. In the process, Coke effectively renewed and revised the law. Though he professed to be merely stating what was, he really settled uncertainty, ended lines of argument, and provided a reformed basis for future development, so much so that students for long failed to see how great the recent changes of the sixteenth century had been. His authority over subsequent generations was, if anything, even more over-

[1] A new definitive edition, to be published by the SS, is being prepared by S. E. Thorne.

[2] See *Bracton's Notebooks,* ed. F. W. Maitland (3 vols, 1897).

[3] *Selected Passages from the Works of Bracton and Azo,* ed. F. W. Maitland (SS, vol. 8, 1894).

whelming than Bracton's had been, and it lasted almost as long. But he was a less agreeable man than Bracton and more concerned to bulldoze his views into general acceptance; especially his pretence that he had only summarised the facts of the past was to delude historians for long into many serious errors; and he badly mis-stated some parts of the law. At the same time, it must be stressed that Coke was a better historian than those concerned to eradicate his errors have usually been willing to admit. The only modest thing about him and his book was the epilogue to the first volume in which he showed himself sincerely awed by the task he had undertaken. His achievement of it must forever excite admiration.

Lastly, among the materials of the law, one may refer to certain treatises which, though more in the nature of literary productions than designed to teach or assist lawyers, do throw light on the law itself. Into this category fall three well-known publicists of the fifteenth and sixteenth centuries. Sir John Fortescue, chief justice to Henry VI but also a member of Edward IV's Council, wrote a Latin treatise in praise of the laws of England designed for the latter monarch's son,[1] and an English polemic in favour of England's form of government,[2] which—in part because in his day they were exceptional—have attracted more praise than intrinsically they deserve. Christopher St German, a leading practitioner in the law, turned pamphleteer in his old age; his best-known treatise, the two volumes of *Dialogues between a Doctor of Divinity and a Student* [of the common law][3] are at heart a rather tendentious piece of propaganda for the excellence of English law and its superiority to the law of Rome. Less committed was Thomas Smith, first Regius professor of civil law at Cambridge and secretary of state to Elizabeth I, whose English work, *De Republica Anglorum*,[4] written for some enquiring French

[1] *De Laudibus Legum Anglie*; best edition by S. B. Chrimes (Cambridge 1942).
[2] *The Governance of England*; best edition by C. Plummer (Oxford 1885).
[3] Published 1528 and 1530; both have been edited several times. A new edition by T. F. T. Plucknett for the SS was in preparation at the time of Professor Plucknett's death; it is to be hoped that it will be completed and published.
[4] Best edition by L. Alston (Cambridge 1906).

friends, contains some matter on the law. From books such as these (and similar productions survive in sixteenth-century manuscripts) one may learn something of an otherwise obscure subject: the cast of mind behind the common law and the opinion held of it, as distinct from what it really was.

Once printing became commonplace, the profitability of legal works showered the market with aids to students and practitioners, with general and particular treatises, and with combative works designed to advance the cause. But these, readily accessible, should not hide the great mass of the genuine materials produced by England's law and courts from which the history of the law must really be reconstructed. And while these materials are, in the first place, naturally vital to that special branch of history, the essential importance of the law in the social and political life of those centuries ensures that virtually no aspect of historical study can afford to ignore the sources of the law. At all points the historian, in his efforts to understand, comes up against the need to grasp the details of an activity which played such a large part, active or passive, in the lives with which he is concerned. Moreover, these materials constantly provide him with unexpected details, with the first-hand evidence of life, with social or economic facts not to be found elsewhere. Above all, perhaps, since aside from theology only the law called upon men to think, reflect, argue and compose professionally, the materials of the law supply an exceptional way into the minds of those centuries. What people did is recorded in many places; what and how they thought is much more difficult to discover. Assuredly, the lawyers thought and argued in a peculiar fashion, in the conditions set by their avocation, but at least we can learn a great deal about it. Of other men's thoughts on their society and government, if any there were, we are, as a rule, quite ignorant, at least before the end of the fifteenth century. It must be a matter for argument whether the very legalistic light in which, in consequence, we tend to see the thought of those times is real or merely a distortion filtered through the bias of the evidence.

CHAPTER 7

Books and Writings

The lawyers' 'books of authority' were not, of course, the only writings of these centuries of relevance to the historian. Indeed, all books concern him; and law books and chronicles have here been treated separately only because, from the historian's point of view, they form special cases—books linked with particular aspects of study and categories of material. But all the works written and put out in those centuries are, among other things, also materials for historical study, so much so that when historical sources are mentioned the layman may think first of books. To many people, 'research' in the humanities means reading books. That this is a very inadequate view has by now become plain. Nevertheless, writings constitute an historical source with a great many applications; and one posing more problems of interpretation than is commonly realised.

From the point of view of written works, the years 1200–1640 fall naturally into two parts. The division is marked by the introduction of printing which constituted one of the major revolutions in the history of mankind. Books were written before printing was invented, and in quantity at that; but the printed book differs from the manuscript book in two ways fundamental to its role as historical evidence. Printed books transmit their authors' intentions with much greater accuracy, and they are produced in such quantity that survival becomes much more assured and availability (including potential influence) enormously enlarged.

In copying manuscripts, even careful scribes make mistakes, and most scribes were not all that careful: books produced before the invention of printing usually pose the first and fundamental problem of textual restoration, and it does not much matter whether what survives are manuscripts only or early printed versions. The same thing could also happen with the printed book proper, especially with such relatively unregarded productions as plays or poems; everybody knows the difficulties encountered in discovering exactly what Shakespeare wrote from the rough and ready versions put out in print. But what is an exceptional problem to the student of printed books is the commonplace occupation of him who endeavours to edit the works of men who did not know of printing; and he is often hindered as much as assisted by the editions made in the early printing days when many books of the past, of which no manuscript now exists, were rescued from oblivion. As for availability and survival, the point needs no elaboration: medieval libraries were bound to be puny by comparison with what libraries have since become. Printing also made books markedly cheaper, though books are about the only thing that, in terms of real money, has drastically fallen in price since the sixteenth century.

Still, the urge to write is so well entrenched in the human mind that long before authors could be sure that their works would endure or stand a chance of being widely read they wrote at length and in great numbers, and in two languages. Latin was reserved, on the whole, for works of learning or for works on such subjects as husbandry or accountancy written by learned men: but most writers were learned, in a technical sense. The vernacular—French, superseded by the early fourteenth-century by English—served for entertainment as well as for books designed for popular use in devotion, politics or instruction. By the fifteenth century Latin had become what it was to remain to the end of our period—the language in which an international body of scholars addressed one another. By this time most serious and virtually all imaginative writing used English.

The output was enormous and varied. The standard bibliographies, which are much fuller for vernacular than for Latin writing, supply hundreds of titles in such categories as tales and romances, politics and satire, religious instruction and service books, devotional and homiletic literature, bible translations and commentaries, lyrics and drama, natural science and medicine, history and law, general information and handbooks.[1] Some works, no doubt, have disappeared. Fortunately the early-sixteenth century discovered a passionate interest in the literature of the English past, an interest mainly called forth by the sudden danger of destruction that arose from the government's attack on monasteries and colleges, the main preservers of manuscript libraries. The manner in which the early printers—especially William Caxton—set about turning old manuscripts into new printed books indicates that the concern was not new in the 1530's, but it grew urgent when it became apparent that in the Dissolution of the Monasteries many rare and often precious manuscripts might be lost. John Leland, who secured from Henry VIII a commission to visit the scheduled houses and list their holdings, did a remarkable single-handed job, and his attempt to compile a dictionary of English writers contributed to the successful enterprise along the same lines which was undertaken by John Bale, the bitterly protestant bishop of Ossory (1495–1563). Bale's *Index Britanniae Scriptorum*, in its published versions, turned into a strikingly partisan production, with venomous attacks on the enemies of the faith (as he saw it) and extravagant praise for its friends. But the basic compilation, which remained in manuscript until published in 1902,[2] is devoid of such flourishes and demonstrates the man's careful scholarship, especially in that he recorded the source of his information. His dictionary amounted to an alphabetical list of authors (alphabetical by first names) with all the works ascribable to them that he could find, and with notes that show him getting his facts from the libraries of univer-

[1] J. E. Wells, *A Manual of Writings in Middle English 1050–1400* (New Haven 1916, continued in nine supplements 1919–51. The ninth is by other hands; the eighth contains an index to the first eight supplements). This catalogue lists and, up to a point, discusses all middle-English writings that have got into print, single lines as well as complete works; occasionally it extends beyond the year 1400. *Cambridge Bibliography of English Literature*, vol. 1 (600–1660), ed. F. W. Bateson (Cambridge 1940); vol. 5 (Supplement 600–1900), ed. G. Watson (Cambridge 1957).

[2] John Bale, *Index Britanniae Scriptorum*, ed. R. L. Poole and Mary Bateson (Oxford 1902). This is a better list than the versions put out by Bale himself.

sities, cathedrals and private owners, as well as from the shelves of booksellers.

In the modern edition, this *Index* makes over 490 pages, though, of course, quite a number of Bale's writers belong to the period before 1200. Nor is he always correct; some of his names are inventions, some of his ascriptions are inaccurate, and he did not by any means find everything. However, his net was cast very wide, for he included sermons and letters and similar brief pieces. Thus (though this is strictly outside our period) he included among his authors '*Henricus secundus Anglorum princeps eruditus*', a generosity which few would copy today when we hardly think of Henry II as an author, on the strength of a letter 'to the princes of the East' which he claimed to have found 'in an imperfect chronicle of England'. He compounded his generosity by mistakenly dividing the one letter into four, thereby making the king into the patron saint of all who inflate their personal bibliography by dubious means.[1] Men in public life appealed to Bale: he included even the Protector Somerset, ruler of Edward VI's England, because, he says, he had found a translation by him of a French sermon 'in booksellers' shops'.[2] But he had a proper sense of balance: Chaucer's writings fills three and a half pages.

Bale worked in the 1540's, and his list therefore extends to include a mass of writers of recent date who had benefited from the invention of printing. It thus overlaps with the modern catalogue of books printed in our period, the famous *Short-Title Catalogue*, universally (in the appropriate circles) known as *STC*.[3] This volume, which neatly covers the years of our enquiry, lists 26,143 items, but the fact that the last author given is the Swiss reformer Zwingli reminds us that what is listed are books printed in England, not only printed books written by Englishmen. There are also hundreds of items, such as royal proclamations, which do

[1] Bale, 157.

[2] *Ibid.*, 69.

[3] *A Short-Title Catalogue of Books printed in England and Ireland, and of English Books printed abroad, 1475–1640*, ed. A. W. Pollard and G. R. Redgrave (London 1926).

not belong to the sort of literature that forms the subject of this chapter. Nor is the *STC* perfect; a new edition has been in preparation for many years but is now, it seems, being delayed by the unfortunate death of its guiding spirit, William Jackson, lately a professor and librarian at Harvard University. Nevertheless, the *STC* shows clearly how massive this category of 'historical materials' is: something like 20,000 books published in England in the first 165 years of printing. This total is well below a single year's production today, but that only makes the source more valuable than it would nowadays be. And the catalogue includes only things known now to exist.

The *STC* forms the foundation of the two books in which H. S. Bennett analysed the facts of early book production.[1] His categories are still much the same as those discovered in medieval manuscript literature, and this is so because in fact these writings, both printed and unprinted, cover effectively all the categories possible: religion, law, education (textbooks), medicine, arithmetic (with astronomy and popular science), geography, history, news (current affairs), and literature proper. Religion supplied the largest part of the output—just about half the total—for the term includes not only the bible and commentaries, sermons and homilies, books of devotion and mysticism, guides to the faith for clergy and laity, edition of early Fathers and later schoolmen, but also the official instructions and the vast controversial literature called forth by the Reformation. The least satisfactory category is the last, for works of imaginative writing were certainly treated with less care than books with a more practical appeal, and more is probably lost. For stage plays, invaluable work has been done in collecting, scrutinising and publishing the evidence, especially in the six volumes which E. K. Chambers devoted to medieval and Elizabethan plays (the latter includes Jacobean).[2]

What was written by Englishmen in these four and a half

[1] H. S. Bennett, *English Books and Readers 1475-1557* (Cambridge 1952) and ditto, *1558-1603* (Cambridge 1965).

[2] E. K. Chambers, *The Medieval Stage*, 2 vols (Oxford 1903); *The Elizabethan Stage*, 4 vols (Oxford 1923).

centuries can therefore be discovered with relative ease; the question what was read is much more difficult to answer. For one thing, of course, books read in England included books written elsewhere, from Plato's dialogues to Montaigne's essays. All the literature of the world's history, so far as at any given time it was known, was theoretically available to the English reader, and at one time or another in this period no doubt all of it was read. A more suitable enquiry would concern itself with the problem of what books are known to have been around and therefore within the reader's reach, the problem of libraries.[1] Here information is hard to come by and thoroughly unreliable. Private libraries have left almost no evidence behind. It is likely that few individuals possessed books, though from the later fifteenth century onwards books begin to make their appearance in wills; men who did own them were either professionals—clergy and scholars—or very occasionally a wealthy patron. Lay book collectors emerge as virtually a new class of men in the reign of Elizabeth when the ideal of the gentleman-scholar began to gain ground, though by that time also men of lower standing were acquiring both education and books.[2]

The main libraries which might tell us what people could have read were those of institutions. Some of them still exist, especially at the colleges of Oxford and Cambridge, though there are also such libraries as those of St George's Chapel, Windsor, or at Lambeth Palace. But even there, unless that rarity, an old library catalogue, survives, it is usually very difficult to discover what was in the collection at some date in the past. Durham Cathedral forms an exception. Not only do many of its medieval volumes still exist, now in the care of the University, but medieval library catalogues, too, survive. The most important of these is dated 1416; it rests on earlier lists and notes what had become of some of the books no longer (even then) in the main library—

[1] There are some informative essays in *The English Library before 1700*, ed. Francis Wormald and C. E. Wright (London 1958).

[2] See e.g. Ruth Kelso, *The Doctrine of the English Gentleman in the sixteenth Century* (Urbana 1929); L. B. Wright, *Middle-Class Culture in Elizabethan England* (Chapel Hill 1935).

some, for instance, had gone to the Cathedral's hostel at Oxford. Its approximately 500 items include bibles with commentaries, works of the Fathers and schoolmen, sermons, saints' lives, histories, poetry, some ancient authors (Cicero, Sidonius, Quintilian), philosophy, medicine, grammar, canon and civil law, and psalters.[1] In the absence of similar evidence it is hard to know how typical this institution in the far north may have been; what can be reconstructed for other places is certainly less impressive. An attempt has been made to sort out the question for Oxford, but on the evidence available the author cannot get very far.[2] For such information as we have on pre-Reformation libraries we depend very largely on the work of John Leland who in his travels round England and the doomed monasteries made lists— very probably quite imperfect lists—of what he found.[3] He was concerned to record things of value, but he was not so selective that his figures become totally misleading. In general, however, he recorded very few books in most libraries: Peterhouse (Cambridge) stands out with over 100 volumes, whereas so ancient an abbey as Malmesbury had only twenty-four and the great church of St Paul's in London only twenty. The books are not only few but predictable and by no means always specially valuable: mostly theology (compendia rather than important original works), sermons, a little history, some science and medicine. Even if we allow for the gaps in our knowledge, we may still incline to think that the libraries of medieval England were in the main small and undistinguished, though manuscripts were always, of course, relatively rare and expensive. The effect of printing on book-buying and book-collecting may well have been immediate, but the size of libraries did not increase until after the Reformation.

[1] *Catalogi Veteres Librorum Ecclesiae Cathedralis Dunelm* (London: Surtees Society, 1838), 85ff.

[2] N. R. Ker, 'Oxford College Libraries in the Sixteenth Century', *Bodleian Library Record*, vol. 6 (1959) 459ff.

[3] J. Leland, *Collectanea*, ed. T. Hearn, 6 vols (London 1770). Most of his surviving lists of books are in vol. 4. Some more are found in manuscript, and there is other information. All of it so far known is assembled in *Medieval Libraries of Great Britain*, ed. N. R. Ker (London 1964).

While the company of authors in those centuries bears some sort of comparison with modern conditions, readers were proportionately far fewer and more select.

The historian concerned with books should treat them in two ways—as physical objects and as containers of information. In the first aspect they yield knowledge concerning their production and the book trade. Very little seems to have been done about this before printing began; though some work exists on medieval *scriptoria* and scribes, this has not been systematised, and if there was anything resembling an organisation for the manufacture and distribution of manuscript works in medieval England it seems to have escaped the notice of historians.[1] One of the remarkable things about printing is the way in which almost overnight it produced practices and conditions which in essentials have altered little since. Within two generations of Caxton's setting up of his press at Westminster, printers (who were also publishers) had established themselves as a regular trade, booksellers had set up permanent shops (especially in St Paul's Churchyard), books were being ferried to and fro among the countries, and the technical terms of the trade—type, copy, proof—had made their appearance. Bibliography—the technical study of the printed book—is a highly specialised form of learning, useful in the first instance to its practitioners but of wider assistance to other historians too.[2]

The trade has been provided with its directories,[3] and since

[1] On the continent, both the manufacture and the distribution of manuscript books was in places well and commercially organised (e.g. Margaret Aston, *The Fifteenth Century*, London 1968, 69ff), but I know of no evidence that this happened in England.

[2] The specialist journals often contain important articles of use to historians. See particularly *The Library*; *Transactions of the Bibliographical Society*; *Transactions of the Cambridge Bibliographical Society*; *Publications of the Oxford Bibliographical Society*; *Huntington Library Quarterly*.

[3] E. G. Duff, *A Century of the English Book Trade* (London 1905); *The Printers, Stationers and Bookbinders of London and Westminster* (Aberdeen 1899); *The English Provincial Printers, Stationers and Bookbinders to 1557* (Cambridge 1912). With the foundation, in 1557, of the Stationers' Company something like order and organisation—but also control—took over: C. Blagden, *The Stationers' Company: a history 1403–1959* (London 1960).

printing is, among other things, an economic activity, information on general problems of manufacture and wealth can be obtained there. The reasons why books got written may sometimes be discovered from prefaces. Caxton, in particular, who through his activities as a translator supplied much of his own copy, always explained at length why a certain work was being put into print; he used his prefaces and epilogues as substitutes for modern publishers' blurbs and appreciative reviews all in one.[1] Thus we learn that he printed *The Sayings of the Philosophers* because Anthony, Earl Rivers had made a translation and sent it to Caxton to be checked and published; and we know that the printer recommended the book for its usefulness to those in need of a working stock of prudence. *The Order of Chivalry* he translated himself, at the request of an unnamed 'gentle and noble esquire', and advertised it as a work much needed by an England fallen away from the ideals and exercises of knighthood. The physical make-up of a book may assist in discovering the history of its composition. Type-faces and ornaments can tell about the printers involved or (by their visible deterioration) about the sequence of printings; this sometimes corrects false literary evidence. Thus G. Pollard eliminated a legendary early edition of Edward Hall's *Chronicle* by analysing the types used in the extant early copies, with the result that he rearranged the probable order of precedence among certain writers.[2] More commonly such reconstructions depend on internal evidence, on the dissecting of what the writer says with a view to learning not about the meaning of the book but about its history: thus the whole interpretation of Thomas More's *Utopia* has been profoundly altered by J. H. Hexter's demonstration that the book was written at

[1] *The Prologues and Epilogues of William Caxton*, ed. W. J. B. Crotch (London: Early English Text Society, 1928).

[2] G. Pollard, 'The bibliographical history of Hall's Chronicle', *Bulletin of the Institute of Historical Research* x (1932), 12ff. However, errors do not vanish so easily, especially as Pollard's article seems to include one or two as well. The spurious 1542 edition, which he rightly demolished, seems to have gone, but the very entry in Read's *Bibliography* which mentions Pollard's article (entry no. 306) invents another spurious edition for 1547.

different times and not in the order in which it was finally put together.[1] If an author's manuscript survives, comparison of it with the finished product can naturally be most effective,[2] and even if a book was never printed a manuscript of it may tell much about its birth and development, which in turn can throw light on its meaning, context or influence.[3] The laborious and rewarding bibliographical and textual work done on the dramatists, often sidling along the precipice edge of wild conjecture but often precise and solid, has done a great deal not only to restore the text but also to sort out chronology and authorship.

Whether we have what an author wrote or dictated, or only a copy in manuscript or print, the physical entity that is a book should be remembered for the information it may yield. However, unquestionably the main interest of historians, as of others, is in what was written, in the contents of a work. The history of culture, of education, of ideas, of literature and art obviously depends on the products of these activities, which are books. If we want to know what people thought, reasoned, believed, hated, attacked, feared, enjoyed, we rightly go to their surviving writings, though—as we shall see—we possibly go there a little too trustingly. For the medieval period, books are also an important source for the history of painting, since miniatures and other decorations form a great part of the extant art of the age.[4] But the contents of books can yield other benefits to historians. Chaucer and Langland, Spenser and Shakespeare were, of course, poets concerned to tell stories, express experience, and produce works of beauty, but they were also men of exceptional sensitivity living in their world and reflecting it. One can learn a lot about political attitudes, social conventions, religious commonplaces from writings which were not designed to reveal such matters at all and

[1] J. H. Hexter, *More's Utopia: the Biography of an Idea* (Princeton 1952).

[2] E.g. Richard Morison's tracts can be usefully compared with earlier drafts (W. G. Zeeveld, *Foundations of Tudor Policy*, Cambridge, Mass. 1948, 179ff).

[3] See my analysis of the manuscript of Thomas Starkey's *Dialogue between Pole and Lupset* in the forthcoming Proceedings of the British Academy (1969).

[4] Below, 232.

from writers unaware that they were telling about them. In the absence of specialist literature, the history of medieval social conditions or political opinions relies heavily on the works of the poets, of Chaucer, Langland or Gower.[1] Again, there are dangers in this which shall engage attention in a moment. Yet however exceptional a fourteenth-century peasant the author of *Piers Plowman* may have been, it would be silly not to listen to the rare voice of an articulate peasant of the day commenting on his world. The tax-collector who wrote the pilgrims' tales on the road to Canterbury may have been untypical of his profession, but should we for that reason refuse to see that road and those pilgrims through his eyes? In any case, there is no escaping it. Imaginative literature—prose, poetry, drama—describes the reality that lies behind the record; it has its own literal rightness; and the historian will be wise to listen. He will be even wiser if he avoids the professional disease of always listening as an historian and at times attends as a man himself gifted—if gifted he is—with imagination and a receptive ear.[2]

Books further introduce their authors, and in periods when too few people stand forth as individuals the presence of men whose minds and quirks come across the centuries has its own usefulness, especially since some of them—by no means all—were men worth knowing at any time. Prefaces and casual references can supply biographical details: it is a pity that Shakespeare never wrote the sort of treatise on the sacraments or pharmacology or horses which commonly tempted its dull author to present his piddling life to the reader. Roger Ascham introduced his *Scholemaster* with a convincingly life-like account of the conversation which led to the writing of the work. Thomas More started his *Utopia* with the story of the embassy that took him to Flanders and followed this piece of accurate autobiography with the imaginary meeting with

[1] M. McKisack, *The Fourteenth Century* (Oxford 1959), 527ff.

[2] A good deal of literary history is awful—destructive of the very literature it tries to enhance. Criticism (in the technical sense employed by literary scholars) can be worse. But historians' treatment of poets and writers is often no better. To seek to extract 'historical evidence' from Chaucer or Shakespeare is legitimate; to treat them as historical documents is not.

Ralph Hythloday from which the book developed. Details of the lives of other people may occur. In particular, there are the dedications which sixteenth- and seventeenth-century writers were wont to include, either to acknowledge the past help or to solicit the future favour of some man of influence. This last is still a little-explored source of historical knowledge which can lay bare a good deal about the political groupings and social alignments of the age. Dedications are obviously not to be taken at face value: a man is not on oath when flattering a patron. Treated critically, however, they can tell much about the persons involved, and above all they can be used to trace literary coteries, links between individuals, the position of the powerful—monarchs and ministers—in the organising of literature, political or not. That first systematic manipulator in England of the printing press, himself no literary man, Thomas Cromwell, occurs in dedications and prefaces; though no one has yet assembled the information to study his use of patronage, the job has been done for Queen Elizabeth's favourite, the earl of Leicester.[1]

The uses of books and writings are so obvious, and this material has been used so regularly,[2] that there is no need further to expatiate on this theme. What is more important is the fact that the difficulties of interpretation inherent in published matter of this kind are as a rule insufficiently appreciated. As source material, books seem straightforward enough—accessible, reproducible, understandable, technical only to the professional bibliographer, a source with which no one can go wrong. Often enough, all this may be true, but it is demonstrably not always true. There are some real pitfalls in the road travelled by the historian who uses learned or devotional or imaginative literature for historical purposes; and since some of them seem to be little known it will be useful to discover the limitations of this source by considering them.

---

[1] Eleanor Rosenberg, *Leicester: Patron of Letters* (New York 1955).

[2] It might, however, be remarked that there is an unfortunate tendency for historians to be either 'book-men' or 'records-men', each slightly contemptuous of the other.

In the first place, it is far from easy to be sure that all the available material is known and being used. Oddly enough, this becomes a bigger problem once one enters the age of the printed book. Unknown, or at least unedited, medieval manuscripts, at best available in a single copy and hidden in remote places, do exist, but 500 years of editorial activity have left few such, and those probably not very important ones. The flood of books which printing unleashed, on the other hand, has imposed much neglect on what does not happen to be in print. Throughout our period, writing for the press was far from commonplace, and many significant works were still, in fact, written to be circulated in manuscript. It appears that down to the early seventeenth century at least, a slight prejudice still attached to any gentleman who published his book, and men of standing continued to prefer the pen to movable type, a harmless piece of snobbery which, however, limited the influence of their writings and still hides some of them. Occasionally such pieces were published quite soon after they were written (though not immediately): Sir Philip Sidney's *Apology for Poetry*, intended as a manifesto and programme, saw print in 1595, seven years after its author's death and some fifteen after it was first read in his private circle. Other books took longer. Sir Robert Filmer produced his *Patriarcha*, a tract on royal power, in about 1635 and showed it around among his friends in Kent; when finally, in 1680, it appeared in print the whole situation had altered so much that Filmer was never properly appreciated or assessed until the 1950's.[1] The best seventeenth-century analysis of mercantilist politics, Thomas Mun's *England's Treasure by Forraign Trade*, appeared in 1664, some forty years after it was written; the best-known treatise on the royal Exchequer, published in 1658, was written nearly a century earlier, a delay which resulted in the wrong author being assigned to it.[2]

At least these manuscript treatises were put out within a

---

[1] See the edition by Peter Laslett of *Patriarcha and other political works of Sir Robert Filmer* (Oxford 1949).

[2] See above, 183.

moderately reasonable time from their date of composition; many others, sometimes as important, were selectively published in the eighteenth, nineteenth and twentieth centuries, or never published at all. Thus Thomas Starkey's interesting political pamphlet, *The Dialogue between Cardinal Pole and Thomas Lupset* (the title itself being invented in the nineteenth century), was edited for the press—not very well—in 1871;[1] yet the State Papers of Henry VIII, among which the manuscript was found, contain many other tracts, memorials and pamphlets at least some of which would merit print almost as much as this best-known product of a busy period. In the eighteenth century, various editors brought out volumes of old writings, as in the *Harleian Miscellany* or the *Somers Tracts*, but while some of the things they picked up are interesting and weighty, they represent a very accidental selection from what is available. Francis Hargreave's two collections of legal writings[2] do not include two early-Tudor products of greater value than much that he did print: Richard Morison's attempt to codify the common law, and John Hales's defence of a system then under attack. This list could be prolonged interminably: the point should be clear. What is in print does not equal what was written, and since a good many people at the time did not suppose that the purpose of writing was to appear in print it does not follow that the printing press may be used as a barrier between what matters and what does not. Anybody wanting to understand the thought and culture of the period—or to study a particular problem of intellectual history—would do well to search manuscripts as well.

Books and tracts themselves, printed or not, pose some obvious problems. Quite often the author is not known, and the attempts to reduce the large bulk deposited in the 'anonymous' pigeon-hole frequently lead to disputes. These may be aggravated by doubts about seemingly well-established ascriptions. The number of 'real' authors proposed in place of the obviously unqualified William

[1] By J. W. Cowper, for the Early English Text Society.
[2] *Collectanea Juridica*, 2 vols (London 1791–2); *Collection of Tracts relative to the Law of England* (Dublin 1787).

Shakespeare is well known, though few people seem to be aware of the extent of that literary craze or to have ever looked at the disturbing aberrations which its products enshrine. But while one need not go so far in following the principle of Ockham's razor as some Baconians do when they make Francis Bacon the author of everything that was written in his lifetime (and some would include stuff published after his death), one may still note, for instance, the recent endeavour, probably sound, to reduce three sixteenth-century writers to one—Sir Thomas Smith, Queen Elizabeth's secretary of state.[1] The ostensible place and date can be as uncertain as authorship. The age was one of ideological warfare and repression, and many books, escaping the censor by being printed abroad or on a secret press, pretended a false place of origin. It will be obvious how important correct attributions to writer, date and place can be in assessing the meaning of a book. Of course, in the great majority of cases no such difficulties arise, but when they do they are fundamental and must be solved.

All these are well enough known problems, though one frequently finds even good historians sidestepping them. Still, literary scholars, bibliographers and textual critics, hard at work on their materials, stand by to assist the historian. Within limits, catalogues of manuscripts and calendars of collections help him to avoid the ignorance which results from using published material only. There remain deeper and subtler difficulties which arise in particular when historians concern themselves not with one writer or with one work but try to use writings for the purpose—the far too frequent purpose—of discovering the 'mind' of an age, for distinguishing the commonplace and generally accepted from the unconventional and exceptional.

In the first place, there is the problem of the books that were written and are lost. That medieval manuscripts were especially liable to this kind of death has already been mentioned. The student of the middle ages is better off than the student of anti-

[1] Mary Dewar, *Sir Thomas Smith* (London 1964). Mrs Dewar makes a good case for ascribing to Smith not only the *De Republica Anglorum* long recognised as his work, but also the economic and the monetary treatises hitherto supposed to be the work of John Hales and Thomas Gresham respectively.

quity—all scholars, as a matter of principle, ought once a year to observe a minute's silence in sad remembrance of the double burning of the great library at Alexandria—but he still lacks many things that he would like to have. Moreover, the losses are not random but subject to a double bias. The authority of the Church imposed at least a measure of orthodoxy even before the Reformation, and books unpleasing to the hierarchy are much less likely to have survived. Only Thomas Cromwell's interest in a book useful to his policies led to the digging out and publication (in an English translation) of Marsiglio of Padua's great *Defensor Pacis*, written 200 years earlier in the 1330's, disapproved of by the papacy, and nearly lost through neglect. Wycliffe's writings survive: at least, enough of his terrible prose exists to illumine his thought and assuage whatever regrets may be felt at the possibility that once there was more of it. But Lollard writings in general are patchily preserved, and all heresies are relatively hard to document—often only (very unsatisfactorily) from the statements of opponents.

This same bias can affect the printed book. From Luther's revolt onwards, control of the press, censorship and licensing, and book-burning gradually came to be commonplace all over Europe, and if England burned relatively few books, official censorship established itself there sooner and more efficiently than in most other countries. Certainly, the censorship was never totally efficient, and heterodox publications—heterodox in religion or politics—continued to appear, but it need not be doubted that matters of this kind survive in disproportionately small quantity. Any attempt to assess the state of opinion or general tenets by weight and numbers alone, or to take these elements in the equation into account at all, misleads. It is necessary, but also extremely difficult, to make some allowance for the fortunes of books, whether accidental or purposeful. *Habent sua fata libelli*— and the commonest of them is to be misinterpreted, misunderstood and misplaced by the unimaginative scholar.

The other bias, starting, so to speak, from the opposite end, can lead to the same mistake. Books survive most probably for one of two reasons: because they are so important and so beautiful that they never cease to be read, or because they were published in so large an imprint that accidents cannot destroy them all. That is to say, the bias of survival works in favour of the great book and the very commonplace book, the genius and the journalist. A simple acceptance of either as in some way typical could again distort the result. In practice, scholars have been more prone to concentrate on the genius. Journalists—the running products of the contemporary scene—are, of course, more ephemeral; they are also, as a rule and after the event, less interesting to read. Nothing in writing palls so quickly as the journalism of a past age. One presumes that a compilation like Fabyan's *Chronicle* was read, since it was published and published for profit; today it is hard to see why anyone should have given good money for it. Even those Elizabethan writers, like Thomas Nashe or Richard Greene, whom the books always describe as 'journalists of genius' are nowadays more likely to bore than entertain, and whether they even inform is a matter of difficult historical assessment. The thought that medieval mystics like Richard Rolle or Julian of Norwich were once popular authors calls forth respectful admiration but certainly no urge to emulate. These things are always true, and the journalism of any age will readily supply parallels.

Thus the historian resorts to the great book which either by the force of its thought or the beauty of its language transcends the limits set by fashion and actuality. This is particularly true in the history of political ideas. There were no political writers of note in England between John of Salisbury in the twelfth century and Sir Thomas More in the sixteenth, and very little has in consequence been written on this theme. The alleged prominence of Sir John Fortescue in the fifteenth century is that of a mole-hill on a very flat plain; and the passion with which lesser men like Thomas Starkey and Christopher St German in the reign of Henry VIII have been analysed results less from their quite respectable production than from their rarity value.[1] However,

---

[1] F. L. Baumer, *The Early Tudor Theory of Kingship* (New Haven 1940); W. G. Zeeveld, *Foundations of Tudor Policy* (Cambridge, Mass. 1948); A. B. Ferguson, *The Articulate Citizen and the English Renaissance* (Durham, N.C. 1965).

in this area of intellectual history as in any other, the historian, remembering the bias of his sources, should try hard to establish a kind of norm before he attempts to assess individuals; and in order to discover his norm—in order to discover what was common coin and common property—he needs to read as widely as possible among the journalists. Even so, the built-in bias may defeat him, for the book so popular or useful as to have been printed in sufficient numbers to overcome its ephemeral contents may itself contain some originality or surprise. The truly commonplace is usually too obvious to say; especially in the days before mass production, every book was at least a little bit of a rarity.

To discover 'the mind of an age' is not an illegitimate enterprise. A given society or company of men and women is bound to harbour some agreed concepts concerning its world, some agreed notions of right and wrong, some prevalent beliefs and prejudices and repugnancies, whatever the range of variety may be at the edges—even at the edge of the individual mind. And a later age, or the product of a later society, can hope to understand that past mind only from the deposits left behind, that is to say, particularly from the books and writings that survive. In learning from them, however, the historian should be much more cautious, much more precise, much less schematic and pattern-making, and especially much more aware of his problems of evidence than (to judge from even impressive books in this genre) he usually is. One of the more influential modern historical works is J. Huizinga's *The Waning of the Middle Ages*, an attempt to understand the spiritual and intellectual malaise which, the author argued, affected the fifteenth century. In that familiar title (a fair translation of the Dutch original) neither the two nouns nor the implications involved in their juxtaposition are, very probably, justified, and an age is presented under a banner which could not conceivably have meant anything to itself. The concepts and the interpretations assumed as well as explicit were excavated from a very restricted range of sources, and they misrepresent very gravely at least a large part of the reality that was the fifteenth century. Huizinga's book is a work of art, but as history it needs as much criticism as the sources themselves.

Another familiar example of this sort of insufficiency—partiality rather than error being responsible for the trouble—is provided by the notion that 'order and degree' dominated all thinking in later-sixteenth-century England. This idea was first given impressive shape and an historical genealogy in A. O. Lovejoy's *The Great Chain of Being* (Cambridge, Mass., 1936) and then received wide currency in E. M. W. Tillyard's *The Elizabethan World Picture* (London 1943). Even commonsense suggests that commonplaces are repeated most insistently when they in fact encounter disagreement or hostility, and while no doubt there was much stress on order and all that in Elizabethan thinking, the trouble for many men lay in the increasing difficulty of maintaining that order. Other pervasive themes of thought can be traced, as for instance notions of rulers' responsibility to the ruled, which have nothing of the hierarchic degree about them; and though radical rebels may not have been numerous they were too many to be totally overlooked. The *Mirror of Magistrates* (1559), a popular collection of tales in prose and verse, is far from certain that superiors must always be obeyed in their God-given authority; and while nowadays Shakespeare's *Richard II* is usually treated as a portrayal of divine-right monarchy, Queen Elizabeth was aware of rebellious implications in the play which made it a dangerous thing to stage on the eve of Essex's rebellion.

Some of these difficulties can certainly be avoided by concentrating on the individual writer or idea, abandoning the attempt to see either writer or idea as part of a whole historical scene. This is legitimate in a limited sense—certainly legitimate at the level of doctoral dissertations—though the many exercises in intellectual history which make nonsense of the enterprise by treating their subject in the isolation usually reserved to the butterfly on its impaling pin should act as a warning. Yet even in this use of books, well done or not, the problems of the evidence arise and are too often ignored. Before the originality or personal contribution of any writer can be assessed, his debts to others—both to individuals and to the common stock of ideas—have to be established; and this is often so difficult as to undermine the whole argument. The practice of the time encouraged and applauded wholesale borrowing and verbatim transcription: to use what earlier writers had written showed commendable humility. However, there were no proper rules about acknowledging such borrowing, and among the hardest things to trace are the sources a man used and the influence on him of what he read. Edward Hall, the chronicler, was quite exceptional in giving a bibliography of 'the authors as well Latin as other out of which this work was first gathered and after compiled and conjoined'—an honest description of a method still sometimes employed by historians. References to authorities, usually given in marginal notes, are not uncommon in books of this period; though they are pretty haphazard and often confined to the writers thought specially impressive—that is, Scripture and the early Fathers—they offer some guidance to what the author had read. Sometimes, another man would be explicitly quoted in the text. However, all this leaves the main question of borrowing and influence largely unresolved. Together with the difficulty, already noted, of establishing what people *could* have read, this should enforce great caution on the historian trying to trace the movement of ideas or to ascribe originality to his author. With respect to this last, there is the further obstacle that what may at first seem original may turn out to be a commonplace of the day; the only cure for this problem is wide reading and a thorough acquaintance with general notions current at the time.

All these are, in fact, the difficulties of all intellectual history, or the history of ideas, a form of historical writing much more popular among beginners than the results justify. Its practitioners have too often treated books as the straightforward historical material which they are not. While books provide evidence for aspects of human activity which the rest of the source material discussed leaves dark, they yield the truth only to the enquirer who understands that, like all source material, they pose technical problems and need to be correctly criticised. One must discover the cause and the manner of their origin; must give proper weight to the author's purpose and knowledge; must cautiously analyse his relationship with his age and his past. The physical make-up, quantity, distribution and survival of books can all provide illuminating help to the comprehension of their contents; while, on the other hand, the limitations forced upon them by the fact that they are the product of a personal and an historical situation can also impede a full understanding and trap the unwary.

CHAPTER 8

Non-Documentary Sources

Historical evidence comprises all the past products of human activity which still survive. In the main this certainly means those written materials which common opinion tends to treat as all the evidence, but there are other relics which tell the historical story, though it should be said that they rarely take one very far except in conjunction with documents. Nevertheless, they add elements of their own to what the historian can tell.

In the first place, there is the land itself.[1] In historical times, the foundation, so to speak, has not changed noticeably; the geological and physical realities have remained unaltered. There has been a little loss from coastal erosion; occasionally, even a town has disappeared, like Dunwich in Suffolk. Some land has been added by draining water-covered areas, and much of that work was accomplished in the period of our survey. The marshes known as the Somerset levels were recovered in the middle ages, mainly by the labours of Glastonbury Abbey; the marshes of the Thames estuary around Plumstead and Woolwich were drained under Henry VIII; and the biggest job of all, the draining of the Lincolnshire and Cambridgeshire fens, was under way before 1640. But, such relatively small modifications apart, the outline and the underground construction of the land have not changed, and a good knowledge of these facts is necessary for an understanding especially of agrarian history. Until quite recently, historians have been too readily satisfied with a totally unreal division of the country into a highland and a lowland zone; there have been conventional terms like 'the north' which threw together the desolate fells of Cumberland and the sophisticated agriculture of

[1] For the good introductory survey see W. G. Hoskins, *The Making of the English Landscape* (London 1957), a general volume intended to go together with a counties series of which few parts have so far appeared.

the Vale of York; analyses of crop-growing or manorial structure took hardly any account of the soil or climatic conditions which determined what could be and what was done. Even those who realised that England packs into a small compass a quite exceptional variety of genuinely different regions, too often failed to make room for this fact in their study of economic or social history. Here R. H. Tawney's famous advice to historians, to exchange their books for their boots, has done nothing but good. A modern history of agricultural change can begin by listing forty-one separate 'farming countries' of England, some of them only a few square miles large but all sufficiently distinct, for reasons of geology and geography, to set different conditions for human use.[1]

However, while these basic terms may have remained the same through history, the surface appearance of the land is another matter. Few areas of the globe have been so thoroughly remodelled by man; few are left with so little wild—that is, untouched—land. The appearance even of the barren uplands of Wales or Lancashire, of the seemingly wild moors of the south-west or north-east, owes everything to human activity—to forest clearance, peat-cutting and sheep-farming, for instance. A good deal of this goes back a very long way, into prehistoric times, but the process never ceased; and at all times the evidence presented by the landscape has been obliterated by further work on it. It may indeed be true that the area of cultivated and occupied land has barely been enlarged since the eleventh century (in a time in which the population has grown twenty-five-fold),[2] but within that area the changes have been enormous. A very well-known example is the replacement of the open fields, farmed in common or—as in other parts of the world they still are—owned and farmed in severalty, by fields enclosed with hedges, stone walls, or more recently wire fences. It is no wonder that this transformation has been credited with far too much importance in the history of agriculture and landowning, for simply as a matter of outward appearance it made the biggest conceivable difference. Though

[1] E. Kerridge, *The Agricultural Revolution* (London 1967), ch. 2.
[2] R. V. Lennard, *Rural England 1086–1135* (Oxford 1959), 3.

enclosing had gone some way by the middle of the seventeenth century, the real remodelling of the landscape took place after about 1720; modern England looks totally different from that which passed through our 450 years, and the historian can only rarely rely on the present aspect of the landscape as evidence of past conditions.

The land, as has been said before, is a palimpsest, a progressive record of activity, in which new effects overlie earlier states at every point. As a rule those new effects tend to destroy those earlier states, and this is particularly true of habitations, of houses in towns and villages where every rebuilding is likely to remove the earlier evidence altogether. Once inhabited sites have been abandoned, for one reason or another, all traces on the ground are at first sight lost; only large buildings like castles or monasteries will leave even ruins behind. Even where the village or town still stands, rebuilding has continuously and greatly altered it; in our period, it should be noted, English towns and isolated houses, too, underwent very widespread and total reconstruction in the century from about 1540 onwards, so that very little trace of medieval building survives.[1] 'Palimpsest' is therefore not exactly the best metaphor, for in a palimpsest the later accretion only lies over the earlier record; it does not destroy it. In the main—and in view of the weight nowadays given to the techniques of recovery to be mentioned in a moment—centuries of human labour on the land, on fields and meadows and buildings, have destroyed the bulk of the potential evidence. What remains is rare, scattered and haphazard, and there are risks, not always realised, in generalising from the occasional survival to the totality of past fact.

Nevertheless, there remain traces of the past to be discovered among the changes, and the methods to be employed are of three kinds: inspection on the ground, aerial photography, and archaeology. All three depend for their proper effect on being used in conjunction with documentary evidence, with maps, surveys and descriptions, but in turn they greatly contribute to

[1] Hoskins, *Landscape*, 124.

the knowledge that may be derived from these documents. Despite what has been said, a walk over the ground can still recover much of the past reality. Roads, in particular, are extraordinarily enduring things; even where they have been abandoned, they often leave unmistakable traces in grass lanes or lines of trees. All over the country, one may track old roads either because they are still in use or because at a point where the metalled surface turns one way, the remnants of its now unused predecessor are visible in another direction. The city of London was burned in 1666 and bombed in 1940–1; yet its street plan differs very little today from that shown on Tudor maps. But fields also often present evidence, especially where such unvarying conditions as the run of a river or the lie of a hill determine the shape of the arable. Inspecting the territory is something that the historian of economic developments and cultural change can always profit from.

Above all, buildings survive in many places, especially if they are large and important. Cathedrals, churches, castles, monastic buildings, great houses, and the many town and country houses that have never quite disappeared provide evidence to the historian.[1] They do so, however, subject to certain weighty

[1] There are many studies of cathedrals and great houses, ranging from coffee table books to architectural histories. For churches see the highly antiquarian but tolerable introduction by M. D. Anderson, *Looking for History in British Churches* (London 1951). For castles see S. Toy, *The Castles of Great Britain* (London 1953) and B. H. St J. O'Neil, *Castles and Canon: a study of early artillery fortifications in England* (Oxford 1960). A good treatment of rural buildings, especially houses great and small, for part of the period is found in *The Agrarian History of England and Wales*, vol. 4, ed. J. Thirsk (Cambridge 1967), chs 10 and 11. I know of no absolutely comprehensive treatment of towns and town houses, though every place has its own guide books and descriptions. The massive volumes published by the Royal Commission on Historical Monuments will, when complete, provide a full survey. So far the Commission have published (1910–62): Hertfordshire, Buckinghamshire, Essex, London, Huntingdonshire, Herefordshire, Westmorland, Middlesex, City of Oxford, Dorset, City of Cambridge, City of York (Romans remains only). For the present more complete, and altogether immensely useful is a series of handbooks, *The Buildings of England*, ed. N. Pevsner, published by Penguin Books.

limitations. It would not be unfair to say that the evidence is the more certain the less complete the survival is. Ruins do represent the traces, in varying degrees of perfection, of the past fact, whereas buildings still in use embody as a rule a good deal of rebuilding and additions, or for that matter subtractions. Thus the monastic relics are 'real' in a sense in which cathedrals not always are, so much so that one historian could assert, somewhat flippantly, that only the Dissolution of the Monasteries preserved them from the drastic rebuilding and destruction which changed so many continental monasteries from gothic into baroque structures.[1] Where substantial parts remain, as in the Yorkshire abbey of Fountains or the Gloucestershire house at Tintern, the joke has some substance, but the remains of Glastonbury Abbey of St Augustine's Priory at Canterbury leave everything to the imagination. Cathedrals, on the whole, stopped being tampered with before the end of our period, though some nineteenth-century restoration (as in the piers of Durham Cathedral) can be responsible for what the casual observer may think ancient, and anciently intended, effects. Even castles have their histories. The great fortresses built by Edward I to control Wales are nowadays partly ruins and partly in use as offices, but in general they preserved the original appearance. Elsewhere any castle that still looks whole is certain to have been continuously repaired and rebuilt; the past reality is in a way better represented by the grass-grown walls at Kenilworth than by the well-preserved habitation at Arundel. Even the coastal forts built by Henry VIII, one of the major achievements of sixteenth-century fortification anywhere (modern, efficient, a real breakthrough into the first age of artillery), have been remodelled over the centuries. Thus St Mawes near Falmouth still looks essentially as it did when first built, but the Kentish forts at Deal and Sandwich, reconstructed in the eighteenth and nineteenth centuries, do not. They continued to be part of the coastal defences of England, whereas the Cornish forts ceased to be so used.

[1] G. Baskerville, *English Monks and the Suppression of the Monasteries* (London 1937), 277f.

Houses, whether great or small, are particularly subject to the consequences of human needs and tastes, and the great building programmes of three periods in particular (1540–1640, 1700–50, since 1850) have removed the evidence for the habitations of the lower orders and gravely affected even those of the aristocracy. There are few great houses in existence with substantial pre-Tudor parts. The splendid Derbyshire mansion of Haddon Hall is exceptional in being largely of fifteenth-century construction (or restored in style); the Manners family, having other houses, used it little before the Gothic revival of the late-eighteenth century, so that it was never remodelled and 'modernised' as other great houses have been. At Hampton Court, a Tudor core is surrounded by later additions, some of them replacing the original structure. At Audley End in Essex, the vastest Tudor pile of them all was in the late-seventeenth century reduced to one-third its size by a sensible owner. Even those well-known Elizabethan manor houses which now survive here and there as substantial farmhouses are naturally very rarely in their original state, and town houses have suffered everywhere from pulling down and reconstruction. Of course, every old building contains visible traces of the past; thus, for instance, the guildhall at Guildford, behind its eighteenth-century façade, is an almost unaltered fourteenth-century building. But in many cases, where an old building has been done up throughout on the basis of older work, it can take real learning, not superficial inspection, to restore the original in the mind.

In this task of reconstruction both of landscape and buildings, the historian is assisted by written evidence of two kinds. He has the contemporary evidence of maps, extents and surveys already mentioned, from which—applying his documents to his inspection of the ground—he can often recover the old lay-out of fields, the run of roads, the disposition of houses and other structures. And he may be helped by descriptions made before the changes occurred. In this connection it is important to note that just before the great transformations interest quickened in the topographical record. The sixteenth century provided a good deal of writing of this kind. At the head one must place the account kept by John Leland as he travelled the country in the 1530's, in his effort to save the memory of things about to disappear.[1] As the art developed, histories and descriptions of counties became commonplace and often very good; at their best, combining topography with history and economic analysis and literature, they culminate in the works of Richard Carew and William Lambarde.[2] However, from the point of view of historical evidence these works are most useful when most professional and least literary, and here pride of place belongs to an eminent Elizabethan surveyor, John Norden, who planned a series of volumes to cover all England, an over-ambitious undertaking for one man, as it turned out. Still, he succeeded in dealing with at least six counties—at least because other anonymous surveys might possibly come from his pen.[3] Norden's method was systematic, useful, but often tedious: he went from place to place, noting details and distances, and he supplied good maps. A typical entry in his Norfolk survey reads:

Brampton Church: *Rectoria valet* £4. *Decima* [the clerical tax called the tenth] *10s. Patronus Mr. Jacobus Brampton*; *habet mansum cum 16 acris terrae.*

In the chancel on a stone the portraiture of one in complete armour between two wives, the epitaph subscribed:

Of your charitie praye for the Soules of John Brampton esquier & Thomasine & Anne his wives the which John departed the 4th day of our Lord God 1575 on whose soules Jesu haue mercy [followed by a heraldic description of the coat of arms].[4]

[1] *The Itinerary of John Leland in or about the Years 1535–1543*, ed. L. Toulmin Smith (6 vols; London 1906–10).

[2] R. Carew, *The Survey of Cornwall*, ed. F. E. Halliday (London 1953); W. Lambarde, *A Perambulation of Kent* (2nd and best ed: 1596).

[3] John Norden, *Speculum Britanniae*. He published his descriptions of Middlesex and Hertfordshire (London 1563); those of Cornwall, Essex and Northamptonshire were published later from his MSS (1728, 1840, 1720). An anonymous *Chorography of Norfolk*, ed. C. M. Hood (Norwich 1938) is convincingly ascribed to him.

[4] *Chorography of Norfolk*, 88.

This sort of thing preserves detail which is either gone altogether or so nearly obliterated as to make reconstruction impossible without Norden's assistance. He is more readable but less useful in more lyrical passages, as when he describes the husbandman, standing at Harrow-on-the-Hill and seeing the fields around ready for the harvest, who 'cannot but clap his hands for joy, to see this vale so to laugh and sing'. Still, it's worth being reminded of what at one time one could see from the top of that hill.

Written materials give shape and help to what may be learned from the surviving facts of land and buildings; they are more essential still in assisting the historian to recover additional facts which no longer lie on the surface. For apart from what can at once be seen, the past labours of man on his surroundings have left traces which special techniques can still reveal. Since the second world war, aerial photography, in the hands of a few enthusiasts, has added a surprising amount of knowledge. Photographs from the air can be taken either from directly overhead or at an oblique angle. The first method reveals the ground plans of buildings, ruins or field systems better than maps or surveyors' reports can do; the second, by giving relief to otherwise unremarkable features, can bring out unsuspected detail quite invisible on the ground.[1] This technique can, for instance, give the best possible conspectus of existing cities and show the past structure surviving inside the later growth.[2] It can precisely outline the plans of a monastic ruin of which hardly anything appears above ground.[3] Above all, it can rediscover the lost fact. Soil once disturbed never behaves in quite the same fashion again, and if a built-up area is restored to farmland traces of the foundation trenches once dug will remain for ever, to reappear as markings on pasture in a dry season or as lines in growing crops if the land is used as arable. These markings, which can be seen only from the air, often

[1] M. D. Knowles, 'Air Photography and History', in *The Uses of Air Photography*, ed. J. K. S. St Joseph (London 1966), 127ff.

[2] See e.g. the revealing illustration in W. G. Hoskins, *Old Exeter* (London 1952).

[3] M. D. Knowles and J. K. S. St Joseph, *Monastic Sites from the Air* (Cambridge 1952).

compose the unmistakable ground plan of houses or greater establishments. Thus the site of the monastery at Sempringham, foundation house of the Gilbertine Order, was completely lost to memory till it was rediscovered on some rough ground. Trenches dug in the war revealed the spot, and when, after the war, the land was sown with crops the outlines of the monastic buildings showed up clearly from the air, despite the earlier ploughing.[1] Similarly, the outlines of open fields, now broken by hedges or roads, can often be restored from the air, sometimes because a characteristic 'ridge-and-furrow' pattern, usually ascribed to medieval husbandry, is seen to run across later divisions in uninterrupted continuity to the extent of the ancient fields. An attempt has been made to provide an aerial description of the whole of medieval England (this being defined as the England which passed away in the changes of the late eighteenth century); the books shows fields, villages (fabric, multiplication, disappearance), towns, planned towns, industrial and extractive features (stone quarries, iron pits, lead mining, etc.), and such miscellaneous features as roads and bridges, all analysed historically, that is to say, through the changes affecting them.[2]

To photography from above may be added the help of digging below. Post-classical archaeology[3] is still a young science, but its principles and practices are being worked out. The rediscovery and restoration of Nonsuch Palace, an Elizabethan monstrosity now totally demolished, is probably its best-known achievement so far,[4] but it has done much revealing work in both towns and countryside. The war, once again, helped by here and there overcoming the main difficulty encountered—the fact that most of the sites worth exploring are covered by modern buildings still in use. A good deal of medieval London was investigated before the post-war rebuilding again covered up the newly revealed

[1] Knowles, in *The Uses of Air Photography*, 132.

[2] M. W. Beresford and J. K. S. St Joseph, *Medieval England: an Aerial Survey* (Cambridge 1958).

[3] The subject is to be fully covered in another volume in this series.

[4] John Dent, *The Quest for Nonsuch* (London 1962).

traces.[1] Lost villages lie more commonly under field and pasture, and here some digging has been done. Combining the three techniques of walking the ground, photographing from the air, and digging beneath the fields, with a study of the documents, Professor Beresford has attempted to plot and describe the areas of habitation once in existence and since abandoned for a variety of causes—plague, exhaustion of the soil, enclosure of fields and destruction of houses, emparking and movement to larger centres of population.[2] Though most of England's villages and towns are very old and have proved very enduring, there has also always been wastage, from the villages destroyed by the Cistercians when in the twelfth century, they formed their great sheep-runs on the Yorkshire moors, to the effects of industrialisation in the eighteenth and nineteenth centuries. The recovery of these sites, with many details, has been a real addition to historical knowledge, made possible by the new techniques of aerial photography and archaeology.

However, this sanguine picture needs a lot of modification. New techniques are not everything, and the first flush of enthusiasm can be as misleading as it can prove helpful. Both aerial photography and archaeology suffer from a defect serious in the study of history: they lack the dimension of time and their findings are consequently often very hard to date. This does not matter so much when what is investigated is the site of a single monastery, vouched for by the record and plainly outlined on the ground. Even then, it may be impossible to know the stages by which the place was built or the time at which this or that part of it was abandoned, before the final suppression in the 1530's. The picture usually presented by these recent studies tends to show the range of buildings in a single totality which as such never existed. The lines of streets or roads may or may not be of

[1] W. Thomson Hill, *Buried London* (London 1955) describes some of the discoveries made in bombed areas of London, though he concentrates on Roman remains.

[2] M. W. Beresford, *The Lost Villages of England* (London 1954). Many of the places in question were small hamlets of a few houses only.

similar dates: the photograph cannot tell. The foundations of ancient buildings, long demolished, may be found in the city of London; the foundations do not make it easy or even possible to say to what century they belong. Add to this the fact that most medieval building was not in stone but in much more perishable material, and it becomes plain that the uses of archaeology, too, must be limited. It is, for instance, often possible to discover post-holes outlining a wooden structure, but quite impossible to say whether the holes were dug in the middle ages or in prehistoric times. Great caution—greater caution than one usually encounters —is required in the interpretation of these data, and despite all the exciting additions to knowledge made by the spade and the camera the historian needs to stick closely to the familiar datable and organisable material—to his documents—if he is not to be led astray.

He also needs to understand very precisely how the features revealed came into being. The outstanding example of possible error is provided by the problem of 'ridge-and-furrow', already referred to. Over large parts of the Midlands, but elsewhere too, the land now appears to lie in raised ridges, running parallel, with regular dips in between, a rolling effect readily recognised by the eye on the ground and even more apparent to the leg muscles. At one time it was vaguely supposed that this represented a system of drainage, ancient or more recent but probably very ancient. Then aerial photography showed the ridges running across post-medieval features; it showed that groups of them lay side by side with other groups of parallel ridges running at different angles; and reference to old maps demonstrated that in some cases the pattern so revealed could be identified with the old pattern of open fields divided into individual strips, the ridges in many instances appearing to be of the width of the strips drawn on the maps. It was consequently concluded that the pre-enclosure field system lay here preserved. The ridges, it was thought, represented the furlongs or ploughlands of medieval husbandry, and a full plotting of these features would enable the historian to plot the whole of the medieval arable and even to calculate the number of peasant families.[1] At that stage it was supposed that the furrows had nothing to do with drainage but rather resulted from a system of strip ploughing which threw the earth inward onto the strip, gradually building up the ridge—a mere by-product of a regular activity which in the outcome outlined the unit of land as clearly as though it had been fenced.

The larger dreams of discovery were from the first rendered less probable by the well attested fact that many parts of England never possessed open fields and gave no sign of ridge-and-furrow. Worse still, the simple conclusion, with its exciting possibilities for historical statistics and agrarian history, suffered from its author's ignorance of husbandry practices. A devastating analysis of the real, and very diverse, situation came to the conclusion (tongue in cheek) that 'all that the evidence of ridge and furrow proves by itself is that the land was at one time thrown into ridge and furrow'.[2] The critique showed that the continuous ploughing presupposed by the earlier theory would have created mountain ranges some eighty feet high across the fields, and it described the various forms of ploughing demanded by and practised on different types of land: the raising and 'slitting' (ploughing down) of ridges, cross ploughing, ploughing for drainage and exposure to maximum sunlight. Contours and soil conditions had as much to do with the existence and direction of the ridges as conditions of tenure or the open field. The land has had to be ploughed this way and that so often and for such a length of time that the patterns discovered by the photograph are rarely to be thought of as very old: 'most ridge and furrow . . . in the English countryside today is the result of fairly recent ploughing, not so much medieval as nineteenth century, and mostly in enclosures'.

This promising controversy turned out to be stillborn, and it is not clear where we stand today. As recently as 1966, Professor

[1] M. W. Beresford, 'Ridge and Furrow and the Open Fields', *Economic History Review*, 2nd Series, i (1948), 334ff.

[2] E. Kerridge, 'Ridge and Furrow and Agrarian History', *ibid.*, iv (1951–2), 14ff.

Knowles could simply reassert that most of the ridge-and-furrow pattern is certainly 'the unintentional outcome of medieval husbandry',[1] but in fact no one seems to have controverted Dr Kerridge's arguments. The coincidence of some of that pattern with old field plans suggests that even if the ridge-and-furrow is recent the old fields may still be outlined by it, but this is not a very useful piece of knowledge because the maps themselves had provided it, too. And, as Dr Kerridge says, enclosures also are not permanent; some of the field patterns clearly describe not open fields but earlier enclosures since rearranged. In short, it would seem that, for the present at least, the exciting possibilities of ridge-and-furrow as a tool of historical analysis must be reduced to order: every instance must be treated on its merits, and nothing general or generalised can be inferred. The chances, on the whole, are that air photography has shown up the recent and not the ancient shaping of the countryside, not an entirely surprising conclusion.

Similar problems attend the discovery of lost villages. That many such lost places can be and have been identified is unquestionably true. But who are we to tell when they vanished? Archaeology offers little help because the dating techniques of the archaeologist, which depend on artefacts and cannot ever be very refined (except when datable coin hoards are unearthed, and even then they are hard to interpret because hoards are collected over a period of time) do not apply at all in this instance where the spade discovers very few things to which dates might be assigned. Professor Beresford confidently ascribed the disappearance of most of his lost villages to the era of the early enclosures, between about 1450 and 1520, but this has raised widespread doubt. Many more than he allows very likely succumbed to the Black Death of the fourteenth century, a traditional explanation which he was at pains to play down; others again lasted longer than he supposed and only went under when eighteenth-century noblemen built their great parks. The approximately sixty deserted villages by now discovered in Leicestershire do seem to fall into the Beresford

[1] In *Uses of Air Photography*.

pattern,[1] but Leicestershire was the county most fully affected by fifteenth-century enclosures and almost certainly not typical of the country at large. The fact that there is controversy certainly does not necessarily prove one or the other party wrong, but it demonstrates that the question very much remains to be pursued further. Dr Hoskins called for a more precise chronology of medieval pottery to give archaeology some safer means of dating its finds,[2] but in view of the facts that medieval pottery was simple and relatively primitive, and did not, it seems, change much in the passage of time, this may prove a hopeless quest. What remains are the documents, available in such quantity, a piece of equipment unknown to the traditionally successful areas of archaeological exploration—prehistoric and classical times.

Thus it follows that for the historian of our centuries aerial photography and archaeology offer valuable assistance, but no more. So far their gifts have resembled those of the Greeks, and a good deal more criticism is needed before their precise import may be judged. With all their deficiencies, and attractive though the exhortation to exchange books for boots may be, the documents remain paramount. To be accurate, books as such offer little enough help, but the joys of tramping fields and roads, or of flying over the countryside, are more likely to benefit the searcher's health than his knowledge. The signposts point firmly to neither libraries nor the out of doors, but to the dust of muniment rooms.

The fields they plough and the houses they build are not, however, the only relics of their possessions that men leave to posterity. Something may be learned from the things they made and used. Agrarian tools, household furniture and implements, the tools of trade, the equipment of the table, tapestries and hangings, all these contribute to historical knowledge. Often the knowledge seems a little unexciting to the more intellectual mind, though the popularity of books on 'everyday things' shows that

[1] W. G. Hoskins, 'The Deserted Villages of Leicestershire', *Essays in Leicestershire History* (Liverpool 1950), 67ff.
[2] *Ibid.*, 107.

there is an interest available for them. These matters as a rule satisfy the antiquarian instinct in man—the desire to see and handle objects seen and handled by remote ancestors. They provide a physical manifestation of the past and therefore a positive proof of history—and one more readily comprehended than illegible manuscripts—of the kind that the more concrete mind requires. And there is certainly some romantic—justifiably romantic— satisfaction in a relish for such things. Museums, especially local museums, are full of them; the great houses, whether used as museums or not, provide quantities. Nor is the appeal exclusively to a sense of romance. Social history of a more powerful kind benefits from a study of surviving tools and equipment. If one is to understand how people lived and what they could do, the instruments, necessities and comforts at their disposal have to be known, and they can be fully known only by inspection. Medieval agriculture may be studied from the documents which describe its organisation or show its profit, but if one is to judge it properly one needs to see also its ploughs, harrows and sickles. The historian of medieval cathedrals or sixteenth-century mansions should have a clear understanding of the saws and sawpits, carpenters' tools, stone-shaping tools, and scaffolds employed; and while pits get filled in and scaffolds taken down, the rest may often still be seen under glass. Until one has actually studied a distaff and a spinning-wheel, the difference which the second made to the production of yarn may remain very unreal. And so forth. 'How our ancestors lived' is not only an amusing enquiry, to be satisfied by gaping round ducal bedrooms and wandering through the reconstructed street in York's municipal museum, but a serious matter to any historian who wishes to elucidate his social, economic, political and constitutional problems within a comprehension of living conditions and active potential provided by his knowledge of artefacts. How far can one really get in, for instance, assessing foreign policy without a full understanding of the means of communication available and the time it took to get despatches from A to B?[1]

[1] E.g. J. Crofts, *Packhorse, Waggon and Post* (London 1967).

The information, once again, is not, however, as good as might be wished. Two facts distort survival. In the first place, the exceptional is more likely to be preserved than the commonplace, the precious than the worthless. We do possess ordinary tools, cheap eating irons and knives, pewter utensils, plain benches, and such like, but we have much more of fine hangings, gold and silver plate, superior furniture, and especially the clothes of the rich rather than the poor. Much of what the bulk of people used has gone and has to be imagined. And secondly, the later has too often demolished the earlier. Thus there is hardly any furniture now in existence that dates from before the reign of Elizabeth. Plate was always being melted down, to be spent or remade, and jewellery broken up; again, what survives dates at the earliest from the sixteenth century (and there is not all that much of that). Clothes wear out, and fire takes care of household goods. These are obvious points. Even as, with the exception of cathedrals, churches and castles, few pre-Tudor buildings survive, so their appointments have mostly gone. This does not matter too much, for occasional survivals will do to illustrate their kind, drawings and pictures fill in some of the gaps, and the more simple, while being more likely lost, is also more readily imagined. Trouble arises, as so often, if people forget chronology and apply analogy. The changes of the last 150 years have been so enormous that there is a danger of lumping together everything that came before about 1800 and to suppose that pre-industrial farm tools and primitive machinery did not change over the centuries. Alternatively, the historian can easily go wrong if he looks at some relatively pre-industrial society and imagines medieval England to have been like Rumania in the 1930's or (worse) West Africa today. The fact that reaping by scythe was, it seems, virtually unknown in England before the sixteenth century might act as a warning; but one can still encounter the sort of attitude which supposes that the 'primitive' manufacture of wheels and waggons described by George Sturt as the practice of late-nineteenth-century Surrey[1] goes back to the dim past, whereas it is in fact most

[1] G. Sturt, *The Wheelwright's Shop* (Cambridge 1923).

improbable that any such wheels or waggons were ever made in our period at all.

Of all the things that men make and use, money is possibly the most revealing and, since in the years under review money meant coins, also the most enduring. The coins of England have been quite thoroughly studied, which is not to say that disputes do not still occur, and numismatics is a special branch of learning.[1] It is, however, a branch of real importance to the working historian.[2] In the first place, since coins represented the means by which men articulated their economic activities, economic history cannot afford to ignore them. Their quantity, variety and quality tell much about wealth and the ups and downs of the nation's economy. There are important inferences to be made from such facts as that England, like most of Europe, had only one coin—the silver penny—till the middle of the thirteenth century, that no gold coins were struck until the middle of the fifteenth, or that from the later fifteenth century onwards many varieties of European coins were current among English merchants. It is obviously significant that throughout the middle ages the fineness of English coins (the proportion of silver in the alloy) remained stable, until in the first half of the sixteenth century debasement by stages reduced it to a deplorable state.[3] The historian of trade, prices, and government finance needs to know about coins, but he should be aware that they present technical problems, even of terminology, which have to be understood. It is easy to make mistakes. Many coins bore very similar names—there were

[1] For the best descriptive list see G. C. Brooks, *English Coins from the Seventh Century to the Present Day* (3rd ed; London 1952); and for general guidance to the subject, P. Grierson, *Bibliographie Numismatique* (Brussels 1967: an enlarged version of a pamphlet published in 1952 under the title *Coins and Medals: a select bibliography*).

[2] P. Grierson, *Numismatics and History* (Historical Association Pamphlet; London 1951).

[3] See A. Feavearyear, *The Pound Sterling* (2nd ed; Oxford 1963). The Tudor debasement remains a much discussed problem; for a recent contribution see C. E. Challis, 'The Debasement of the Coinage 1542–1551', *Econ. Hist. Rev.* 2nd Ser. xx (1967), 441ff.

several crowns, ducats, escudos and so on minted in various places and current at the same time—or, alternatively, several names occur which represent only one actual coin, as with the angels and nobles that confuse the issue between about 1470 and 1510. The problems of weight and fineness have to be understood; coins should be seen, not only read about. In addition, coins by themselves are poor historical material; they must be used in conjunction with the documentary evidence of mint records, merchants' papers, public proclamations, and other materials bearing on their production and use. However, the technical problems need to be resolved, not ignored, and coins do offer a most useful additional instrument of analysis to the economic historian.

Other forms of history, too, can benefit from them, though more marginally. There is comment on the government and administration of the thirteenth century in the fact that the coins of Henry II did duty for over a century after their issue, as in the fact that that 'imperial' king, Edward I, decided at last to strike his own. The designs of coins illustrate policy and purpose, especially from the fifteenth century onwards when new designs, influenced by the Italian Renaissance's rediscovery of ancient practices, began to make their appearance in England. Coins are among the most generally distributed objects on which designs can be impressed; in a semi-literate society they are among the best instruments of government propaganda, and they were so used. Henry VII's sovereign, a splendid coin, showing the King wearing a closed or imperial crown, points to a deliberate glorification of the monarchy of which there is little evidence in the record.[1] The coins of Henry VI show very clearly how dynastic claims and national concerns could be exhibited to the people in a painless form: the King's position as sovereign of both England and France, and the political consequences which flowed from that claim, are graphically illustrated in the design.[2] All coins deserve careful scrutiny for

[1] P. Grierson, 'The Origins of the English Sovereign and the Symbolism of the Closed Crown', *British Numismatic Journal*, xxxiii (1964), 118ff.

[2] J. W. McKenna, 'Henry VI of England and the Dual Monarchy: aspects of royal political propaganda 1422–1432', *Journal of the Warburg Institute*, xxviii (1965), 145ff.

the symbolism they carry; there is nothing accidental about the dies from which they were struck, and the historian would do well to distinguish the original and purposeful design from the conventional. Monarchs on horseback, reverse designs of trading ships or coats of arms, all carry their message; political thought as well as public need went to the making of coins.

Coins are also, of course, works of art and can be used in the study of the history of art. They do not carry genuine portraits before the reign of Henry VII, one of whose coins reproduces a very remarkable portrait of the King, much the best likeness that we have of him. Though his successors employed less successful engravers, the tradition of actual portraiture so started has never ceased; the change from a conventionalised 'kingship' to individual personality itself indicates an interesting fact of history. But coins are, naturally, only a small part of the evidence produced by art. Even for royal portraits they are rarely the best. An unexpected source was discovered in the plea rolls of the Court of King's Bench where the initial letter of the covering membrane encloses, in Tudor times, a lifelike drawing of the monarch. These pictures provide a continuous and datable series, a most valuable tool for the chronology of drawing and an illuminating commentary on the history of sixteenth-century art.[1]

The main sources of art history, however, are more conventional and better known. They are the surviving products of the artists' work, among which buildings must, in our period, take pride of place.[2] Medieval art in England is mainly architecture and sculpture.[3] The great cathedrals are the supreme monument of that art, and in the first place they are the triumph of architect and builder. Much of their sculpture has, in fact, disappeared because Protestantism quarrelled with the saints' statues that filled

[1] Enna Auerbach, *Tudor Artists* (London 1954).

[2] There is a good and well illustrated introductory survey in Doreen Yarwood, *The Architecture of England from Prehistoric Times to the Present Day* (London 1963).

[3] Joan Evans, *English Art 1307–1461* (Oxford 1949); L. Stone, *Sculpture in Britain: the Middle Ages* (Harmondsworth 1955); G. Webb, *Architecture in Britain: the Middle Ages* (2nd ed; Harmondsworth 1965).

so many now empty niches; but some remain, as do secular statues like the royal monuments in Westminster Abbey. There remain tombs and gargoyles (sometimes actual portraits, especially of the craftsmen employed on the job), and there remain the carvings on choir stalls and misericords. The last—the carved undersides of tip-up seats—are particularly fascinating because they range well outside the pious purposes of the building. With their animal scenes, homely caricatures of housewives, and occasional obscenities they offer a precious comment on common ways of life and thought in the middle ages for which, naturally, very little evidence survives even in the literature of the period.

Medieval painting in England is of two kinds. Illuminations in manuscripts are the best preserved example of it and the most important, demonstrating a tradition of miniature painting that culminated in the great Elizabethan and Jacobean miniaturists (especially Nicholas Hillyard and Isaac Oliver) and amounted to a native tradition of line-drawing readily distinguished from continental miniature painting.[1] Illustrations in manuscripts are evidence for more than the history of art. They show clothes, equipment, buildings and other common articles of life. Borders of realistically drawn plants and animals can be of interest to the historian of agriculture and of science, and the former will be even more interested in the depiction of farming activities. Every book on medieval rural life is liable to reproduce the scenes of sowing, reaping and threshing which decorate the Luttrell Psalter. These illuminations were intended to adorn the book but also to provide the additional information which book illustration still offers, and they can therefore still be used for their original purpose of giving a graphic understanding of the details mentioned in the text. Outside books, painting has not survived very well, except in the stained glass of which the best kind, that produced in the decades round the year 1500, was in fact nearly always the work of foreigners, especially Flemings. Wall paintings in churches and old houses are mostly found in a fragmentary state; what can

[1] O. E. Saunders, *English Illumination* (2 vols; Florence and Paris 1928); M. Rickert, *Painting in Britain: the Middle Ages* (2nd ed; Harmondsworth 1965).

be discovered is not very impressive.[1] A recent addition to the materials of art history and, even more, social history, are medieval 'graffiti', casual and usually rough scrawls or incisions on walls which do tell something of common notions, preoccupations and even (up to a point) of literacy. They present problems of accurate reading, interpretation and dating which have not yet all been solved.[2]

As the fifteenth century passed into the sixteenth, the materials produced by art changed significantly. Churches and cathedrals were still building—the finest monument of late-gothic art in England, King's College Chapel at Cambridge, was not completed until 1515—but as the chief concern of architects they were making way for private houses and mansions, itself a social fact of prime importance; and among the visual arts, sculpture was being replaced by painting.[3] The sixteenth and early-seventeenth centuries were a great age of portraiture, and even though the outstanding artists came from abroad—Holbein, Van Dyke—their products illumine both the art history and the social history of England. The native tradition continued to derive from illumination and specialised in miniatures, but both painting and miniatures specialised in faces. The assertion of the individual—of the individual stressing his place in society and wanting to communicate the facts of his appearance to others—spread from royalty to quite inferior degrees in the body politic. Men and women had their portraits painted and copied for sending to friends and business connections; from the courtiers of Henry VIII onwards, Englishmen and women suddenly become physically real in ever increasing numbers. The fact must be read in conjunction with the sudden appearance, in bulk, of private letters and other personal material. The people of the middle ages were, of course, also individuals and usually quite well aware of

[1] E. W. Tristram, *English Wall Painting of the Fourteenth Century* (London 1955).

[2] V. Pritchard, *English Medieval Graffiti* (Cambridge 1967).

[3] J. Summerson, *Architecture in Britain 1530–1830* (4th ed; Harmondsworth 1963); E. Waterhouse, *Painting in Britain 1530–1790* (Harmondsworth 1953).

their separate identities. Only deficiencies of evidence have led to theories which see them as consciously concerned to sink into membership of corporate institutions. Yet that the outburst of portraiture and letter writing represents a much heightened self-awareness and a transformation in social values is also true. The materials of human art throw light not only on the history of art but also on spiritual concepts, habitual thought, and modes of life.

All the materials discussed in this chapter have two things in common. From the historian's point of view they are somewhat unconventional, relatively rarely used, yet capable of adding dimensions to his understanding which the conventional sources of history do not offer him. On the other hand, their use is very limited, and they yield even their information at all satisfactorily only if used in close conjunction with the documentary evidence. The historian should study the physical appearance of countryside and buildings, should handle coins, should investigate carvings and illustrations. But he must not fall victim to the pleasures of the physical and visible object, or to the propaganda of fashion and the excitement of a 'new' source. The written record dominates not only by its quantity but also by the fact that it alone answers the historian's proper questions accurately, fully and imaginatively. The good historian uses everything that has survived from the past, but he recognises that soil and stone and metal and pigment achieve meaning only under the dominant rule of parchment and paper.

CHAPTER 9

English History 1200–1640

A few years ago, an eminent historian of recent times committed himself to the view that 'what we know as the facts of medieval history have almost all been selected for us by generations of chroniclers who were professionally occupied in the theory and practice of religion'.[1] All that has here been said forms a somewhat sardonic commentary on this text. Even the chroniclers tell us far more about matters in which their professional interest as clergy played no part than the usual disparaging phrases about monkish historians would suppose. Unlike Mr Carr and those who share his relativist view of history, they were not burdened by an attitude which denied the possibility of historical knowledge; instead, as best they might, they presented all the details of their past and of their own time that they could gather. However, the modern historian is so far from being compelled to rely on them that his characteristic fault nowadays is to ignore them unduly; a preoccupation with 'records' has imposed the peace of neglect upon the narratives written in those 440 years. The records, as we have seen, are indeed extraordinarily voluminous, various and informative. Despite the many deficiencies and hidden dangers which have been noted, that must be one's first impression. A casual glance suggests that any question can profitably be asked and all kinds of history be written, even though here and there gaps in the material will leave an answerless blank. It is therefore worth consideration whether this is true, or whether the precise structure of the surviving evidence imposes severe restrictions upon the product. What sort of accounts can we write, what have we written and should we write, about this long and important stretch of English history?

In the first place, it has throughout been the contention of this

[1] E. H. Carr, *What is History?* (Harmondsworth 1964), 14.

book that the materials considered consist overwhelmingly of official records, that is to say, of deposits created by governmental action of one kind or another. The biggest part comes out of the archives of the national government, the King's administration, but the archives of the Church and of lesser authorities add sizeable quantities and are, in every sense, as official as the central records. This state of affairs is by no means universal: in the evidence, for instance, available to the historian of ancient Rome, of the earlier middle ages, or of recent centuries, the proportion of official records is for different reasons much lower. The period covered by this book does therefore have this unity that it is exceptionally dominated by official records. And even though the official records in question are various and flexible, even though they offer answers to many sorts of questions, this dominance has undoubted consequences for the kind of knowledge we can acquire.

Because of the state of the evidence, we are always bound to see these centuries from above, from the position of rulers and administrators. Only very occasionally can we take our stand with those who suffered rule or even rebelled against it, but even these exceptional points of vantage are often provided by official records and coloured accordingly. Not that this fact produces a monolithic outlook. Because English government was throughout this time bound by law, by legalism, and by physical problems of control, the sources do not put us in the position or acclimatise us to the minds of despots; the diffusion of authority through the nation, and the existence of representative institutions able to give voice to protest, diversify the 'from above' character of the official record and offer a constant reminder of the difficulties of government as against its opportunities. But this means only that we are able to see the system of rule in its right light, not that as historians we are freed from dependence upon the agents of rule. Up to a point the historian can create his own liberty by the use of his proper imagination; even when confined to the products of authoritative action, he can make the effort of understanding events and people from a position of subjection, of being governed. Indeed, most English historians, obeying the instinctive directives of their whig and liberal traditions, have commonly adopted attitudes at least mildly hostile to the ruling forces and have shown a pretty inadequate grasp of the problems involved in the exercise of power. Dominated by their sympathies rather than their records, they have inclined either to the story of increasing political liberty—the story of successful radicalism—or to a criticism of a social order allegedly hostile to the mass of the people, a criticism which has produced some strange sentimentalities about the middle ages and some rather one-sided accounts of early capitalism.

However, even in these reactions away from the official point of view, historians have had to submit to the control of the evidence produced by the system they disliked and attacked. Or rather, they have too often been able to free themselves from this control by simply ignoring the evidence. The difficulties created by the inescapable bias in the sources are no doubt best resolved by forgetting the first rule of sound study—namely, that all the available evidence must be read—but this is a freedom for which it is hard to feel much respect. A good example is offered by some studies of the condition of State and Church which, since the official materials are recondite and mostly unprinted, have relied on the small section of the total evidence which is not official record, in the main accepting the words of observers—men led to record themselves by a uniform bias—without question.[1] This is as inadequate as, alternatively, a total neglect of such critical material would be. Modern critics of King John, of the fourteenth-century Church, of Henry VII's policies, or of the Elizabethan clergy have far too frequently simply repeated the criticisms offered at the time, without looking at the evidence in a systematic manner. It should be stressed that their conclusions may nevertheless be accurate enough: in asking people to read the official records one is not trying to force them to accept official points of view. Yet when the proper course is followed, too many of the

[1] The poor practice of some historians may help to explain why Mr Carr believed the materials of medieval history to be confined to the hand-outs of ecclesiastical chroniclers.

entrenched legends are forced into oblivion to allow any comfortable supposition that a partial use of the evidence will after all do. To depend on the venom of a chronicler in assessing John's treatment of the Church, or on the resentments of tax-payers in judging Henry VII's fiscal policy, when so much other evidence exists by which to measure these understandable attitudes, is to write history without respect for the past. Such history is equal to that written in the news pages of the *Daily Mirror* and the leader pages of *The Times*. The historian who frees himself from the bias produced by the dominance of the official record by leaving it out enters a worse bondage—the bondage of deliberate ignorance.[1]

The proper use of the historical imagination follows upon a thorough acquaintance with the materials and a sound understanding of the bias which they contain and impose. And here it is important that the official records, as we have seen, are full of evidence for what one may call unofficial history, for details of life in which government and its purposes play a small part or none. The court records, in particular, while they testify to the actions and advantages of the rulers who held the courts, mainly illumine the needs and activities of the ruled who resorted to them. Court records compose so large a part of the extant evidence (even though it remains an insufficiently exploited part) that we do really come to know a remarkable amount about all sorts of people throughout the social scale. Here, as everywhere, however, the conventions of that dead society also interpose a barrier and a bias. A society organised hierarchically, in which equality was not so much resisted as thought naturally impossible, will necessarily leave better traces for the top of the tree than for its roots and most of the trunk, and while this condition makes possible an accurate understanding of the social relationships of the past it certainly differentiates between the few about whom we know

[1] For attempts to test, enlarge and revise standard interpretations of familiar themes see e.g. J. E. A. Joliffe, *Angevin Kingship* (London 1955); J. C. Holt, *Magna Carta* (Cambridge 1965); G. R. Elton, 'Henry VII: Rapacity and Remorse', *Historical Journal*, i (1958), 21ff, and 'Henry VII: A Restatement', *ibid.*, iv (1961), 1ff.

much and the many of whom we know little or sometimes nothing. Nevertheless, at some point or other we can get into that society at all levels; despite its bias, the evidence makes sure that our writing of history is not confined to the upper classes.

Records that are overwhelmingly the product of rulership need not, therefore, confine understanding to the behaviour of the rulers, and our records do not do this. Such records are, however, liable to include two further inadequacies, and these do occur here. Even about the facts of government—using that term in the widest sense—they tell only what concerned that government itself; and, being official, they are likely to be in the main impersonal.

The facts of medieval and early-modern government include, in the first place, a more restricted sphere for government action than has since become customary. The record is so heavily biased, and the historical works written have therefore been so much concerned with government and administration, that people think of those centuries as centuries of intensive government and forget the quite narrow limits of the area which it occupied. Even a government as energetic as that of Edward I or Henry VIII penetrated far less deeply and above all much less constantly into the lives of the nation than does government in the twentieth century, and its records therefore leave unexplained many aspects of life which modern government records would illumine. We have noted, for instance, that we know almost nothing about so basic a fact as the production of manufactured goods in this period because the recording agency was concerned only with that part of the goods which was exported and therefore earned customs revenue. We shall never cease to debate the problems of medieval agriculture, not only because the evidence is in places ambiguous but even more because the record preserves systematically only one aspect of it—the income it yielded to rentiers. Above all, we lack anything resembling a sound basis for statistical studies of all sorts, in part because evidence survives haphazardly, but in the main because it was created by record-keeping agencies who had no interest in collecting the facts we need. Of course, facts concerning population, resources or production are to be found scattered through the materials, but systematic surveys are very rare, so that historians try to help themselves out with the dangerous weapons of analogical reasoning and the theoretical construction of figures to fill gaps in series. As it is, English history has exceptionally benefited from the government's occasional ability to carry out a real survey (of Crown assets), but between Domesday Book in 1086 and the *Valor Ecclesiasticus* in 1535 no government attempted anything so extensive as a national record.[1]

I am not denying that the materials that do exist sometimes serve to answer these quantitative questions that historians are being told by sociologists and others are the only useful questions. Some reconstructions that have been attempted are impressive, and we may be only at the start of the story. But it must be very firmly said that thanks to the facts of evidential survival it will never be possible to provide even remotely satisfactory answers to all the questions which modern historians, moved by modern interests in demography and sociology, would like to ask. Only investigation will reveal where the real limits lie—though I will risk a guess and conjecture that they will be found to enclose a very small territory—and unfortunately, though understandably, investigators do not like to feel that their labours have turned up nothing but an impasse. In consequence, investigation is likely to produce not the humble recognition of limits but a quantity of overconfident and highly dubious generalisations based on insufficient evidence helped out by rash statistics and preconceived notions.[2] I am sure that we are still a good way from the frontiers which the state of the evidence sets to knowledge, but I am also

---

[1] In the thirteenth century, general enquiries into Crown rights yielded returns which came close to such a record, but they do not survive complete (Helen Cam, *The Hundred and the Hundred Rolls*, London 1930, 27ff).

[2] There is a good example in J. C. Russell's ambitious *British Medieval Population* (Albuquerque 1948). Miss McKisack (*The Fourteenth Century*, 558) calls it 'a stimulating essay' and warns that it needs 'cautious handling'. But the fact is that its conclusions are either wrong or misleading and its methods misconceived; and it is better to say so.

sure that historians anxious for these 'fundamental' answers about society and population should from the first accept that their real knowledge will always be very limited, that this is so because the evidence imposes its control, and that an admission of ignorance is better than the construction of inaccurate tables and graphs. The inaccuracies are often striking and do real harm.

The impersonality of the official record, even though the veil is occasionally lifted and even though other materials at times remove it, has similarly restricting consequences. The very many people whom the historian encounters in his researches are, as a rule, knowable by their externals only—age, sex, habitation, occupation. We have a massive collection of passport descriptions without even passport photographs. Of course, there are exceptions, and the higher up the social scale one moves the more one is likely to learn. However, it remains true that private lives remain obscure, private opinions and motives are rarely discernible. This is no age for biography—which is not to say that biography cannot ever be written inside it. Biography, to be worth doing, depends a great deal on some evidence for the subject's life before he is fully formed, or at least on some of the facts of childhood and adolescence. The state of the evidence in this era means that such facts can only survive for those known from birth to be important, for princes and their families. With very few exceptions, people below that level did not record themselves until they were old enough to make a personal impact, and that means too old to leave behind evidence for their formative years. Virtually all the books that masquerade as biographies of individuals in the years 1200–1640 (or at least down to about 1550) either give an account of the subject's public life (which is history, not biography) or assist themselves inordinately with conjecture. Even as mathematical statistics cannot operate without a sufficient basis of mathematical data, so psychology cannot do much good in a vacuum of psychologically interpretable fact. I have said that there are exceptions, but historians would once again be wise to recognise that the evidence at their disposal makes the biographical method, however popular, just about the least useful for a proper understanding of this part of the past. There is certainly no need to eliminate people from the story—far from it. They come, recognisably individuals, even from the official record, but they are not so largely described that biography is the way to success.

Even more serious is the fact that the official record is a record of official intent and action only. It rarely admits the facts of deliberation and decision-making. What moved people to action, what purposes they intended, what personal interactions lie behind their doings, are things that far too often have to be conjectured from probability and cannot be based on documented certainty. The conjecture may well be convincing, but the most convincing conjecture has before this been disproved by the discovery of new facts. In this business, the historian's two main tools of analysis are themselves somewhat suspect. He is likely to assume that those whom a given action can be shown to benefit were themselves responsible for it, and he is prone to ascribe initiative and originality to those who nominally controlled action, that is kings. No doubt he will frequently be right in either assumption, but the fact that at times he is demonstrably wrong should act as a warning on the many occasions when he makes his two equations—beneficiary equals initiator, ruler equals motivating mind—without any evidence to support it. Of medieval legislation we rarely know more than that the law was made; are we wise to identify as its originators those interests that gained advantage from it?[1] Henry VII is credited with a deliberate economic policy, Henry VIII with devising the policy that led to the break with Rome; in neither case—to put it no more strongly—is there sufficient evidence to allay doubt.[2] It is natural, and creditable, for historians to want to know the why and how as well as the what, but once again, they need to respect the limitations to understanding and explanation set by the

[1] Helen Cam, 'The Legislators of Medieval England', *Law Finders and Law Makers in Medieval England* (London 1962), 132ff.

[2] G. R. Elton, 'State Planning in Early-Tudor England', *Economic History Review* 2nd Series, xiii (1961), 433ff; 'King or Minister? The Man behind the Henrician Reformation', *History*, xxxix (1954), 216ff.

evidence and to accept that in matters of policy-making, personal influence and initiative, and the growth of policy they are very often bound to remain ignorant.

At this point, however, it is necessary to make some distinctions. The years 1200–1640 may be the era of the public record, but the record is not uniform. The consequences of the fact that the narrative sources are least satisfactory for the fifteenth century have been noted; the deficiencies of the record material add to this. The official records of the State are quite full and consistent throughout the thirteenth and fourteenth centuries, but begin to get dilapidated in the fifteenth; there is a period (*c.* 1470–1540) during which they are confused and confusing, with old series running to a stop and new ones beginning in halting fashion; moreover, they become very much more formal from about the middle of the fourteenth century onwards. And round about the reign of Henry VIII quite new sorts of materials—letters and papers of all kinds, printed books—make their appearance in quantity. The whole period therefore falls into three parts in which the evidence differs sufficiently to affect the historical knowledge possible.

From the reign of John to the 1340's we possess good narrative sources and relatively informal—that is, flexible—public records, but very little else. The history of those years can be written very well at the level of politics, public action, government, law, and administration, and quite well on aspects of economic activity; now and again, personality stands forth clearly. From then to the beginning of the sixteenth century, the growing formality of the record and the decline in narrative sources, inadequately compensated for by casual evidence (despite the Paston, Stonor and Cely letters) render all historical description less full and more conjectural, reduce the precision of constitutional and administrative history, complicate understanding of the economy—in short, introduce greater difficulties without, however, altering the real areas of past life which are open to historical investigation. The last section of our period brings a real transformation. Although the bulk of its evidence remains in the official records of all kinds, the increasing volume of more private and less formal material entirely alters the historian's methods and knowledge. Of the things he can know about the middle ages none disappear, though details of government and law are, at least so far, more obscure. To these traditional themes he can add insight into individual personality, the prehistory of political action, a much fuller grasp of social and economic problems, and an understanding of cultural and intellectual activity which is rarely possible before. None of the things which the new type of evidence opens to the historians from the 1530's onwards is absolutely dark for the previous three centuries, but the new evidence adds so much potential history that a quantitive change becomes a change in kind. Not for nothing did historians of the Tudor and Stuart periods manage for generations to do their work without ever paying much heed to the official records. They ought not to have done so, but one can understand a temptation which for the medievalist simply does not exist.

Thus even though the period 1200–1640 has a real single character by comparison with what came before and after, a character determined by the historical sources available for it, there is inside it a seeming break of major proportions. The state of knowledge typical for what may concisely be called 'medieval history' is replaced by one much more like that available for 'modern history'. The point should reflect upon the common debates as to the 'beginnings' of modern history. No one now would wish to assign a particular date to that tenuous event, and historians are only too easily impressed by the fact that attitudes and habits once thought of as medieval or modern are readily enough traced as starting much sooner or enduring much longer than these distinctions would seem to imply. Yet the surviving historical evidence points a firm finger to the generation of the early Reformation when the older type of public record began to give way to another, and when great additions of a non-official kind were made to the historian's larder.

Of course, there are those who would wish to deny the occurrence of any serious or deep-searching alterations in the body politic in the sixteenth century—who see it as still very much in accord with its past and resist the notion of 'a Tudor revolution'.[1] To them it may well appear that the contrary view rests simply on the accidents of evidence-preservation and on an unimaginative acceptance of the materials as governing historical interpretation. But this will hardly do. Historical evidence is sometimes destroyed or preserved by mere accident, but it is not so created, nor, in this case, does its survival in bulk depend on accident. On the contrary, what an age leaves behind of itself is one of the soundest indications of its purposes and attitudes. The messy state of the public records between the accession of Edward IV and that of Edward VI is not an accident, but the direct consequence of administrative changes, of the attempt to create strong government first by traditional and then by revolutionary means. The appearance of the State Papers, and the proliferation, from about 1550, of private papers result from genuine changes in the politics, the society, and the mind of England. The 'modernity'—if that be the term—of post-Reformation England is not the illusory creation of record-keeping but a fact adequately reflected in the state of the historical evidence. Like so much else, the developed use of the printing press and the sophisticated correspondence of Thomas Cromwell point to the 1530's as an age of profound change and innovations. Nor is this fact disposed of by the survival of some 'medieval' conditions in the state of the evidence: all that this proves is the obvious and never doubted truth that the full transformation was the work of generations, of a century and not of a decade.

So much has now been said about the limits and deficiencies of all the evidence discussed in this book that it becomes once again necessary to emphasize how very full it really is for all these centuries, and how much history can be written about them. Above all, much the biggest part of the materials that survive

---

[1] See e.g. the controversy in *Past and Present*: P. Williams and G. L. Harris, 'A Revolution in Tudor History?', 25 (1963), 1ff; G. R. Elton, 'The Tudor Revolution: A Reply', 29 (1964), 26ff. Further contributions *ibid.*, 26 (1963), 110ff; 31 (1965), 87ff; 32 (1965), 103ff.

was not created for historical purposes: it was not designed for the writing of history but for various purposes embedded in the life of the times. It can therefore be restored to that life and can tell at length and in detail about many things beyond the merely political interests of the historians who practised in those years. Since the official record predominates, it is easiest to write the history of government and administration, and a good deal of this has been and is being done. Nor is there anything lowly or inferior about these studies of offices and officers, episcopal government or manorial courts. Not only do they treat of matters important in themselves; it is also vital to remember that only competent studies of this kind make possible a proper understanding of the records which they use and are therefore a precondition of any other uses to which these records may be put. Since the official situation depended so much on the relationships which gave structure and solidity (as well as conflict) to society, social studies—patronage and service, the execution of policy in private hands, the place of order and degree and the attitudes derived therefrom—are also obviously possible, though the amount of work done on all this is not so far very large. Government was for ever searching for money, and the position enjoyed by rulers at all levels depended on wealth: hence economic history has every opportunity to benefit from the records, and has taken it. Government was law: the history of law, lawyers and law-courts could be written both better and much more fully than has so far been done, and this is rather urgent. Intellectual history, the history of all sorts of ideas and currents of thought, is less well served before the sixteenth century but can at all times do something.

In fact, there is no question that any historian, dead or living, has ever tried to ask which he was wrong to ask of the materials surviving for English history between the accession of King John and the outbreak of the Civil War. Some questions, perhaps, have not yet been asked at all, and many have certainly not yet been put to every part of the period. We need much more work on administration and government, especially in the fifteenth century and from 1558 onwards. That there is still no history of the Tudor Privy Council will surprise only those who have never looked at the evidence available for such a history.[1] The financial problems of English governments remain in great part unstudied.[2] Much more should be done about the organisation of the Church at all levels. Above all, there are the records of the common law for whose proper exploitation one would like to breed a race of Maitlands. Similarly, almost every serious problem in the history of agriculture, trade and industry should still attract attention, either to fill in for periods insufficiently understood or to reconsider, from a much larger coverage of the material, many of the answers at present thought reliable. Altogether, the traditional forms of historical studies, themselves the products of the most obvious implications of the record, are so far from exhausted that generations of scholars will be able to live productively and (one hopes) happily without ever troubling themselves about an original approach to their materials. And they will be no less useful for that, nor less worthy or intelligent.

Yet the evidence can also call forth more novel ways of using it. For example, the increasing refinement of socially analytical tools—forgetting the crudities of class, recognising the role of myth or convention, using the connections between faith and social standing—can only benefit from a precise attention to the materials produced by processes quite unaware that obvious facts of social life were being recorded for the benefit of historians to whom they are no longer obvious. An historical study of thought which abandoned the 'great man', 'great book', or 'great idea' approach, or one which considered not only (in the traditional way) the setting in time of intellectual activity but also its links with the agencies of power and resistance, with the means of

[1] G. R. Elton, 'Why the history of the early-Tudor Council remains unwritten', *Annali della Fondazione Italiana per la Storia Amministrativa*, i (1964), 268ff.

[2] Only F. C. Dietz, tackling the years 1485–1640, has attempted to provide total figures and a general survey, and he is shot through with error. We also need more books like R. Ashton's *The Crown and the Money Market 1603–1640* (Oxford 1960).

production and the distribution of consumption, will greatly increase the relevance of its concerns and deepen its understanding of the past. Even the fundamental studies of population and wealth, beloved by those to whom quantification alone provides historical certainty, are not rendered impossible or illegitimate by the frequent absence of possible statistics, provided they accept their limitations. Sound knowledge can be gained of such matters, and the inspired rashness of the enthusiast or pioneer, however tiresome at times in its assertiveness, should neither hide the good that may come of it nor make one forget the more solid achievements of the careful work-horse.

Thus, all that ever happened in those four and a half centuries may have left deposit in the record, and all questions relevant to the lives lived in that time are legitimate. But the record is very far from complete; it has its limits as well as its problems of comprehension. The historian should ask every possible question, but he must submit himself to the discipline of his sources. He must understand their real meaning and accept their deficiencies. If his very proper questions can receive no answer, he should say so and not try to remedy the lack of the record by spurious or question-begging devices borrowed from other students or invented by himself. If he accepts the primacy of his materials, he will enjoy a form of intellectual liberation: he will cease to thrash about and arrive at understanding. And, in all conscience, there will still be plenty for him to do.

Index

(to materials and sources only)